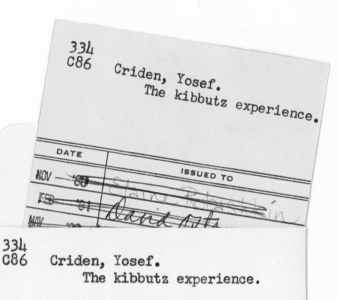

334
C86   Criden, Yosef.
         The kibbutz experience.

DATE	ISSUED TO
NOV '80	Elaine Rotostein
FEB '81	David Litt
MAY	

334
C86   Criden, Yosef.
         The kibbutz experience.

Temple Israel Library
Minneapolis, Minn.

Please sign your full name on the above card.

Return books promptly to the Library or Temple Office.

Fines will be charged for overdue books or for damage or loss of same.

THE KIBBUTZ EXPERIENCE

THE KIBBUTZ EXPERIENCE

Dialogue at Kfar Blum

by

YOSEF CRIDEN and SAADIA GELB

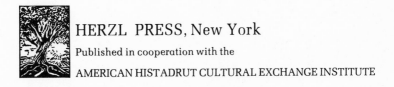

HERZL PRESS, New York

Published in cooperation with the

AMERICAN HISTADRUT CULTURAL EXCHANGE INSTITUTE

To our wives
RUTHIE and HELEN (AYALA)
who loyally accepted the early stages of pioneer life
and learned to be better kibbutzniks than we are

YOSEF and SAADIA

Contents

PREFACE

This is a unique book about that unique phenomenon of Israeli life—the kibbutz. Although much has been written about virtually every aspect of Israel, including the communal settlements, many of the books dealing with the kibbutzim have been the result of the observations of visitors whose comments, with rare exception, were of necessity superficial. The special virtue of the present book is that it was composed neither by journalists eager for a "quickie" nor by traveling social scientists engaged in a brief survey but by two veteran kibbutzniks who left the United States in the forties to be among the early settlers of Kfar Blum. Both, without being dogmatic, are articulate commentators on life in Israel. At the instigation of Jesse Zel Lurie, executive editor of the Hadassah Magazine, Yosef Criden and Saadia Gelb agreed to talk spontaneously about the kibbutz experience. The results were 16 hours of taped dialogue, complete with typical Criden humor and Gelb's sociological insight. The generous assistance of Rabbi Philip S. Bernstein made the transcription of these tapes possible.

A word about the authors: Yosef Criden, born and raised in Buffalo, studied engineering in California and dreamed of "being a doctor, a farmer, a lawyer or what have you." He went on aliyah with his Brooklyn-born wife, Ruth, in 1940, as one of the original settlers of Kfar Blum. Before the group actually settled in Upper Galilee, Criden worked as an engineer with a fishing fleet in Haifa. Like many a kibbutznik, he devoted years to military service, as a transport expert and sometimes as an education officer with Nahal, the pioneer youth formation that trained its members for border kibbutzim. All told, Criden spent 17 years in military service, first with the British during World War II, then in Hagana and ultimately in the Israel Defense Forces. Besides trucking, he has managed Kfar Blum's factory; his hobbies are reading, writing and music; mostly, however, he is a story-teller.

Saadia Gelb was born in Poland in 1913, coming to America at the age of 12. He studied in the public schools of Minneapolis, and graduated from the University of Minnesota in 1934 with a master's degree in social work. At the same time, he had been studying at the famed Minneapolis Talmud Torah, where his father was one of the outstanding teachers. He received a rabbinical degree in 1943 at the Jewish Institute of Religion while also studying at the Graduate School for Jewish Social Work. During World War II, he took various courses in engineering and machine shop, in preparation for settling in Israel. In 1947, with his wife Helen, and three children, he joined Kfar Blum, where he has since worked as farmer, fisherman, hotel keeper and kibbutz secretary and treasurer. He has hosted countless youth study groups and individual intellectuals from abroad, as well as trade unionists and ordinary tourists; with his particular verve he has introduced them to the meaning of the kibbutz and described in practical terms the way of life at Kfar Blum.

Both authors, long-time friends of the writer of this preface, were active in Habonim, the Labor Zionist youth movement, which sent a nucleus to help establish Kfar Blum. Despite the fact that the kibbutz is named after the late French Prime Minister Leon Blum, its membership was largely "Anglo-Saxon," a mix of American and British Habonim; as years went by, groups from other parts of the world joined. Yet, a distinctive American character persists at Kfar Blum, even to the second and third generation. Yosef and Saadia, their children and grandchildren, are testimony to the vitality of the kibbutz experiment.

It was hoped that this volume would appear on the 30th anniversary of the founding of Kfar Blum. However, the Yom Kippur War intervened. Saadia's letters, written after the attack on Israel in October, 1973, indicate how the kibbutz movement rallied to the national defense, giving more than its share of the population to the roster of dead on the Golan Heights and the Suez Canal.

I should like to express my appreciation to Marie Syrkin, editor, and to Gertrude Hirschler, assistant editor, of the Herzl Press, for editing the taped dialogue for publication without sacrificing its spontaneity and maintaining fidelity to the text. The Herzl Press and the American Histadrut Cultural Exchange Institute have cooperated in making this intimate account of the kibbutz available to the English-reading world.

NAHUM GUTTMAN

New York
November, 1973

INTRODUCTION

FROM MAVERICK TO MOVEMENT

The kibbutz movement is now in its third generation. Reaction to it has run the gamut from ridicule as an unnatural, "utopian" delusion, to condemnation as a selfish and amoral, if not immoral, society, to enthusiastic acceptance of the kibbutz as the ultimate in pioneering idealism and self-sacrifice. Though the kibbutz arose as the logical form to fulfill both the national and social goals of the young pioneers who with equal fervor sought to rebuild a Jewish homeland and to create a new society, it was not only an ideological but a pragmatic response to the demands of the Palestine reality—the only practical solution to the unique problems of a labor force composed of former intellectuals untrained for agricultural work and an economy lacking the funds necessary for settlement on, and development of, the land.

But the kibbutz, product of need though it was, was not an inevitable response to that need. There had been other forms of settlement. The kibbutz took the form it did because there was an ideal behind it, and a philosophy, derived in part from Jewish tradition, as Martin Buber recognized almost thirty years ago: "In the spirit of the members . . . ideal motives joined hands with the dictates of the hour; and in the motives there was a curious mixture of memories of the Russian *Artel*, impressions left over from reading the so-called 'utopian' Socialists, and the half-unconscious after-effects of the Bible's teachings about social justice."

Nachman Syrkin, one of the chief contributors to the ideological structure of the Labor Zionist movement—and therefore, to the State of Israel itself—was certainly more than half-conscious of the role of the Bible in Jewish thinking, his own included, when he characterized the Jews as "a people faithful to

5

the Torah and prophets, whose entire history was nothing but an unending struggle of the prophetic ideal for realization." In his ideological groundbreaking study, *The Jewish Problem and the Socialist Jewish State* (published in 1897), Syrkin excoriated the political Zionism of his day, which was "striving for a Jewish state based on the rights of private property." To him it was "inconceivable that people will agree to the creation of an autonomous state based on social inequality, for this would amount to entering into a *social contract of servitude*. No new social contract will ever come to be unless its foundation is freedom." For that reason, it is "only by fusing with socialism [that] Zionism [can] become the ideal of the whole Jewish people." He posited the creation of a classless society and national sovereignty as "the only means of completely solving the Jewish problem." With the legacy of Judaism as his point of departure, Syrkin argued that the high values of socialism, its concern for human dignity, were identical with the ethical values of Judaism, and that "a Jewish State without the elements of social justice would be foreign to the Jewish spirit, while social equality alone would be of no redeeming value to the Jewish people unless it struck roots in its own soil." In sum, as Syrkin insisted throughout his life, "there can be no Zionism except Socialist Zionism."

Syrkin, then, was the initiator of the kibbutz movement while Ber Borochov, another synthesizer of Zionism and socialism, founded the Po'ale Zion organization, which transformed a philosophy—or a platform—into a program of action.

Another seminal influence was that of A.D.Gordon, who not only preached the "religion of labor," the importance of agricultural work as the road to man's spiritual renewal, but practiced what he preached: Gordon was almost fifty when he arrived in Palestine and became an agricultural worker. For eighteen years he worked in the fields by day and wrote his essays by night, and was a source of inspiration and encouragement to many younger and stronger than he.

Israel, of course, was not the birthplace of the kibbutz form of society. There were communitarian societies in Europe in the Middle Ages, and in the United States in the eighteenth and nineteenth centuries. There are Hutterite settlements in Canada and the United States today, and Bruderhof communities in Paraguay, Uruguay and the United States. But the kibbutz differs dramatically from them in that almost all these settlements outside of Israel were religious sects with religion the basis of and the reason for their establishment, while the kibbutz movement in Israel is almost entirely a secular movement, with strong nationalist and political flavor. Even in the religious kibbutzim religion is not the reason for choosing the kibbutz form of life but an expression of their members' commitment to Jewish values beyond those of the secular kibbutzim.

In any event, neither the Hutterite nor any of the other communitarian settlements abroad had any influence upon the kibbutz movement in Israel, although the kibbutz does appear to have inspired at least some of the communes which have waxed and waned in the United States in recent years. Few of these have lasted very long because they lacked the motivations which made the kibbutz a means of achieving national, economic, and social goals instead of being simply a negation of society. The American communes are isolated both from one another and from the rest of society: in Israel the various kibbutzim, from the very outset, tended to band together into movements, culminating in a Federation of Kibbutz Movements. As an integral part of the labor movement, the predominant sector of Israeli society, the kibbutz was not only not isolated from society, but played a major role in the national and social revival of Palestine.

The kibbutz is, essentially, a group with common economic, social and political ideologies. It was founded on the idea of Jewish farmers working nationally owned land through collective ownership by the whole group of all the means of production —soil, equipment, livestock, and so forth. The commune itself controls purchasing, production, marketing, consumption—including housing—the rearing and education of the children, cultural recreational and all other services. No wages are paid: every member is expected to work according to his ability, and has all of his basic needs met in return. There is complete equality of both rights and obligations. A necessary corollary to the requirement of self-labor was the rejection of all hired labor, a

principle accepted by most kibbutzim. According to the model
rules for kibbutzim, drawn up as the kibbutz movement grew, a
member leaving the kibbutz is not entitled "to withdraw any
private belongings or monies which he may have turned over to
the kibbutz when accepted as a member," (unless specifically
provided for in a written agreement between him and the kibbutz
at the time of his entrance). In theory, at least, the kibbutz forms a
single estate; its community, a single large household which is
responsible for the needs of every member. The individual family
remains unaffected economically by illness, invalidism or the
death of the head of the family.

The leadership is democratically elected and enjoys no special
privileges; management of the various branches of the kibbutz
economy rotates, and all decisions on the economic, social and
cultural life of the kibbutz are made by the members themselves.

The first attempt to establish a kibbutz—or kvutza, as it was
called initially—was at the Sejera training farm run by the Jewish
Colonization Association. In 1907–8 members of Bar Giora,
forerunner of the self-defense organization HaShomer, (which
was, in turn, followed by the Haganah) were given an opportunity
to cultivate a tract of land collectively. The commune lasted only
a year and a half, but it did prove that collective farming was
feasible.

A subsequent attempt was more successful. In 1908 the World
Zionist Organization opened a Palestine office in Jaffa, under the
direction of Dr. Arthur Ruppin. The following year the Palestine
Office established the Kinneret Farm, near Lake Kinneret, for the
training of agricultural workers. There was constant tension
between the farm manager and the workers, who finally went out
on strike when the manager refused to permit them to visit a
comrade lying gravely ill in the hospital in Tiberias. Dr. Ruppin
decided to give the workers an opportunity to prove that they
could work the land collectively, and more efficiently, without
outside control. Six men and one woman undertook the
responsibility on a one-year trial basis. After an unequivocal
success—they finished the year with a surplus despite their
inexperience and the illnesses which plagued them—it was
decided to make the arrangement permanent, and to replace the

first experimental group with permanent settlers. On October 28, 1910, ten men and two women took over the land at Umm Juni, later renamed Degania and famous today as "Mother of the Kvutzot."

The training farms at Kinneret and Merhavia were also transformed into kibbutz settlements after Degania had demonstrated how successful the collective could be, particularly in view of the unhappy history of earlier noncollective agricultural settlements.

The first agricultural settlements—also founded by seekers of social justice and equality—were the product of the First Aliyah which brought to Palestine 23,000 immigrants between 1882 and 1903. Russian Zionist youth, mainly university students, organized the "Bilu" movement (acronym for the Hebrew slogan, "House of Jacob, rise up and go forth," from the Book of Isaiah) and dedicated themselves to the idea of actual settlement of the land by Jews.

Though these young people dreamed of cooperative effort, the realities of Palestine defeated them. They lacked basic agricultural skills, were ravaged by disease, and were desperately under-financed: they had left Russia with little more than their fare. To keep body and soul together they were compelled to hire themselves out as ditch-diggers to Mikveh Yisrael, the first agricultural training school for boys, which had been established a dozen years earlier. Some of them held these jobs for two years, until additional Bilu members arrived and they settled on a tract of land at Gedera. Others joined the early settlers of Rishon LeZion, which had been established in October, 1882, just two months after their arrival in Palestine. They sowed wheat in land suitable for vines, and their first harvest was a failure. They were saved from bankruptcy by Baron Edmond de Rothschild of Paris, who responded to their appeal for help with 30,000 gold francs for deep-well digging, to relieve their fatal water shortage. But the grant did not solve their other problems—lack of experience, unfamiliarity with the soil, and lack of means to sow another crop. Rothschild came to their aid again, and was soon supporting a number of villages, all on a one-crop economy based on grape and wine production. To bolster the shaky economic foundation,

Rothschild built two large wine cellars, which became the single largest consumers of the settlers' grapes. But the settlers remained dependent on the whims of nature and the fluctuations of the market. Because the labor needs of their one-crop settlements varied seasonally, they began hiring cheap native labor, and gradually gave up working the land themselves.

When the first young socialist-inspired Zionists began arriving in the country, with the Second Aliyah some twenty years later, they found a Jewish community which lived mainly in the cities, in very much the way Jews had lived in the diaspora: by trade and minor business enterprises. The few who remained of the original Bilu settlers operated farms with cheap Arab labor; their sons were trained as artisans and professionals. The country was barren, and denuded; it could be reclaimed only through the personal labor of pioneers who would not follow the course taken by the Biluim. The only possibility of success was through cooperation; individuals could not undertake the task.

The failure of the original settlers to produce an effective agricultural base for a renascent Jewish people, their failure to transform themselves into a Jewish peasantry rooted in the soil, opened the way for the kibbutz movement. The early settlers had demonstrated what not to do; the newcomers would have to find another way—and they did.

Degania, and all subsequent collectives, including the additional forms which developed later—the *moshav shitufi* (collective smallholders' village) and the *moshav 'ovdim* (cooperative smallholders' village) were built on Jewish National Fund land. The Jewish National Fund (JNF) was created by the Zionist Congress in 1901 as a land redeeming and reclaiming agency, with the view to securing a national land reserve for Jewish settlement in Palestine. The only land available for sale was in the waste and sandy areas, the ownership of which was concentrated in the hands of a few Arabs, mostly absentee landlords. Such land was not attractive to private purchasers and it was therefore necessary to mobilize national funds for the redemption and reclamation of the land for Jewish settlement.

During its first two decades, the JNF operated on a small scale, limited by the scarcity of funds. In 1922, however, the Keren

HaYesod (Foundation Fund) was established as a separate agency for financing settlements and, together with the rapidly growing JNF funds, made possible large-scale land purchasing and reclamation activities. The Jewish National Fund is required to hold the land it buys in eternal trust for the entire Jewish people, a principle which has been reaffirmed by the government of Israel despite some pressures to raise money by selling portions of these lands to private purchasers.

The idea of national land, which strongly appealed to all sections of Jewry, was the first major step toward realization of the dual goal of national and social reconstruction. Without JNF land there could have been neither large-scale settlement nor the development of the moshav and kibbutz villages.

At a conference of agricultural collectives held in 1920, the 40 collectives participating had a total of 660 members, and more than half of these groups had fewer than a dozen members. Today there are about 235 kibbutzim in Israel. Their total population is over 100,000, including members and their children, parents of members, groups in training and other categories of permanent residents. The largest of the kibbutzim have populations of more than 2,000; some, as few as 100. In the majority of kibbutzim the population is between 200 and 700.

Many of the features of kibbutz life which are taken for granted today grew out of internal kibbutz confrontation with the problems of everyday life. Full communism, for example, was not initially practiced: members of Degania received monthly wages of fifty francs from the Palestine Office. Some paid it all into the kvutza treasury, others retained part of their wages for the purchase of shoes and other clothing, and for other purposes. No kibbutz member receives wages today.

The principle of the equality of women was another question which was not answered overnight—and has, in fact, not been resolved to this very day. Were the women to be "equal" as members of the kibbutz, while they remained tied to the "traditional" occupations—in the kitchen, the laundry and care of the children, or were they to labor in all branches of the kibbutz economy, alongside the men? Communal rearing of children became a part of kibbutz life, and the women proceeded to fight for assignments in agricultural work. They won and were successful in many branches of agriculture, but the battle did not stay won: within a very short time kibbutz members were to complain that the women had to be prodded to take advantage of their rights; the women seemed to view housework in the kibbutz as their refuge. As a result, "a division of functions crystallized— housework for the women and agricultural work for the men."

Joseph Bussel, a founder of Degania, summarized the purpose of the kvutza and hinted at the attendant problems when he said that the goal was to "enable us to decide how to run our own lives and to create economic equality and equality between the sexes." To this day the last remains a problem despite the constant attention it has been getting. Another basic principle was the rejection of hired labor, viewed as the exploitation of man by man.

The example of Degania was followed by the kvutzot established during the ensuing decade, even to limiting the size of the kvutza so that it might function as a moderately-enlarged "family," what they called an "organic" community. Two years after the establishment of Degania, Kinneret and Gan Shmuel were founded, and during World War I, Ayelet HaShahar, Kfar Giladi, Mahanayim and Tel Hai were set up.

During the years of the Third Aliyah (1919–1923) a major deviation from the Degania model appeared on the scene: the large kibbutz. These new collectives refused to limit their population to a small group of likeminded pioneers; they were prepared to take in any and all sincere workers capable of living a communal life. To distinguish between the two, the smaller collectives retained the kvutza designation, while the larger adopted the term kibbutz (both terms deriving from the Hebrew root for "group" or "collective"). In modern times, the vagaries of usage have led to the dropping of the original term altogether, and kibbutz is now the accepted term for all the communes.

While the term is universally accepted, the principle is not: Degania gave up part of its land for the formation of an additional kvutza rather than take in the additional members they would have needed to cultivate all of the land originally assigned to them. Stubborn adherence to principle, whether philosophically or pragmatically arrived at, characterized kibbutz thinking from the very earliest days and, in some instances, hampered adjustment to changing conditions. One of the very basic requirements of kibbutz life, for example, the rejection of hired labor, was severely threatened in the 1930's and is again under fire today.

In the first instance the kibbutz had to resolve the conflict between the ban on outside workers with the needs of the immigrants arriving from Europe, who needed housing and employment and had a new language to learn as well. Under the pressure from the leadership of the Yishuv, the kibbutzim accepted a compromise under which the new immigrants were housed and clothed, worked a half-day and attended classes the other half. No wages were paid. The broader demands of "general welfare" and the "national interest" won out over the narrower claims of kibbutz ideology, albeit not without a struggle.

A more recent compromise on the same question derived from purely pragmatic considerations: the industrialization of the kibbutz has resulted in a shortage of kibbutz labor. Therefore many kibbutzim have had to choose between hiring workers from the outside and either limiting their industrial expansion or even closing down some existent enterprises. A glance at the Appendix to this volume will indicate what choice they made. With close to 250 enterprises in over 160 kibbutzim, kibbutz industry already produces 7 per cent of the national industrial product. Of this, 25 per cent is exported; in 1972 kibbutz industry brought in over $45 million. It was simply not possible—certainly not practical—to return to the original, purely agricultural kibbutz economy.

Not that the kibbutz remained purely agricultural for long. By the early 1930's industry had been introduced into some of the kibbutzim, albeit as a marginal activity, theoretically to take up the slack during the less busy seasons on the farm—almost as a make-work program to keep everyone occupied. But no modern factory with a production schedule can rely on seasonal unemployment on the farm for its labor force; it must work on a year-round schedule. Furthermore, its labor force becomes increasingly more sophisticated and specialized as kibbutz industry becomes more complex, since it requires skills the average kibbutznik does not have. Industry could not remain a part-time objective.

In spite of initial difficulties, kibbutz industry has been growing steadily. One stimulus to that growth was the increase in farm productivity on the kibbutz as a result of improved agricultural technology. A second is the fact that farm work stresses physical fitness, while the kibbutz population, on the average, is getting older every year. Industry thus can provide jobs for physically disabled or elderly members. (Industrial workers on the kibbutz are on the average five years older than those in agricultural branches). For women, in particular, industry offers productive work commensurate with their physical strength, and while they are a minority in kibbutz industry, as they are in kibbutz agriculture, they constitute a much larger minority in industry. Add to these inducements the fact that in Israel industry is more profitable than agriculture, and pressure for increasing industrial activity in the kibbutz becomes compelling.

A spin-off from this trend in the kibbutz economy is a change in kibbutz attitudes towards higher education. Whereas most kibbutzim had been reluctant to let their youngsters go to college, for fear that they would become "over-educated" for life in a comparatively simple agricultural economy, they now want their children to take advantage of the opportunities for higher education so as to bring added skills back to the kibbutz. The extent of this shift in kibbutz attitudes may be seen most dramatically in recent proposals to establish a special kibbutz university for graduates of the kibbutz secondary school systems.

A recent study of kibbutz industry reached some very interesting conclusions: In addition to being economically successful, kibbutz industry is more efficient and more profitable than nonkibbutz industries; one-third of the plants have been able to avoid hiring outside labor, the others have accepted hired labor as inevitable despite the ideological objections to such labor; industry has helped significantly in providing jobs for the older members.

One anticipated problem has turned out to be less serious than had been feared: a managerial class has not developed, and rotation of workers in the offices of kibbutz industries is as prevalent as in the farm branches. An unanticipated benefit of kibbutz industry has been the success of workers' participation in management programs, a concept whose time has not yet come, to any appreciable degree, in non-kibbutz factories.

The growth of kibbutz industry has reversed, for Israel at least, a historic trend which has had devastating consequences throughout the developed countries of the world. In the 19th century, the Industrial Revolution drained the villages of their labor force and lured the young away from the farms. The rush to the towns for new jobs resulted in the proliferation of dreary factory-towns with the appalling misery which characterized them, while the villages became desolate and impoverished. The kibbutz brought industry back to the village. As in so many other elements of kibbutz life, reality outstripped theory and kibbutz industry flourished both because of its own dynamism and because the demographic reality of kibbutz society required it. It would be difficult to determine whether kibbutz industry's greatest contribution has been in providing jobs for those incapable of work in the fields—women, the aged, the poor in health—or in providing jobs for new immigrants, for whom a long period of agricultural training and physical conditioning is neither practical nor desirable. Furthermore, kibbutz industry can absorb the talents of young kibbutzniks whose horizons have been broadened, and whose skills have been diversified by their years of army service outside of the kibbutz and by study at the universities. It may well be, then, that kibbutz industry is playing a major role not only in the economy of the kibbutz but as a deterrent to the flow of younger people out of the kibbutz.

The introduction of new ideas and new practices was not the fruit of isolated kibbutz agonizings over principle versus pragmatism but flowed from the interplay of ideas between kibbutzim within the associations which were formed early in the development of the kibbutz movement.

In the late 1920's an attempt was made to unite all of the kibbutzim in one institutional framework. It failed because of substantial differences in the social origin and cultural background of the settlers, and serious differences as to the place of the kibbutz in political life. In May, 1923, a United Kibbutz Movement held its first and only meeting. Within four years the movement had separated into three camps, each with its own federation.

The immediate issue at that 1923 meeting was that of the small versus the large kibbutz, but the wide-ranging discussion disclosed a general concern over the very viability of the kibbutz as a socio-economic form. One of the founders of Kiryat Anavim complained of the tendency of the kvutza to stifle individual initiative. He went on to say that "even in the small kvutzot ideology is decreasing and institutionalization and degeneration already are visible. The struggle for existence kills energy and community apathy is increasing." In December of that same year, Yitzhak Tabenkin of En Harod reported a marked decrease in the total population of the kvutzot. "The movement is crumbling with appalling speed," he said. "There is not one kvutza which has not lost some of its founders. . . ."

Similar prophecies of doom were periodically made, only to be proven false by the kibbutzim as they continued to grow and proliferate.

The first countrywide organization, "HaKibbutz HaArtzi-Ha-Shomer HaTza'ir," was organized in April, 1927, at a conference in Haifa. By 1973 it had grown to include 75 kibbutzim with a total population of 31,055. Member kibbutzim of the movement retain their internal autonomy in all areas of social, economic, cultural, political and educational activity, in line with principles laid down by the movement as a whole: the kibbutz is an instrument for the realization of Zionism, the waging of the class struggle and the building of socialism. It is also an end in itself, the archetype of the socialist society. Limits were put on the size of kibbutz population. The Kibbutz Artzi program included the development of friendly relations with the Soviet Union and the goal of a binational (Arab-Jewish) state. The realities of intensified Soviet hostility to Israel, however, particularly since the eve of the Six-Day War, and the absence of any Arab response to the binationalist idea, effectively nullified both of these ideals.

In August, 1927, the same year in which HaKibbutz HaArtzi was founded, a second national organization appeared on the scene: HaKibbutz HaMeuhad. Based on En Harod, the movement called for large kibbutzim, with no predetermined limits set to membership, open to all comers and not limited to graduates of any particular youth movement. They were to engage in agriculture, industry, and handicrafts, and expand as rapidly as possible in order to absorb new immigrants. While the largest of the Kibbutz Artzi settlements eventually grew to 300 members, Yagur, one of the founding kibbutzim of HaKibbutz HaMeuhad had 1,007 inhabitants by 1941 and over 1,200 by 1970: Giv'at Brenner, founded in 1928, already has a population of over 1,700. Today, the movement's 58 settlements have a combined population of 26,000.

In contrast to the broad autonomy of members of HaKibbutz HaArtzi, kibbutzim of HaKibbutz HaMeuhad are autonomous only in matters of administration and finance, while the movement is the arbiter of ideology.

The principle of the economic independence of each kibbutz, while universal today, was accepted only after bitter debate. En Harod was the focus of the struggle, which occurred in 1922, just one year after the kibbutz had been founded by members of G'dud Ha'Avodah, the Labor Brigade named in honor of Joseph Trumpeldor. Leading members of the Labor Brigade insisted that En Harod's current expenditures should be controlled by the national executive of the Brigade; the majority of the membership of En Harod insisted that all operational decisions should be made by the kibbutz itself. Acceptance of self-rule for En Harod set the pattern for the kibbutz movement as we know it today. Haim Barkai points out that the debate at En Harod was strongly influenced by a similar controversy in the Soviet Union at the same time, and many of the leading personalities favoring centralization left the kibbutz and returned to the Soviet Union, where they were ultimately liquidated in the course of Stalin's purges.

The largest of the kibbutz movements, with 85 affiliated kibbutzim and a total population of 32,000, is the youngest movement, although it includes some of the oldest kibbutzim as well as some of the newest. "Ihud HaKvutzot VeHakibbutzim" was founded in 1951, through a merger of the much older "Hever HaKvutzot" (founded in 1925) with "Ihud HaKibbutzim," which was formed in 1951 when a group of kibbutzim seceded from HaKibbutz HaMeuhad over political and educational differences. Since 1951, the movement has grown steadily. Five of its affiliates belong to the No'ar Zioni movement, and three to the strictly Orthodox Po'ale Agudat Israel. The former are associated with the

Independent Liberal Party; the latter's association with the movement is purely economic.

The Religious Kibbutz Movement—HaKibbutz HaDati—was organized in 1935 by four religious pioneer groups from Poland and Germany. By 1948 they had succeeded in establishing twelve kibbutzim. Six of these were at the very periphery of the Jewish area, completely surrounded by Arabs, and were destroyed during the War of Independence. Three of them were reestablished as moshavim, and after the Six-Day War, the remaining three were reestablished as kibbutzim, with many of the children of the original kibbutz members who had been killed in the destruction of their kibbutz constituting the new settlers. HaKibbutz HaDati has grown to thirteen settlements today, and in addition maintains two Nahal settlements in the Jordan Valley.

The basic principle of the religious kibbutz is "Torah Va'Avodah," religious commitment accompanied by self-labor. After a lengthy period of stagnation which ended in the 1960's, they are among the most flourishing kibbutzim in the country.

While all of the kibbutz movements are theoretically autonomous they are, in fact, subject to the guidance of, and closely linked to, the four Labor parties:

Ihud HaKvutzot VeHaKibbutzim—Mapai
Hakibbutz HaArtzi—HaShomer HaTza'ir
HaKibbutz HaMeuhad—Ahdut HaAvodah
HaKibbutz HaDati—HaPo'el HaMizrahi

While the political linkage would tend to be divisive, there has always been pressure from within the movements for an overall framework, some kind of umbrella organization. Hever HaKvutzot in 1925 was the first such attempt; a second was made in 1936 when B'rit HaT'nua HaKibbutzit (Federation of Kibbutz Movements) was formed in an attempt to unify at least HaKibbutz HaMeuhad and Hever HaKvutzot. It languished, however, until its reformation in 1963 as a federation in which all of the kibbutz groups participate. It represents the kibbutz movement vis-a-vis the government with regard to political and monetary problems; it concerns itself with agricultural and economic services for the entire movement, handles cultural and educational projects and studies sociological problems within the kibbutzim. At the same time, the younger kibbutz generation is far less doctrinaire than its forebears and therefore less subject to the intensity of feeling engendered by differences in kibbutz ideology or political philosophy, differences which had led to dramatic conflict and splits within some kibbutzim, as happened in the 1930's at Bet Alpha and Ramat Yohanan. Bet Alpha had been the first of the HaShomer HaTza'ir kibbutzim, but included among its founders and a substantial number of its members many who did not accept HaShomer HaTza'ir ideology. The tensions engendered by the political conflict poisoned the social atmosphere as well, and it was only by effecting an exchange of populations with Ramat Yohanan, where a similar struggle had developed, that the destruction of the two kibbutzim was prevented. HaShomer HaTza'ir members from both kibbutzim were concentrated at Bet Alpha; Ramat Yohanan became a kibbutz of Mapai, Israel's dominant labor party.

A decade later, in 1944, and then again in 1951, there was a split in Mapai. Old, established and flourishing kibbutzim, such as Givat Haim, Ashdot Ya'akov and En Harod were actually divided and separate settlements set up. The reasons for these splits are totally irrelevant to the contemporary kibbutznik, who is faced with altogether new and different problems.

The image of the kibbutz, for one thing, has changed. Granted the success of the kibbutz economically: with only 3.8 percent, perhaps a little less, of the total Jewish population of Israel, the kibbutzim produce half of its food; that same 3.8 or less percent also turn out 7 percent of Israel's industrial product. But the kibbutz no longer plays as dominating a role as it once did on the political scene or in the contemporary mythology of Israel.

More than a quarter of a century has passed since eleven kibbutzim were literally planted, overnight, in the Negev, to establish the Jewish presence there. "Homah Umigdal"—Watchtower and Stockade—was a glorious chapter in kibbutz history. These groups pushed forward the borders of Jewish settlement and provided defense against Arab attacks and British hostility; they created the Palmach (the commando force of the Israel Defense Army); in 1948 they held back the Arab invasion, while the young Israeli army was shucking its swaddling clothes. Today the creation of new kibbutzim is far less dramatic, and requires neither outwitting the British nor outmaneuvering the Arabs, and defense is in the capable hands of Israel's army, navy and air force. The great days of "Aliyah Bet," the "illegal" immigration to whose success the kibbutzim contributed so much, have also receded into the haze of history.

It has been calculated that in the 1950's the proportion of kibbutzniks in positions of power was over seven times their proportion in the population as a whole; in the 1970's it has declined to four or five times their share of the population. The kibbutz still contributes a disproportionate share of leadership to the military and to management. Though simply being a kibbutznik is no longer synonymous with being a member of Israel's elite, the moral and political influence of the kibbutz movment in Israel is still far more pervasive than the number of members would indicate.

It is obvious that there would have been no Israel today without the kibbutzim, which reclaimed and rehabilitated the land, developed a broad spectrum of agricultural products, established the Jewish presence up to the very borders of what was to become Israel, and provided leadership and manpower for the army even while it fed the population at large. It should be equally obvious that the kibbutz still has a crucial role to play in the future. The kibbutz remains a source of ideals and a focus of idealism; it can still play a major role in the absorption of new immigrants and the development of new industries. and it still provides a way of life infinitely more attractive to idealistic youth than the city life against which so many are rebelling today. Some of the glamor may have worn off, economic values may have changed somewhat and the structure of kibbutz life itself modified—not a few of the kibbutzim no longer relegate the children to special dormitories, but house them with their parents—but the kibbutz remains a unique institution, with a remarkable record.

Writing on the subject, Michael Curtis summed up the achievement of the kibbutz as

> Self-sufficiency without greed or materialist spirit; coopera-
> tion without a coercive apparatus; equality without a

reduction of cultural or intellectual standards; freedom without disorder; work with neither boredom nor need of incentives; self-expression without licence; specialization without stratification; guidance of public opinion without repression; moral concern without dogmatism; industrialization without urbanization; rural life without idiocy.*

Georges Friedmann sees the kibbutz as "Israel's most effective contribution to the millenary messianic promise of justice and peace", and adds that this contribution is in large measure due to "unbelievers inflamed by the same ardor that consumed Isaiah."

MORDECAI S. CHERTOFF

---

*ISRAEL: Social Structure and Change, edited by Michael Curtis and Mordecai S. Chertoff. New Brunswick, N.J., E.P. Dutton and Co., 1973.

1

WHO BECOMES A KIBBUTZNIK?

You are probably going to ask us why we are writing this book.
We are writing it because there is something about our
experience that is of great interest. You have no idea how many
visitors we get: students of the New Left, the Old Left, trade union
members—from America, Europe, North and South America;
singly, in groups—without end. People want to know what makes
us tick.

SAADIA

Some of the people are delightful. Some are snoopers. Some are
intolerable. Some ask very intelligent questions; they observe and
learn. Some, of course, see nothing, hear nothing, and go home
with the same distorted picture they had before they came here.

There is another reason: We ourselves are troubled by many and
profound uncertainties and we believe that perhaps by verbaliz-
ing our experiences, by describing our situation as we see it, we
may be able to find the answer to some of our problems. I think it
would be unfair for us to say that we now know it all. Today,
thirty years after it all began for me, I would like to say that for my
part I am happy and I am convinced I did the right thing. But the
questions I have had over the years have multiplied, and I do not
know whether we will be able to answer them all. Perhaps the best
way to start our book is by setting down the questions others have
asked us and the things which we ourselves already know.

YOSEF

I think it would be a good idea to begin by describing what you
see when you get off the bus here at Kfar Blum.

Ours is a setting which people sometimes describe as a country
club. There are spacious lawns, beautiful trees, a magnificent
swimming pool, and a wooden-bench sauna. There is a fine,
well-equipped high school—which serves not only Kfar Blum but
the entire surrounding area—and a nature study house. There are
comfortable living quarters, handsome dining halls, and farm

***Our
Kibbutz***

buildings of every description. There is a factory, there are sidewalks, there are nooks where people can sit, and places where you can go for a walk in the evening. There are tennis courts and fish ponds, and orchards and fields stretching out in every direction. The River Jordan flows right through our kibbutz.

On one side we have the Golan Heights from where the Syrians used to look down upon us. (Today, when we see the lights up there, we know they are our own people.) On the other side, you can see the hills of Lebanon. We sit in one of the most beautiful valleys in all of Israel, the Huleh Valley.

It is hard to compare Kfar Blum today with what it was like in the beginning. The house I live in sits on ground which used to be under water ten months out of the year, because this was once the northern end of the Huleh swamp. There was a period when we had 100 per cent malaria. Not today. We have no mosquitoes; flies are rare. The only animals we have running around are the children's pets—the dogs and the cats. The place is quiet and beautiful. That is how it is today.

When we first came to Kfar Blum back in 1943 there wasn't a tree for twenty-five miles around. Out in the fields there might be a lone tree, probably somewhere near the grave of an Arab holy man. The Arabs and the Bedouins who drifted into the area with their goats learned that there was a great deal of good to be gotten out of trees. The leaves were food for the goats, the branches could be used for fuel, and the bark yielded various dyes and medicines. Unfortunately the goats, after finishing off the leaves, started eating the bark also and that was the end of the tree. The next year the Arabs came back and took away the dead wood to use as fuel. The Arabs never thought in terms of reforestation, and so, over the centuries, they gradually denuded the land and the famed cedars of Lebanon survived only in legend.

When we set up our kibbutz the first thing we did was plant trees. Every year on *Tu Bishvat*[1] we added another grove. Today, we have thousands of trees here at Kfar Blum, and we have come to a point where at times we find it necessary to cut down some of them.

---

[1]The Arbor Day of Jewish tradition on the 15th day of the month of Shevat, which usually falls late in January or early in February.

Eretz Yisrael in the old days was nothing but swamp and   SAADIA
wilderness, so when Theodor Herzl started to dream of building
up this brand-new Jewish state of ours even he thought in terms of
agricultural settlements to reclaim our soil. Franz Oppenheimer[2]
then conceived the idea of cooperative settlements.

In 1909 Arthur Ruppin[3] decided that a model farm should be set   ***The Early***
up in Kinneret—near the Kinneret of today, on the Sea of Galilee.   ***History of***
Some of the people who trained on that model farm thought: Why   ***the Kibbutz***
not get together and settle down some place on a permanent basis,
with all of us sharing in the work and in the profits from our
labor? The idea of settling down in one place was something
revolutionary, because these trainees came from a workers'
movement which saw itself serving the land as a "mobile"
pioneering force.

You must remember that many of the workers who founded the   YOSEF
first kibbutzim came to Palestine from Russia where a revolution
had been put down only a few years before—in 1905—and where
the revolutionary spirit was still very, very active. So these
pioneers also considered themselves revolutionaries. To them,
their pioneering work in Palestine was part of that revolution.

Let us get back to the mobile pioneering force. The idea was to   SAADIA
wander from place to place to put yourself at the service of the
nascent Jewish society, whether it was to drain swamps or to open
up a new valley. But as these young nomads reached their early
twenties, some of them felt that perhaps it would not be such a
bad idea to settle down somewhere. There were some who
frowned upon that: They felt that settling down would deprive
them of the freedom to serve wherever they were needed.

Anyway, a man named Yosef Bussel[4] and eight others got
together and obtained[5] a tract of land at Umm Juni, on the east

---

[2]Economist, sociologist and Zionist (1864–1943). Oppenheimer's ideas greatly
influenced the development of the cooperative settlement in Israel.

[3]Organizer of agricultural settlements and member of the Zionist Executive
(1876–1943).

[4]Pioneer Labor Zionist (1891–1919). He was instrumental in formulating the
theoretical and practical principles of kibbutz life.

[5]From the Palestine Office of the World Zionist Organization.

bank of the Jordan. There, at Umm Juni, was founded the first of
our kibbutzim, or collective settlements. It was named Degania
Aleph. "Degania" was for the cornflowers which are abundant in
the Jordan Valley. "Aleph" meant that this was supposed to be the
first in a whole string of Deganias: Degania Aleph, Bet, Gimmel,
Daled,[6] and so on. But the settlers never got beyond Degania Bet.
The people who set up Degania Bet were even more revolutionary
than those at Aleph. They said that what they were doing at
Aleph—sharing all the profits among the members of the
group—was not going far enough. The people of Degania Bet
wanted to establish "a total, true collective," as they put it. So, if
you really want to know the story of the kibbutz movement, it
begins with Degania Bet.

The kibbutz movement is now roughly sixty years old and we
have evolved to a point where Yosef Bussel would not recognize a
kibbutz if he saw one.

YOSEF   Let me add something about the early days. As I have said
before, the pioneers who founded Degania in 1912 were under the
spell of the revolutionary spirit. Therefore anything that smacked
of the bourgeois world was abhorrent to them. The women, for
instance, said that a female who adorned herself to attract men
was acting contrary to the laws of nature. However, you must not
think that there was no sex life in those kibbutzim—because there
was. Otherwise Degania Aleph would not have been followed by
Degania Bet and all the rest!

But the early kibbutzniks felt that people must live as close to
the earth as they possibly could, even to the point of resembling
the earth in the clothing they wore. They wore khaki clothes and
nothing which could be construed as personal adornment. The
women tied their hair back to keep it out of their eyes. A room was
simply a place you slept in. You lived, worked and ate together.
You took your meals in the communal dining hall. All the
equipment was owned communally, and you even used the
amenities in common as much as possible. Take clothing, for
example. Nobody had clothes of his own. All clothing was cared

---

[6]The first four letters of the Hebrew alphabet also stand for the numerals 1, 2, 3 and
4.

for and laundered in the kibbutz "clothing center." On Fridays, or whenever it was that they gave out clean clothes, you would go to the clothing center and say, "I need a shirt size such-and-such and a suit of underwear." (They did not have socks in those days.) You were not supposed to say, "I want this, and not that, because this looks better on me." You wore clothes because you needed them for the protection of your body, not to enhance your appearance.

Those early pioneers were true idealists. They wanted to build a new world, where people would not exploit one another. In their view, the way to achieve this goal was through a communal society, which they saw as the ultimate ideal for a proper and more equitable way of life, something in which I personally still believe today. Of course, they went just a little too far. In time, certain things in the kibbutzim changed. People today tell us, "Well, you are not a kibbutz any more. You are becoming just like the capitalist world." But that is not true. Of course we like to dress well, to be comfortable, and to have our rooms look nice. We also want to have personal belongings, our own hobbies. But we do not think that this in any way changes the basic ideology of our kibbutz.

By the way, there is a question of nomenclature here. A *kibbutz*   SAADIA is sometimes referred to as a *kvutza*. What is the difference between the two? Actually, very little. The word *kibbutz* simply means "a gathering," a group of people who have gotten together. A *kvutza* is something on the same order. Etymologically, there is no difference between the two terms. There was one slight distinction in the early days: a *kvutza* was supposed to be a small, intimate place, a highly selective group that lived together as one large family, while a *kibbutz* implied a movement which thought in terms of a broader society and industrial growth; it took in people from all walks of life, accepting anyone who wanted to join and who the other members felt would fit in.

Underlying the idea of the kibbutz are two fundamental motives: Zionism and socialism. Unquestionably the more important of the two is Zionism—the desire to build a Jewish state in the land from where we originally stemmed, to return to the place where our ancestors made history, and where we Jews of today and tomorrow will be able to work out our destiny and be a little creative, too.

In talking about the early pioneering days, the turn of the twentieth century, we must remember that there were so few people in Palestine then that it was, for all practical purposes, a deserted and barren land. It is very important to remember this because if the Jewish pioneers would have had to displace an already existing native population, that would have conflicted with the second of the two principles on which the kibbutz idea is based—the humanitarian ideal of socialism.

But as the Jews developed the country, Arabs from surrounding lands began to stream into Palestine. And so a conflict did arise, and exists today. Further on, we will go into some ideas relating to ways of resolving this conflict.

However, the idea of the kibbutz was not just to achieve coexistence between the nationalist aspirations of Zionism and the universal ideals of socialism, but a fusion of the two. The pioneers wanted to create this fusion by practicing what they preached, by expressing their dreams and visions in their day-to-day lives. You could not do that as long as each individual lived for himself. The only way to do it was through the group: You organized a group of dedicated people who would live together, go through struggles together, make mistakes, and evolve a new life-style of their own. That is why there really was no blueprint for the kibbutz. Beyond certain clear-cut, basic concepts, the details developed differently from kibbutz to kibbutz. Naturally, over the years, some of the original naive, idealistic aspirations have undergone considerable change.

Let us look at some of the basic aims of the kibbutz movement. The kibbutz was part of the workers' movement, but its purpose was not to take people who were already workers and to organize them into a collective community. The aim of the kibbutz was to take Jewish intellectuals and turn them into workers. This idea attracted thousands of people. But there were hundreds who quit because they found out it was not for them. Still, if you were to take a census today you would find that perhaps one-third of Israel's present Jewish population had some kind of contact with the kibbutz movement at one time or another.

The kibbutzim, by the way, were never in the urban areas but out on the frontier. This was in keeping with their purpose. Wherever there were swamps to be drained, wherever there was rocky terrain, wherever there was danger of attack from nomads or infiltrators, you had a kibbutz. As a matter of fact, if you look at a map of Israel today, showing only the kibbutzim, you will see that the kibbutzim closely follow the borders of Israel. These outlying places are the most dangerous, the least attractive, and the ones that offer the greatest challenge to people who want to be pioneers.

The kibbutz movement hoped that it would be able to do two important things: one, to evolve a cadre of pioneers devoted to the service of the nation, and two, to turn out a new, better type of human being. In the first aim, they succeeded. But whether their second hope came true—that is a question mark. In the early days, the kibbutzniks really thought that it was possible to change people by changing their way of living. But over the years we have learned that the basic pattern of the human personality is quite firmly set, so that a change in life-style won't make very much difference. Society can help the individual overcome some of his deficiencies, and help guide his behavior. But while it can change his patterns of behavior, it cannot basically change him either physically or psychologically. We should keep this in mind later on when we talk about the kibbutznik to see what he looks like and how he acts.

The kibbutz concept is simple enough to define. But when it is translated into individual lives and daily group interaction, we find that kibbutz life does not always fit the stereotype. It is one of the curious complications of kibbutz living that it is akin to a religious discipline; every aspect of behavior must somehow be squared with the total concept, but it generally is not quite so simple to follow the rules.

At this point you may ask: What kind of people join a kibbutz? Most of the people who came to our own kibbutz from America, England and South Africa were products of Zionist youth movements. We Americans had been members of Habonim and Hehalutz.[7] We came here because we felt that the natural result of

YOSEF

Who Joins a Kibbutz?

---

[7]Labor Zionist youth movements which train their members to live as pioneers in Israel.

our being in the movement was to come to Israel and to live in a
kibbutz. In our kibbutz, and in many other kibbutzim as well, the
nucleus was an organization-oriented group. Many kibbutzniks
came to this country as refugees from Nazism, especially during
the 1933–39 period. Boys and girls were brought to Israel by
Youth Aliyah and sent to kibbutzim for training. They arrived
here at the age of twelve or thirteen and were raised in a kibbutz.
Naturally, a large number of them remained there. Other refugees
came to the kibbutz with their families in the hope that perhaps
this new way of life would be a solution to the Jewish problem.
So, a kibbutz might be started by a group of pioneers who came
from the same country, or perhaps from two countries. They had,
more or less, a common background.

Another source of kibbutz members has been *Nahal,* or *Noar
Halutzi Lohem,* an elite unit which organizes groups of boys and
girls in the pre-military stage as potential kibbutz groups. When
they subsequently join the army, they join as a group, and when
they have finished their three years in the army, they either join an
existing kibbutz as a group or they may set up a new kibbutz of
their own.

SAADIA   You always have to remember that the kibbutz is basically a
creation of youth. It was conceived by young people, it attracted
young people, and it is still a young people's idea.

But now what about the American Jews who came to Kfar Blum
and to many other kibbutzim? For the most part, these included
two types of individuals: those with European backgrounds who
had the same ideas about the survival of Jewish culture and the
same aspirations as their counterparts in Europe, and the
native-born Americans, whose motivation was entirely different
—they were dissatisfied with the social structure of the United
States.

It is customary nowadays to assume that the New Left has
discovered social equality. Some of the college kids today talk as
though they were the first to have reached the conclusion that it is
time to improve society, that it is necessary to have love rather
than hate relationships among human beings. Some of these
youngsters would be amazed to discover that we in the early

1930's went through almost the same stages and the same problems.

When the crash of 1929 shattered the basic optimism of the progressive American capitalists, and it dawned on people that this spiral of getting ahead and becoming rich could collapse, many young people began to consider the issues and purposes of life, the meaning of society, the objectives of personal and social development and the interrelationships between nations. All those big, complicated, insoluble issues plagued the younger generation of 1929 no less than they do the young people of today.

Those of us who were Jews had an added, complicating factor: the rise of anti-Semitism. We saw Hitler in the distance. We realized that we were being hurt not only as human beings but as Jews. We found ourselves at an impasse in American society.

So we had a dream. Why shouldn't we solve several problems at one shot, build a new society, and really take the world by the scruff of its neck and lift it up? We wanted to do all this as Jews; to develop a new country, and establish a haven for refugees and for any others who might want to come. So, we got together and evaluated the fledgling Zionist movements in the United States. When we started to look around we found that they were very small, very poor, and not at all satisfactory. We thereupon decided to establish a movement of our own. In the early 1930's we set up Habonim, an educational youth organization whose purpose was to combine Zionism, socialism and pioneering. We hoped that our graduates would become Zionists, socialists and pioneers.

Of the thousands who went through our ranks, many dropped by the wayside. But enough remained so that those who are here in the kibbutz today have been able to realize an ancient dream. When we came here to Israel we found young people like ourselves, with the same dreams as our own. It was natural for us to join them and to work together with them.

The nucleus of Kfar Blum consists of pioneers from America and England and the Baltic countries. Later on, we were joined by others from thirty-odd countries of the world.

For fully half of its sixty years of existence, the kibbutz movement and its ideology bore the stamp of youth. The big issue today is: Can the kibbutz adjust itself to an aging population? We are quite used to the fact that about every two or three years some journalist writes an obituary about the kibbutz. The earliest of these obituaries dealt with the advancing age of the kibbutz members. Some thirty years ago there were wise observers who said, "It is impossible for the kibbutz to survive. The kibbutz was established by and for young people; obviously, therefore, as soon as the population ages, the kibbutz will die." Since we have refused to die of old age, people have found other possible causes for the imminent demise of the kibbutz.

YOSEF   Margaret Mead, the famous anthropologist, once visited our kibbutz and told us that America began to degenerate when the Americans finished killing off all the Indians. She wanted to know what we would do once we had solved our problems. I think that the problems of the kibbutz are probably no fewer today than they were thirty years ago, perhaps even greater. To the extent that Israel has the right to call itself a young, new and dynamic country, I think the kibbutz can claim the same description.

SAADIA   Youth *per se* is a neutral word. *Youth culture,* which is supposed to connote freshness, vitality, dynamism and life, does not necessarily fit that image. Young people do many foolish things. The early kibbutz did some of the silliest things just because of lack of experience. For example, socialism and the idea of sharing everything brought up the problem of what to do about combs. Combs, after all, were comparatively inexpensive. Could we arrange, we wondered, to buy each individual a comb of his own? Certainly it would have been more pleasant from the esthetic point of view, but socialism forbade it. So we did not buy combs for each individual, and the kibbutz comb continued to go from one *haver*[8] to the next. Perhaps in the early days they even shared toothbrushes, though I find this hard to believe.

People tend to the "old oaken bucket" illusion that the "good old days" were all romantic and good. But I would not like to repeat my early days here at Kfar Blum back in 1947. Mud, swamps, cold, and miserable food. I do not think there is any

---

[8]"Comrade," "friend." The term *haver* (plural: *haverim*) or its feminine form *havera* (plural: *haverot*) also refers to any member of a kibbutz.

romance in that. Youth, in that respect, is a marvelous thing. We can survive anything when we are young.

Don't get the idea that everybody came to the kibbutz for the same reason. Not everybody was an idealist. Today, as I look around and see my own *haverim*—and there are a few hundred of them now—I realize that the kibbutz is a cross-section of society where the people, even though many, or most of them, are idealists, all have the idiosyncracies, the faults and virtues of people in any other form of society, whether it be a big city or a small town, or whether it be in Israel, in America or East Africa. People are people. YOSEF

We came to the kibbutz for different reasons. I came—and I am proud of it—because I had an ideal. I believed in something, and wanted to carry it out. Many came for that same reason. Others came to the kibbutz because they were refugees and had no other place to go. They were looking for a haven and we gave them that.

Some came to the kibbutz because they needed security, and the kibbutz gave them economic security; it gave them a feeling of having a home, a family (many of them had lost their families in World War II) and a place to live. The kibbutz gave them work in which they may not have been interested, but they knew that no matter what they did they would receive the same amount of food as everybody else and they would get their housing by seniority. They would not have to worry about making a living.

There were those who came merely because they were natural-born adventurers; they wanted to try something new. Some came because of personal problems. One woman came because she had recently been divorced; she was heartbroken and she wanted to get away from her old environment. One bewildered widower came because he did not know how to handle his three daughters alone. There was a man who joined because he wanted to be a vegetarian, and a girl who wanted to be a tractor driver. There was a boy who wanted to have a quiet place where he could do his eight hours of work each day and then read a book and not have to worry about anything else. And there was the woman who said, "I want to have children but I also want a career. I don't want to be just a housewife."

There were those who came because they were interested in solving social problems. One man joined because he wanted to participate in this interesting social experiment and in our method of bringing up children. Others came because they had friends here. There were single people looking for a wife, or a husband, and there were drifters who came because they were simply tired of drifting.

What happened to them all? I think that one of the people who made the best adjustment was a man who had not been born a Jew. He was converted fairly late in life. He happened to drift into the kibbutz. He had met somebody and wanted to stay here for a while. In the end he became a kibbutznik. We see this very often. There may be a hippie who says he wants to stay for a few months because he is interested in our work, or in certain people with whom he spends his time. Later, he feels he might like to try it out for a longer period. And then he settles down on the kibbutz; he gets married and starts a family.

Of all those who came, for all the various reasons that I have enumerated—and there are many more—you cannot remember after a number of years what their motive was, nor is it really very important. Since they have accepted the kibbutz for what it is, and they are part of the kibbutz, their contribution is no smaller than mine.

As I have said before, our people have their pluses, their minuses, their idiosyncrasies, and their faults. We even have those who came because they figured this was an easy life; you don't have to work too hard and you get fed just the same. Anybody can go into the dining room of a kibbutz and get food; nobody even asks who you are. The point I am trying to make is this: We are just normal people. The people who live in a kibbutz are not crackpots, nor are they fanatics. They are not characters with fire in their eyes and their heads in the clouds, dreaming dreams all the time. You don't have dreams very often when you are cleaning out a barnyard. Chickens smell. We do most of the work because it has to be done, not necessarily because we like it.

Farming is a mixture of bad smells and back-breaking work—just like almost any other job. I have a feeling that very often visitors look upon us as being somehow superior, or "different" or "weird." But we are not superior, nor are we weird, nor are we really different from anybody else.

Friends or relatives come from America to visit us, and after spending a few hours with us they say, "But you haven't changed. You're just the same as you always were." Why should we have changed? We *are* the same as we always were.

We have learned that the individual who is a 100 per cent kibbutznik may be the one who finally decides that if he cannot have perfection in the kibbutz, he might as well leave and forget about the whole thing. So you will find that a kibbutz will consist of the not-so-100 per centers—individuals who are willing to make compromises, except on essentials, of course. A flexible individual is able to ride out the difficulties. It is the perfectionist, the zealot, who is apt to break. Sometimes he uses it as an excuse for escape; sometimes he really has a crisis in his life; but very few of the perfectionists remain on the kibbutz.

There are now in the State of Israel close to 240 kibbutzim with a total population of roughly 90,000—half adults and half youngsters, if we take age 18 as the dividing line. Of these 90,000, maybe 10 are perfectionists. The other 89,990 are reasonably normal human beings.

2

HOW A KIBBUTZ IS GOVERNED

Most of Israel's kibbutzim are oganized on a national basis. YOSEF There are three major national kibbutz federations and several minor ones. Our own kibbutz, Kfar Blum, belongs to the **The** *Ihud HaKvutzot V'HaKibbutzim.* With its eighty-three constituent **Central** kibbutzim, this is the largest of the three major federations. It is **Organi-** the least dogmatic; it has accepted groups from many different **zations** backgrounds. But it identifies with Mapai, the ruling labor party here in Israel.

HaKibbutz HaMeuhad has fifty-eight member kibbutzim. It stands for active service to the nation, and for strong socialist awareness combined with activism in matters of defense and foreign policy.

The third major federation is the *Kibbutz Artzi* of the left-wing *HaShomer HaTza'ir,* which has seventy-five affiliated kibbutzim and identifies with our Mapam party.

The Liberal (General Zionist) party, which is non-socialist, has its own small federation, to which six kibbutzim belong. Most of the dozen or so religious kibbutzim belong to *Kibbutz HaDati,* which has a working arrangement, but no direct affiliation, with our own *Ihud HaKvutzot V'HaKibbutzim.*

There was at one time a single Communist kibbutz, but to all intents and purposes it no longer exists. The right-wing Herut party also tried to organize kibbutzim but they did not succeed.

The national kibbutz federations all belong to the Agricultural Center, which in turn is part of the Histadrut, Israel's general federation of labor.

The general kibbutz movement has central offices, mostly in Tel Aviv, which carry out a number of functions. Certain technical jobs, such as the purchase of clothing and shoes, can be done by a national office much better than by the individual kibbutz. The central offices have a large clothing center where the purchasing agent or the member in charge of clothing from each affiliated kibbutz can come, see what is available, and get goods more cheaply than he would if he went from store to store. There is a central purchasing department to deal with major items such as fuel, fertilizer, grain and building materials. In this way you can get better credit, and you pay less than you would if each kibbutz were to go out on its own to make these purchases.

The central kibbutz organization also represents its member kibbutzim in governmental bodies and in other activities that have to do with our relationship to the State. However, each kibbutz may also conduct these functions through representatives of its own.

Every kibbutz has a certain amount of autonomy in the overall kibbutz movement and in the national associations. The super-bodies do not interfere with the day-to-day operation of the individual kibbutz.

Perhaps we should point out here that kibbutzim do not have constitutions or by-laws—only rules and regulations about such things as how many hours per day a person should be required to work after he reaches a certain age. By and large, the members live by ideals rather than by codifications of these ideals.

However, not all kibbutzim feel the same way about written constitutions, nor do they all allow their members an equal amount of latitude. One kibbutz movement, the *Kibbutz Artzi*, is more rigid. The *Ihud HaKvutzot V'HaKibbutzim*, to which Kfar Blum belongs, is considered more liberal.

Let me give you a case in point—political thinking. In our *Ihud* kibbutzim a member may be known to support a political party other than the Mapai and vote for it in national elections. The member might even ask the kibbutz to pay his dues to that party because this is the party he wants to support. As long as the party does not represent a real deviation from kibbutz labor ideology, this is his own choice. We believe in "live and let live." There are kibbutzim, on the other hand, which say, "If you want to belong to our kibbutz you must hold our political views, or our religious beliefs."

Incidentally, kibbutzim are not all based solely on agriculture any more. In fact, there are very few kibbutzim today which do not run a manufacturing enterprise of one sort of another. Some of these factories are very big. One kibbutz in the Jordan Valley, for instance, manufactures formica and plywood for the entire country; a lot of it goes for export. Netzer Sereni[9] turns out huge trailers, military equipment and rolling stock for the trucking industry. Several kibbutzim may get together and set up a jointly-owned cannery or knitting mill. There is a paint factory which is owned jointly by a number of kibbutzim. These industries may employ as many as three to five hundred people.

So, a kibbutz needs engineers, teachers, and a great many other specialists. You may ask, then, why all the kibbutzim still belong to the Agricultural Center. It is probably an inheritance from the early days when the kibbutz, in order to exist, had to be primarily agricultural. Too, there was a time when we felt that if you wanted to be a good Zionist, a good socialist and a good kibbutznik you had to be a worker on the soil. But as we drained the swamps, got rid of the mosquitoes and settled on the land near the border or in one of the outlying areas, we were confronted with the problem of reassessing the role of agriculture in the modern State of Israel.

When kibbutz boys like my son came home from the army and took an interest in technical matters, and electronics began to have an ever-growing impact, the kibbutzim began to realize that industry was not a dirty word, and many of them set up factories ranging from small workshops employing three or four people to large industries employing as much as 30 per cent of the working population of the kibbutz.

We are still farmers but we no longer ignore industry. We feel that by being industry-minded we can develop a small plot of land more fully than we could otherwise. Besides, having a variety of trades and industries gives our people additional outlets for their skills and ambitions and so, in the long run, they will be happier kibbutzniks.

As we said a while ago, when we talked about the people who   SAADIA

---

[9]Kibbutz originally founded in 1948 by survivors of Buchenwald. It is named after Enzo Sereni, one of the Palestine parachutists dropped behind enemy lines by the British during World War II. Sereni was captured by the Germans and died in Dachau.

join kibbutzim, a kibbutz usually starts out with a nucleus of young people from the same group, or the same area, or from the same city or country abroad. This nuclear group receives an allocation of land from the settlement authorities—originally this was the Jewish Agency, but nowadays it is the Ministry of Agriculture or the Ministry of Defense. Individuals who want to join this nuclear group after that point have to apply to the group for membership and must be accepted by majority vote.

The   This brings us to the question of how a kibbutz is governed. The
General kibbutz, as you have probably heard many times before, is a pure
Meeting democracy. The governing body of each kibbutz is the kibbutz meeting, or the general meeting, which is very much like the old New England town meetings, where any citizen could come to express his views, air his grievances and raise issues. In almost every kibbutz there is a general meeting once a week, usually on Saturday night. Anybody at the kibbutz, man or woman, who is eighteen or older and has been accepted as a member, can come and vote at these meetings.

One of the functions of the general meeting is to pass on applications for membership in the kibbutz. A prospective member has to be a candidate for a year before his application is voted upon. As a rule, before he becomes a candidate, he has lived in the kibbutz for three months as a "guest." This gives the kibbutz plenty of time to find out whether he is an escaped convict or is mentally or morally unfit—in short, anything that might automatically disqualify him. If he survives these three months, he becomes a "candidate." As a candidate, he has all the duties and privileges of membership except that he cannot vote at the general meetings. During his year of candidacy, the membership committee gets reports from the work committee and from the other kibbutz members about his work, his conduct, and about whether he would really fit in. By the time a person has lived in the kibbutz for a year, the members have come to know him quite intimately, so when the membership committee recommends that a candidate be accepted as a member, the general meeting as a rule accepts him.

A kibbutz in a very real sense is a large family, an "in" group. Accordingly, the membership committee may reject a candidate if, in their opinion, he will not fit into their particular kibbutz—maybe for a reason as simple as age. If most of the members of the kibbutz are twenty-five a person of forty-five may be turned down because he would be too much of a "father figure." Each kibbutz sets its own age limits for new members. A candidate might be found unacceptable because of his personal habits. Nobody will jeopardize a community by taking in a new person who does not seem very savory. In short, the kibbutz has the right to accept or reject any applicant for membership. By the same token, a guest or a candidate may change his mind about staying; members, too, are free to leave at any time. It is a close but strictly voluntary society.

Aside from membership applications, what other topics may be discussed at a general meeting? Just about everything and anything, as long as it has been placed on the agenda and announced in advance so that members with a special interest in the subject will be sure to attend.

I will give you just a few examples of problems that have been brought up at our own general meetings here at Kfar Blum. One of our members had grown a tree and tended it for over five years, but one day the person in charge of construction work said it would have to be cut down because a sidewalk was going to be laid over that particular spot. When the man in charge of construction work came to chop down the tree, our member refused to let him do it. The matter was reported to the kibbutz secretary, who tried to explain to the member that, after all, he had the welfare of the whole kibbutz to consider. Our member, on the other hand, argued: "Why can't you have the sidewalk by-pass the tree, or move it a little to the left? Why does my tree have to be cut down to make room so you can lay a sidewalk?" The secretary answered that he could not allow one member's tree to interfere with the building plans of the kibbutz. In the end, the problem was brought before the general meeting. Unfortunately for the poor fellow, the general meeting ruled that the tree would have to go, and he had to accept that decision.

Then there is the problem of travel abroad. According to our rules at Kfar Blum, individuals who have belonged to the kibbutz for a certain period of time and have not been abroad are permitted a trip abroad, with expenses paid by the kibbutz. But what about a married couple, where both husband and wife have the required kibbutz seniority but where one partner has already been abroad once? The committee dealing with this problem decided that the one who had not yet had his turn could go, but not the other partner. The question was brought before the general meeting, which very wisely referred it back to the committee for further consideration.

At most kibbutz meetings there is a question and answer period, which can range over the whole gamut of life. Why haven't the houses been painted? Since when can the new administration arbitrarily decide to cancel the weekly movie? Can't you do something about the cats?

YOSEF   Sometimes we have a serious, pressing problem, and then we discuss it at the general meeting as you would in a family. There was the time when one of our children had to go to America for open-heart surgery. We had no provision for that in our budget, of course. The little girl and her mother would have to stay in New York for quite some time. How were we going to pay for that? We certainly did not want to go out and ask people for donations to pay for the plane tickets, and so forth. The general meeting decided that we would take the funds out of our daily budget. First of all, every member agreed to give up one day or so of his year-end vacation. Translated into working hours, that took care of part of the expenses. Secondly, we agreed to cut down on certain other expenditures. We would buy one tractor less or make an old tractor do for another year; we would not paint as many houses as we had planned to do that year, and so forth.

Another time, there was a proposal that all the smokers in the kibbutz should cut down on their weekly cigarette rations by 20 or 25 per cent. This raised a tremendous brouhaha at the meeting, for while the non-smokers thought this was a very good idea, the smokers felt that the non-smokers should not be allowed to vote on the issue. After a heated debate, it was decided to put the question to a trial vote. It seemed that the argument was not about the idea of smoking as such; a large majority had voted for the reduced ration and the smokers had agreed to the cut. Rather, the question had been one of principle: Did non-smokers have the right to express an opinion as to who should smoke, and how much?

In addition to acting as the governing body, the general meeting is also the sole disciplinary authority in our kibbutz. We very rarely need such an authority but we feel that when, say, one of our members calls another member a bad name, something should be done about it by the community. There was one case when a fellow hit another man in the mouth—why, I don't remember. Anyway, the matter was referred to a committee, and it was decided that this sort of behavior should be censured in strong terms at the general meeting. That was the end of the matter.

Some people who come to visit us ask how a big community like ours, with hundreds of members, can get along without a police force, or a jail. How do we punish people who do not want to work, or who commit crimes? **SAADIA**

Let us start with the parasites—the people who do not want to work. Let us get one thing straight: The people who live on a kibbutz usually came there because they held certain convictions. At the very least, they came with some understanding of what they were getting into. They knew that in this society certain things were expected of them. They knew that they would have to live with other people, and to put in a day's work. As a result, the vast majority of people on kibbutzim are not free-loaders. The parasites usually stay away. But it is interesting to see what the kibbutz does about those few whom we get from time to time. **YOSEF**

Our chief weapon is public opinion. A person who does not pull his weight is usually looked down upon, even though people may not express it in so many words. He will not be given a position of responsibility. No one will listen to his opinions and he will never become a real "insider" on the kibbutz. We will be polite to him because he is a member of our community, but we will not be overly friendly.

Now, supposing he simply refuses to work, and does not even make the pretense of working. Well, then, first of all, we will ask ourselves: Do we really want him around? Maybe he has a fine wife, who is a hard worker, and two wonderful kids. In that case we may decide that he is a burden we will simply have to live with, a wart on the skin of the kibbutz—unsightly but not really doing much harm. We will keep him here because of his family.

We will try to find out the reasons for his behavior. We will ask the doctor. Maybe there is something physically wrong with him. If he agrees to go, we will send him to a psychiatrist, or to a counselor for vocational aptitude testing. Maybe we just haven't found the kind of work he would really like to do. Perhaps we should try to give him work he will find more congenial. We will give him as much help as we can.

But when it comes down to real disciplining, there is very little we can do. We can invite the problem *haver* to come before the membership committee, and they will ask him what is wrong, and why. If he has any complaints he can present his point of view and the committee will make suggestions. He may be publicly censured at a general meeting. If worst comes to worst, of course, we can tell him to leave the kibbutz. We can give him two, three or four months to shape up or get out. We have very few cases like that, but if we really want to get rid of somebody and he says he does not know what he will do or where he can go, we can handle that, too. We had two such cases here at Kfar Blum; we gave each of them large sums of money and found them jobs and even housing in the city just so they would leave, because they were not doing their share and acting as one should as a member of a kibbutz.

As for criminals, I should say that the incidence of crime on kibbutzim is practically nil. A kibbutz, like any city, town or village, is part of the State and the State has a police force on which we could call to deal with criminals but except for petty thefts—which are very rare—in the quarters of the temporary workers whom we take in from the outside, we have never had to cope with a crime problem. Oh, there is petty lawbreaking galore. For instance, we have tractor drivers who exceed the speed limit or who insist on driving their tractors in the residential areas of the kibbutz. If it is just a youngster of fourteen or fifteen, we let our school handle it. If it is an adult, the farm manager will tell him off, and if he is really a chronic offender we will forbid him ever to drive a tractor again. But we have never needed a police force to settle problems like that.

To get back to ordinary aspects of kibbutz government, the general meeting is the supreme authority in the kibbutz, but it obviously cannot deal with the details of day-to-day activities. The work of supervising the daily functions of the community is divided between the elected officers of the kibbutz and the various committees. *SAADIA*

Let us start with the officers. The number of officers changes as the kibbutz gets older. As long as a kibbutz is young, it must have a very alert and active individual to represent it to the outside. This *bakoah,* or representative, has to deal with the settlement authorities, the kibbutz movement, the Ministry of Agriculture, and so forth. He has to be wherever the planning goes on, to help the kibbutz to get started and to grow. *Officers and Committees*

As a kibbutz matures, the *bakoah* does less outside work and increasingly assumes the function of treasurer. His counterpart acting within the kibbutz is the *merakez meshek,* the general manager, or coordinator, who plans the economic development of the kibbutz. The administrative tasks of the general manager are shared by the *mazkir,* or secretary, who presides over the general meetings, receives official visitors and sees to it that all the committees are doing their job. As a rule, the *mazkir* is an *ex officio* member of all the committees on the kibbutz.

Each kibbutz also has a purchasing agent who goes out to purchase all the supplies needed by the kibbutz, its various working groups, and its individual members. On one trip into town, he may order tens of tons of cement, bags of cattle feed, some spare truck parts—and two dozen shoelaces.

The person who supervises and arranges the daily work schedule is the *sidur 'avodah,* or work manager.

These five officers—treasurer, general manager, secretary, purchasing agent and work manager—along with one, two or more individuals elected at large, constitute the kibbutz secretariat. In almost every kibbutz nowadays it is this secretariat that supervises the daily operations of the kibbutz in accordance with the overall policies laid down by the general meeting. The general meeting, in turn, delegates many of its functions to committees.

There are so many committees in every kibbutz that if you were to describe them all you would have to describe the whole life of the kibbutz community. For example, the economic committee deals with investments, expenditures, the budget and all other matters relating to the economic welfare of the kibbutz. In many kibbutzim the general meeting will only set overall guidelines and approve the annual budget, leaving the economic committee to cope with month-to-month economic problems. The welfare committee is a catchall for anything having to do with the individual member, his personal needs, his grievances, and his relationships with the committees and officers of the kibbutz.

There is a children's committee, a youth committee, and a committee for the care of aged parents.[10] There is also a committee on landscaping, and a committee on housing to allocate living quarters according to the rules set down by the general meeting. There is an athletics committee, and, of course, a cultural committee; culture is a very noble theme in any kibbutz. The cultural committee deals with holiday observance, special events, weddings, and it has charge of the kibbutz newspaper. Speaking of newspapers, there was a time when the entire kibbutz community had to share one newspaper; today there is one copy for every two families. In some kibbutzim every family is entitled to a copy of its own, and maybe someday every individual in the kibbutz will be able to have his own personal copy. You see, the days of the Messiah are coming closer all the time!

YOSEF   I would like to say something about how the various committees of the kibbutz function.

Let us start with the housing committee. Our kibbutz budget allows us to put up only so many new dwellings in a given year. It is the job of the housing committee to decide who is going to move into the new houses and it will submit various building

---

[10]In some kibbutzim, the aged parents of members are invited to live in the community; other kibbutzim send regular allowances to parents living outside the kibbutz and in need of financial support.

plans for the kibbutz to choose from. When the houses have gone up, the housing committee is responsible for the allocation of the dwellings, the painting, minor repairs, and the maintenance of elementary comforts and amenities.

Now let us look at the committees that deal with the problems of individual members. Supposing I feel that I would like to go back to school. (This is not just my personal problem—it involves the whole kibbutz, because the kibbutz pays the tuition fee. We will go into that later.) I would go to the committee in charge of adult education and tell them what subject I want to study, and where. The committee would then decide whether the kibbutz can afford to send me to school, whether I can be spared from my work, and whether they approve of the course or courses I want to take. They would not say no if I said I wanted to study some purely abstract subject, but they would want to know more about my interests and my plans, and perhaps even give me some advice if I am amenable to it. If the committee does not approve of my plans, I can always appeal to the general meeting, which then calls upon the committee to give its reasons for not approving my request. Very often, the general meeting overrules the committee; sometimes, it refers the matter back to the committee for review.

All the committees make a sincere effort to meet the needs of the members. On the other hand, members do not usually come to the committees with proposals that are not important. There has to be mutual understanding of one another's problems, otherwise the whole thing would not work.

What is it like to be a kibbutz officer? Let us start with the SAADIA *mazkir,* the kibbutz secretary. Here I can talk from personal experience because I myself once served a term as secretary of Kfar Blum.

The secretary of the kibbutz is the person who comes in contact **The Kibbutz** with every member, every visitor, and every worker on the **Secretary** kibbutz. At one time it was thought that the secretary could perform these functions in addition to his regular chores on the kibbutz. The original conception of the secretary's job was that he should devote a few hours after his regular workday to attend to the needs of his community.

In the early kibbutzim this was not very difficult. In a small community, where just three or four dozen people get together to discuss everything, and where everybody knows all that has to be done, you do not need anything more. In a new kibbutz, members are involved in every aspect of every problem, so that it really makes no difference who happens to bear the title of secretary; he is simply the individual who has been formally appointed to put the papers into a little order.

But all this changes when that small group grows into a large community, with diversified activities. Take Kibbutz En Harod, for instance, which runs a farm, a factory and an art center, and is involved in any number of outside enterprises—the transport and waterworks cooperatives in the area, the regional dairy, the maintenance of the En Harod natural preserve, various national youth organizations, and the national kibbutz movement. Under such circumstances the secretary's job is not only a full-time one but he must also have a full-time staff to assist him—stenographers, typists, and from time to time extra help to dig the office out of the mountains of papers which have a way of accumulating. In addition, he will need individuals who can be mobilized for special occasions—to receive visitors or to help out in such events as, in our own kibbutz, exhibitions at our museum, and so on.

As complicated as the public relations aspects of running the kibbutz may be, the problems of internal administration are infinitely more complex. Because when all is said and done, the visitors eventually leave; they either liked it at the kibbutz or they did not, but as far as we are concerned, our job is finished. It is not quite that easy with our own members. If a member comes with a complaint one day and he feels it is not being taken care of properly, he will come back the next day and the day after that until he gets satisfaction, or he gives in, or he brings his complaint to the general meeting.

The kibbutz secretary has to hop from the petty troubles of one member to a reception for a representative of the Ministry of Agriculture. He has to conduct the general meeting of the kibbutz and the weekly meeting of the secretariat, oversee the smooth operation of the various committees, manage the office and give out petty cash to the members when they need it. He also has to keep an up-to-date, accurate record of everybody who comes here.

In a period of national emergency we must know about each and every individual who enters our kibbutz, whether he has only come for the day or whether he wants to become a candidate for membership and stay for good.

While the job of the kibbutz secretary carries a lot of prestige and is in fact the highest office in the kibbutz community, it is not at all sought after. When the kibbutz has to elect a new secretary, instead of everybody wanting to be a candidate, the kibbutz has trouble finding someone who wants the job.

If you were to ask me what job in the kibbutz I wanted least, I would say the job of secretary. The secretary's day never ends. He may get awakened at 2 A.M. by someone who wants to report a real or imagined insult from another member, or by the police looking for a missing person or for a suspect who they think may have drifted into our kibbutz. You go to the kibbutz secretary for anything and everything. YOSEF

Perhaps one of the secretary's nastiest jobs is giving out petty cash from kibbutz funds. At any hour of the day or night people come to him and say: "Look, I'm going to town tomorrow on kibbutz business (or personal business)," and he will have to hand out the necessary cash. We do not have a bank in our kibbutz. When the money comes from your own personal allowance, which is provided for in the kibbutz budget, the transaction is relatively simple. There is no discussion, no argument. The secretary has to give you the money. But when someone goes to town and asks for money from the general funds of the kibbutz, it may be a little more complicated. Say, a mechanic has to go to Tel Aviv or Haifa for a day to take in some machine part for repair, or to call for a piece of equipment that has been fixed. He will say to the secretary: "For this trip into town I will need money for three meals, and a place to stay overnight. Obviously, you don't expect me to spend the evening just drifting around; I'll go to the movies. It's a hot day, so I'll buy myself a cold drink. I also will want to get a newspaper and a pack of cigarettes," and so forth. All these arguments sound reasonable and so, again, the secretary will give him the money, in keeping with procedure at that particular kibbutz.

But then there are all sorts of variations and personal quirks.

One man will say: "I'll have to be away for three days. When I come back, my little boy will expect me to bring him something, even if it's only a bag of peanuts or a little toy." Someone else may ask for additional cash because he is going to stop off and visit his sister and he just cannot go there empty-handed, because his sister brings a gift each time she comes to visit the kibbutz.

There are a dozen different kinds of special travel and gift allowances. For instance, people who have grandchildren living outside the kibbutz are given an allowance to go and visit their grandchildren. Someone else needs money to buy gifts for his children, or his mother, or his sister. The day is full of these problems, and a hundred and one others.

Knowing myself, I would say that if I were secretary I would probably stick it out with a smile on my face until about 10 o'clock in the morning. From 10 to 12 I would stop smiling, but I would still be reasonably affable. From 12 to 2 I would start getting a little gruff, and by 2 o'clock I would be shouting at people. At 4 they would probably take me away in a straightjacket.

The secretary has to be a person who can hold the job for a number of years, despite the fact that very often he will be criticized for practically everything he does.

The man who takes the job is considered a hero, but soon he is toppled from his pedestal and shown to have feet of clay by the very people who elected him and who knew this well in advance. Why anybody would want the job I do not know. And yet every time we need a new secretary we somehow find one.

SAADIA   As I have said before, I served my time as secretary, not too long after my arrival here. I think the kibbutz took advantage of the fact that I was a newcomer and did not quite know what was involved. When they impressed upon me that it was my duty to serve as secretary, I accepted and was elected.

For the most part I had no complaints, but some of the members posed problems. While I was secretary, we had a cultural chairman who was full of energy and new ideas. For the first holiday program he undertook to arrange he had plans, people and suggestions. I was very pleased. Here at last, I thought, we had a cultural chairman who would do extremely well. Then, just three days before the holiday, he told me that he had a very urgent personal problem and that he simply could not do anything for the program. He threw the whole thing into my lap. I was disappointed but I felt this was part of the package. This happened on Purim.[11] I made the best of it and somehow we survived that Purim. Then he began to plan for the next holiday, which was Passover. This time he had grandiose ideas. He had organized a committee and he had gotten everything all set. Then, one week before Passover—a repeat performance. Another emergency in his personal life, and once again I had to take over.

But a kibbutz secretary has to accept members as they are. To offset the shirker, there is always one "old reliable." I, too, had such a standby and I knew that I could always count on him in any emergency. I had a serious conflict with myself trying not to take advantage of his good nature and his readiness to cooperate. But the pressures were so severe that no matter how hard I tried, in the end I found myself turning to him all the time, until he began to have the feeling that I was exploiting both our personal friendship and his good nature.

The secretary has the problem of what to do with the people who demand and receive attention. If we were to take the 600 members of our own kibbutz, I think we would find there are 90 per cent who require 50 per cent of the secretary's attention and 10 per cent who require the other 50. How do you handle that 10 per cent? If, as secretary, you are polite and democratic and considerate, that 10 per cent will soon claim not 50 but 90 per cent of your time. On the other hand, if you cut them off brusquely or just bypass them, you protect yourself, but are you really doing your job? They are members who do deserve attention. So the secretary has to find a compromise between the legitimate needs of the members and the need to protect himself.

There are times when the secretary is faced with serious problems that are time-consuming, complicated, and sometimes insoluble. What do you do when a married couple breaks up and the secretary must decide which one of them is to get the room

---

[11]Holiday described in the Book of Esther, commemorating the deliverance of the Jews of Persia from the evil plot of Haman. Purim is celebrated with masquerades and merrymaking.

they shared? The husband and wife came to the kibbutz together and have the same seniority. They acquired their furniture together, and they lived together happily for a long time. But then they decide to separate; these things happen. There is no question that each partner is entitled to equal and satisfactory accommodations. But one of the partners has to pick up and move out of the room. Which one of them is it to be?

If the husband is a gentleman, he may say, "You, my former wife, my future friend—you make the choice. If you want to stay in our room you stay and I will move out. If you want to move out because of the memories, I will stay and you can leave." It is marvelous if the husband is a gentleman. It is almost as marvelous if the wife is a lady and she says, "You, my former husband and future friend—you make the choice."

But very often when it comes to separation, the husband is not always a gentleman, nor is the wife always a lady, but each of them will say, "I'm staying. You get out." Then the secretary is called in to mediate—really not so much to mediate, because neither of the partners wants mediation, but each of the partners wants him to tell the other person to move out.

Sometimes one meeting is sufficient to settle the question. Sometimes it takes three, or five, meetings, and the matter is taken to the welfare committee. And there are cases where it must be decided arbitrarily and one of the partners simply has to yield.

The secretary finds himself in a situation where he cannot even have meals without some urgent problem hanging over him. He sits down to breakfast, or lunch, or supper and somebody comes up to him and says, "Oh, it's good that I caught you. There's something I wanted to ask you." The same thing can happen when he wants go go to bed, or when he wants to lie down for a nap.

But the job has its satisfactions, too. First of all, you are in the center of the community's activities. Everybody in the secretariat knows how the kibbutz is progressing and what the plans are for the future; the people in the secretariat are involved in every important event, with every important visitor and in every important decision. You are not dealing with petty matters. When you draw up plans to pave a new walk you know that this walk is part of an overall layout which will ultimately connect all the walks in the area. When you have a building put up you know how it will fit into the general plan. When you buy a tractor you know how it will fit into the total tractor setup.

Being the secretary, or treasurer, or general manager of a kibbutz means that you will have direct contact with the outside world and meet interesting people.

YOSEF

Other Kibbutz Officers

Speaking of the treasurer, here is a typical discussion with the treasurer. I will ask him: "How are things?" He will reply: "Well, if you want to know the truth, money is very, very tight. I can't get any loans. Interest rates are sky-high. The people on the kibbutz are not working; our cotton fields look lousy. The cost of fuel is going up and I can't get credit, not even for a day. Not only that, the way the apples look, all we're doing is spending money on fertilizer and insecticides. I don't think our crops are going to be any good, either. Our operating costs are too high. Our standard of living is too high. We're eating too much and spending too much on clothes. We can't go on this way. I don't know what's going to happen. Every time I sign a check I have a feeling it's going to bounce. We have nothing in the bank. You want more housing? I don't know what we're going to do about it. I have no funds for housing. . . . All in all, it's been a fairly good year." That is typical.

The general manager does not have it easy either. He assigns a certain tractor to plow a field and then he finds that the tractor has broken down and is in the garage. I remember listening to one little conversation a few weeks ago. The manager was talking to the *haver* in charge of irrigation. He said, "Look, I hear that you didn't turn on the water in Section 6. You were supposed to give me four hours of water at a pressure of three atmospheres—about thirty-five pounds per square inch. What happened?" The *haver* replied, "Well, I would have given you the water at the hours you wanted, between two and six in the morning, but you forgot to have the pipes connected. What did you want me to do, just let the water spill out?" The manager gave him a sheepish look. He had forgotten to assign somebody to connect the network of pipes that were needed.

You get all sorts of problems. You get good years and bad years. The treasurer is the one who has to suffer when you have a bad year. The manager is the one who has to find ways of making up for the loss. Both of them will refuse to admit that we ever had a good year.

There is, for instance, the problem of weather. Early in May, three years ago, there was this discussion on the kibbutz: "Are we properly insured against natural catastrophes—floods, or insects? Let's take out some sort of insurance policy." We looked into the matter and decided that we were adequately insured. But then someone said, "Well, what about hail in the summer, or torrential rain?" "That's ridiculous!" came the reply. "In Israel you don't have hail or rain in the summer." Nobody was going to bother taking out crop insurance for such remote possibilities. That was that. Then, on May 31, a hot summer day when people were walking around sweating, the skies suddenly got dark and at 11:20 A.M. we had a hailstorm, with hailstones almost an inch in diameter. The storm lasted exactly 25 minutes and completely destroyed the apple crop, the pear crop, and the cotton which was just beginning to show its head. The cotton could be replanted easily enough, but every single pear and apple had been damaged. All our Class A fruit became Class B, and most of it turned rotten. We lost the entire crop, a loss of well over a million pounds.

In general, to be a manager or officer of a kibbutz means that the eyes of the kibbutz are upon you all the time. Your behavior must be circumspect wherever you go because you are traveling on kibbutz funds. At one time some people in the city would look askance at kibbutz treasurers. "Naturally," they would say, "When he spends time in town he finds something to do every night of the week—a play here, an opera or concert there, and a couple of movies." But in fact a kibbutz treasurer or any other kibbutz official who is away from the kibbutz on business for any period of time works very hard all day long. While he is in the city he eats at places we call kibbutz restaurants—usually cheap and not very exciting—and instead of staying at a hotel he rents a furnished room, not in the best part of town. At night he goes to bed early because he is too tired to do anything else. At the end of the week he makes the long journey home to the kibbutz, only to get caught up in a series of meetings and reports on the week's

the people in the kibbutz would no more think of giving up the weekly movie show than they would of skipping a meal. As a rule, the movies come from the Histadrut, which has a cultural department and a motion picture office. That office contracts for films which might be of interest to people in kibbutzim, moshavim, or outlying areas. A cultural chairman has available a list of about 800 titles, from which he may choose 52.

But no matter what movie he chooses, the members will have something to say. "Why so many mysteries? Why so many Westerns? Why so many foreign films? Why not more American, or English, or Russian films? Why musicals?" The poor cultural chairman can never be right. This would not be so bad if he did not have other jobs, too. He has to work on programs for holidays and special occasions. He has to make the arrangements for concerts and other performances—get the stage set up, have a reception committee to greet the artists, and arrange for the people who help him in these programs to get time off from their regular work on the kibbutz.

There is an endless variety of detail, as we have said before, and all committee chairmen work mostly on their own time. No matter what a kibbutz officer says, he must be very highly motivated and have a significant degree of social consciousness to withstand the criticism he gets in the performance of his duty, because the kibbutz tends to be very free with criticism and very sparing with compliments. This has changed a little, too, in recent years. The younger generation is much more direct and outspoken than we are. As a result, they are much more harsh in their criticism, but they can also be much more effusive in their praise.

3

WORK AS A VALUE

Probably the most complicated aspect of our entire lives here is labor. You must remember that with us labor is a goal, a necessity, and part of every aspect of our lives. Nevertheless, there are distinctions between labor as a way of life, on the one hand, and labor as an activity necessary for acquiring a certain good, on the other.

As Israel became more affluent and began to produce most of its own goods, many people began to feel that the time had come for them to get something for their labor. The slogan, "I've got it coming to me," has evolved as a distinct antithesis to the pioneering ideal that you have to go out to the swamps and do your share in building up the country. Many people assert that while they did not think in terms of gain to themselves during their pioneer days they now feel they ought to have some reward for what they have done. People who have survived the Nazi concentration camps said, "I've been through hell. I'm entitled."

There is no doubt that even in the kibbutz movement there has been a shift from the self-abnegation of the early days to a more commonplace egoism. But it would be a mistake to think that there was one point at which all the pioneering and sacrificing stopped and the "gimmes" began. The truth is that today the spirit of self-sacrifice and the "gimmes" operate simultaneously on the kibbutz. At what point can we permit ourselves as individuals to benefit from our own labors? Or, conversely, to what extent should we work for the common good without expectation of reward? There is no resolution for this problem because as we increase our potential and develop our economy, we certainly want to share in these benefits also as individuals.

On the other hand, if we individuals take too big a share of these benefits it may threaten the whole economy. Even worse, we may suddenly find that we have forgotten the basic reason for our

SAADIA

"Give and Take" on the Kibbutz

existence: the development of the community and of the ideals for which we organized. After all, our purpose in getting together was to settle the country, to develop it, and to make it possible for others to come. If we were to use up all the fruits of our labors and maybe even go into debt, we would jeopardize our potential for increasing our capital gains, which we need if we are to expand further so that we can absorb new members, including our own children.

YOSEF   Saadia keeps using the term "labor." I do not like this term; it smacks of labor pains, and labor disputes. The basis of our existence in the kibbutz is *work*. We work because we have to, and we judge a man by his ability to work well for the required number of hours—and a little bit more when he is called upon to do so.

Every one of us works willingly; some of us have to do things we do not like but we do them with good grace. This business of "I've got it coming to me; I deserve some sort of material reward," is irrelevant. A person may say, "After so many years of hard work, I would like to have a rest." But the idea that "I've got it coming to me" is not a serious problem in the kibbutz. Our people do not go looking for material gains. Our work carries the same remuneration whether you have been doing it for twenty years and enjoying it, or for thirty years and *not* enjoying it. The coin in which we are paid is the knowledge that we have done our share for our community.

Attitude   An applicant for membership in the kibbutz is judged not only *Toward*   in terms of his social adjustment on the kibbutz but also for his *Work*   ability to put in a good day's work. In the old days an applicant, during his year of candidacy, had to spend some time at work in every kibbutz activity; the idea was to let him prove that he was capable of doing every type of physical labor, of working very hard with a smile on his face and of getting along with the people he is working with. Today we try to employ people in their own trades and professions or, if they have no special training, to place them into jobs for which they are suited. But the point I am trying to make is that the ability to put in a day's work has been perhaps the major criterion by which a candidate for membership has been judged.

We cannot stress that point too much because to this day ability SAADIA
to work and attitude toward work still constitute the most
important single factor in our judgment of the individual.

Only a week ago, a city girl who married one of our boys came
to live on the kibbutz. The girl had been raised in Tel Aviv with
no background of physical work. She did not know what a potato
or a dishrag were nor did she know her physical abilities because
she had never tried them.

One day I said to her, "Never mind, you will learn. At our
hakhsharot[12] back in the States we got many a city girl who didn't
know whether potatoes came mashed, french-fried, sautéed or
boiled." Whereupon she turned on me with great impatience and
said, "My God, everybody here is always talking to me about
work, work, work. Is this the only criterion by which you judge a
person? Doesn't a person's artistic feeling, his emotional makeup,
count for anything? Is work the only thing you people know
about?"

Her emotional outburst was justified in her circumstances
because she found physical work extremely difficult. But unless
one clears the hurdle of work, unless a member proves that he or
she is working to full capacity, he will find that he will never be
completely accepted by the group, no matter what his "official"
membership status. This has nothing to do with production
volume. A person whose abilities are limited but who works to
full capacity within these limits will gain complete acceptance
and respect. Not so the shirker.

A man I know in one of the kibbutzim has made a career of
dodging the total productive capacity contained within him. I
have seen him putter around at a job for two or three hours in
order not to get to the actual performance. In the course of the
years he has become quite discontented because he thought he
was going to outsmart the entire group in the one area about
which we are all very sensitive: namely, doing our share. Yosef
has already described how our kibbutz handles people like that.

When you work in a group, there is a natural human tendency
to feel that you are giving your optimum. "I am really pulling a

---

[12]Plural of *hakhshara*; literally, "preparation." A *hakhshara* is a training center, or
training farm, set up by pioneer Zionist movements in diaspora countries to
prepare young people for a pioneering life in Israel.

big load, but those in front of me and behind me are doing a little less"—this feeling naturally creeps up on you unless you have full faith in the group within which you are working.

One of the reasons why the Israeli army has been so successful is the realization on the part of each individual soldier that those on his left and those on his right are all pulling an equal amount; in fact, they are vying with each other for bigger loads. This was also true in the kibbutz movement at certain periods and it is still true in every kibbutz today during its early stages.

But when a kibbutz has matured and the *haverim* get a little tired and a little more cynical, some people say, "Well, perhaps I really need not exert myself. Perhaps I really should relax." At that point there must be a rejuvenation of the pioneering spirit if the kibbutz is not to perish.

The reason why the kibbutz has survived is simply that at the critical juncture there has always been a return to the initial approach—pulling together for common goals. The problems of work and its psychological interrelationships, its relationship to our economy and to our ideology are all extremely complex. It is possible to develop cultural activities, an educational system and much else. But without the prerequisite of joint productive work the rest will not follow. This should be remembered by all those who want to establish communes and who believe that all they need to do is get together, find a plot of ground and just live. They will discover very quickly that "just living" is not enough. If they do not find a way of pulling together and working for a common ideal they will never be able to "just live"; they will just disappear.

One problem of our work on the kibbutz is that no one sees direct results from his efforts, but only collective results. If I plow a stretch of land, it does not mean that the fruit will be all my doing, because the harvest will depend upon many other workers who will follow me. All I do is drive a tractor. There are so many other people involved before my own plowing is translated into the food I eat, the clothes I wear, and the housing I get, that sometimes the direct connection between productivity and satisfaction is lost. In such a set-up it is possible to develop a notion of the community as the great provider who is supposed to give you everything. Let us say that I have lived in tents for three years and I want to move up to a wooden bungalow, and after a certain number of years to a regular house built of concrete. Instead of having to attend to my needs in an outhouse, I want, at long last, an indoor toilet and a shower. At that point the treasurer's argument that the community cannot afford it will not impress me. I will say, "If you would just economize on the fuel we are using for the tractors and save 10 per cent of our fuel bill you would be able to build me a house." Or, it is very easy to say that there are too many women working in the children's houses taking care of the children, and if you had only one woman for every five children instead of one woman for every four, that saving of labor could help build me my house.

But of course when the same calculation is made by 600 members of a kibbutz for thirty different branches of work, then obviously the saving will have to be divided among the 600 members and all it will come down to is that each one of us will be able to get one extra shirt, a pair of pants or a skirt.

What Saadia is saying is that by working only at one specific YOSEF phase of a job, you lose your contact with the end product; you don't associate the work you are doing with the financial situation, or the income, of the kibbutz. It is very difficult just to plow a field and to associate that with a harvest of corn or cotton which will not materialize until months later.

On the other hand, everybody takes a certain pride in the branch of work to which he has been assigned and in the income which that department is bringing to the community. In every department there is a tremendous *esprit de corps*. The fishermen know that when the market is bad, things in the kibbutz are not going to be so good. The boys in charge of the cotton—and they are the younger generation today—are confident that they are going to have a good year. In the showers, instead of talk about girls, you will hear, "Should we try this new machine?" or "How many pounds per acre do you think we will get out of the crop this year?" These men and women are deeply concerned with what goes on in their branch of activity.

A factory or workshop in the kibbutz has to have regular meetings with all the members of the kibbutz who are working in that factory or workshop because these *haverim* are sincerely interested in what is going on. They want to know whether the work they are doing is worth while or not. You have a feeling of family solidarity. Every department tries to do its very best, and persons working at other jobs may be called upon to help out, if necessary. For example, loading chickens onto trucks for marketing is done in turn by everybody in the kibbutz. You see your name up on the bulletin board as one of the ten people who must show up at 9 o'clock that evening to load the chickens. This is work that I dislike intensely, but it has to be done. My own attitude towards chickens is purely culinary. I cannot work up much enthusiasm for the live bird. Therefore, when I am called upon to load chickens I need to know whether that branch of activity is productive and what its special problems are. In this way I get the feeling that every branch of kibbutz activity belongs also to me. It is a very good feeling.

Each time I enter or leave Kfar Blum I look at the fields and say to myself, "These are our fields. Our cotton looks good. Our orchards look green," and I have the feeling that all of this belongs to me.

SAADIA   Our ideal pattern of work organization—let us take the fruit orchards—would be that every individual in those orchards would be a knowledgeable pioneer, an expert who knows that he is there for the purpose of growing the maximum amount of fruit to feed the population, developing the country, and getting full satisfaction from his agricultural pursuits. In practice, of course, it is quite different. There are people who work in the orchards because they have tried everything else and were not satisfied. There are temporary workers whom we bring in from the outside who are there to do exactly what they are told and to get the work done as quickly as possible so they can go back home to their records, or their volley ball game. There are people who go to the orchards the way Yosef goes to load the chickens onto the trucks. But if the orchards are to survive we must have a hard core of devoted workers, the kind I described at the start. Otherwise the orchard will not flourish.

What is the ratio between those *haverim* who choose a given job because they want to help develop a worthy branch of our agriculture and those who do the same job just on a temporary basis? Theoretically the ratio ought to be at least one to one; at least 50 per cent of the *haverim* should be knowledgeable, and devoted to that particular job. But in practice every department has different ratios and it shows up in the results.

What happens if there just are not enough workers for a job? **Extra** What do you do if the apples have to be picked at the end of the **Work** summer and there simply are not enough people to do the work? For one thing, we can ask any member who has done his own job for the required eight or nine hours to put in another hour or two in the apple orchard. We have devised what we call a "volunteer labor corps." At a general meeting we decide that we are all going to volunteer two extra hours a day, or two extra hours a week, during the apple picking season. Actually, this kind of arrangement is not exactly "volunteering" because once the decision has been made by a majority vote it is binding on every member, whether he agrees with the idea or not.

The arrangement for extra working hours, especially at crop picking time, has been a component of our system for decades. Since many different fruits have to be picked at the same time in the early fall, things get to be quite hectic. So, if you want to see a kibbutznik at his worst, come to look at him late in September when he is physically drained from the strain of the harvest.

Very often the volunteer hours are not sufficient to gather in all the crops. In that event, the kibbutzim have to resort to various ways of obtaining workers from the outside to do the job. The simplest and most obvious way is to hire workers from the Labor Exchange, pay them their wages and that is that. But this has endless complications. After all, the idea of the kibbutz is self-labor. The people of the kibbutz are supposed to do all the work with their own hands and to resort to outside assistance only for tasks which the individual members are absolutely unable to perform. In the early days this only meant engaging professionals—agronomists, doctors, engineers—for specific jobs that required assistance from experts who did not happen to live on the kibbutz. But as for engaging any other outside help, it was clearly understood that it was wrong for a kibbutz to hire workers.

The idea of "self-labor" grew out of the desire to become a

self-contained community as far as possible; but beyond that, there was the ideological argument that to hire a worker meant to exploit him. No matter how high his wages, a hired worker was the victim of exploitation, if not economic then certainly psychological. You had a situation where a "boss" was giving orders, imposing his ideas and his desires upon another human being.

Therefore, if the kibbutz needed additional workers, it tried to increase its labor force not by hiring extra labor but by getting new members. One result of the economic pressure for additional workers was the evolution from the small, select *kvutza*—based on the idea that the community should be small enough to constitute a sort of extended family—to the larger kibbutz. The reasoning was that if we needed more workers but could not get people who would fit exactly into our existing group, we simply had to stop being so choosy about whom we accepted and become a more open community. That is how the modern-day large kibbutz developed.

But even the large kibbutz did not solve the labor problem. There are two kinds of help that are absolutely essential for the existence and prosperity of the kibbutz—first, the specialists, about whom we have just spoken, and secondly, the temporary workers whom we need at special times, particularly during the harvest season.

In order to avoid violating the principle that the kibbutz should not hire paid labor, various kibbutzim evolved arrangements for obtaining temporary workers who did not take pay in the form of direct wages or salaries. These kibbutzim would take in youth groups from various schools as "trainees." Except for the fact that the kibbutz could not give them the same housing as the members, these young people were treated in every respect as members of the kibbutz while they were there. They ate their meals in the communal dining hall, they got pocket money like all the others, went on trips with the others and could attend concerts and other performances held on the kibbutz. In other words, they were guests of the community who worked for their keep. These temporary workers included youth leaders, school children on vacation, groups thinking of becoming kibbutzniks themselves, soldiers stationed in the vicinity, and workers who came from the city especially to help provide the food for the country. In this way there developed a category of temporary workers which did not involve a departure from kibbutz principle because there were no wage payments in actual cash.

By a strict economic accounting, it would probably have been much cheaper for the kibbutz to employ hired labor. Hired workers would have been much more skilled than the "guests"; besides, they would have made no demands on the kibbutz, whereas with volunteer and youth groups at least one member of the kibbutz had to be taken off his normal daily work schedule to take care of the "guests" and to attend to their medical needs.

Just before the establishment of the State, the problem of hired **Hired** labor on the kibbutz seemed well on the way to solution by the **Labor** very simple expedient of cutting down on those crops which required extra man-hours and increasing these crops that needed fewer man-hours of work, so that with proper management it was possible for the members to do the job without outside help.

With the establishment of the State, however, the situation changed. When the State flung its doors open to refugees from every corner of the world there arose the problem of how these refugees would be maintained. It did not take a special genius to discover that the available farm equipment was not being put to maximum use. Tractors could plow additional acreage and harvesters could be used to harvest much more produce than they did. It was considered essential that this equipment should be placed at the disposal of the new State so that the new immigrants could have jobs. In short, it became a patriotic duty for the kibbutz to hire new immigrants as workers. In fact, Ben-Gurion made a passionate appeal to all the kibbutzim to do their duty as citizens and once again show their pioneering spirit by hiring as many immigrant workers as they could.

By this time, however, appeals to patriotism and duty were not considered sufficient, so our very bright Cabinet ministers and government functionaries thought up an added incentive: Immigrant workers, whose wages were six pounds a day, should be assigned to the kibbutzim at one-third the rate, with the government paying the other two-thirds directly to the workers.

In other words, would the kibbutz be good enough to accept workers whom they would have to pay only two pounds a day?

Under the circumstances, the double motive of true patriotism and a very handsome profit was just too much for the kibbutzim to resist. Many kibbutzim, including Kfar Blum, responded to the appeal. All of us have lived to rue the day. We would have been much better off if we had engaged those workers on our own and paid them the entire six pounds per day ourselves. We would have been spared many of the problems that arose as a result.

What was the trouble? Since we had to pay these individuals only two pounds from our funds, we gave them all sorts of jobs which were not essential. We had them do a lot of leaf-raking and landscaping, and we had them clean up old sheds and repair old machinery which we had been about to discard.

From our point of view we were doing our duty to the State. But as far as the immigrant worker was concerned, he may have been a new, uninformed Israeli, but he was no fool. He soon realized that the kibbutz was paying him only one-third of the standard wage. As he saw it, the other two-thirds which he got from the government was not part of his wages for the work he was doing on the kibbutz, but a bonus which the Israeli government paid him, independently of his wages, for having come to build the State.

Inasmuch as he felt he was getting only one-third of the standard wage, he saw no reason why he should do any more than one-third of the work required of him. Net result: Instead of developing good work habits, which the State had hoped they would do, these individuals became sloppy and inefficient. Instead of the kibbutzim deriving economic advantages from the cheap labor, they became involved in projects which were not essential and could well have been postponed.

All in all, the arrangement was not successful. Neither side was satisfied, and in the long run the only party to benefit was the government; since the immigrants were taken care of on the kibbutzim the government gained time to raise funds for building up new industries to absorb the immigrants on a permanent basis. But for the kibbutz, both as an economic unit and as a society, this period was disastrous. Worst of all, of course, was the reaction of the hired worker who suddenly saw the kibbutz not as a socialist utopia but as a capitalist exploiter.

One thing which may perhaps be said in our favor is this: We at Kfar Blum decided—and I think that petty as it may sound, it was a wise decision—that we would not use any hired labor for those activities which involve personal service to members. In other words, the laborers we hired would not be put to work as servants in the kitchen, or wash the dishes, or be asked to do anything that would make them feel they were in a master-and-servant relationship. From the most menial chores to the more sophisticated tasks—we serve ourselves. Hired workers are engaged only in those branches of kibbutz activity where there is no possibility of their work being construed as personal service. They work in the meat packing plant, at landscaping and at loading and unloading in the fields.

Let me point out one more thing. During those days when the country's leadership said it would be a good thing if the kibbutzim hired immigrant workers, Ben-Gurion even suggested that if we took these workers in they might become imbued with the *halutz* ideology and would eventually join the kibbutz themselves. Unfortunately, this did not happen, because the relationship between the kibbutz and these workers was one of employer and employee. As the hired laborers became more and more a part of the working life of the kibbutz, a serious problem arose. Since in many cases these outsiders were a transient population, certain branches of kibbutz activity began to shape up in such a way that the management was in the hands of the kibbutzniks, while the actual work was done by the hired laborers.

A question that arose in every kibbutz and to this day plagues those kibbutzim which still have large numbers of hired employees is this: Will we reach a point where the kibbutznik will be a manager? Will the kibbutz members become a white-collar class, superiors of a proletariat who would not be members of the kibbutz? This idea, of course, is anathema to us.

As if the problem of hired workers were not difficult enough, we now have an even more serious complication: the Arab workers.   SAADIA

The
Kibbutz
and
Arab
Labor
Arab workers in the cities pose no problem. They are citizens of the State of Israel who go out to work at various jobs and live in their own homes. But when an Arab worker comes into a society that is so open and yet so closed as the kibbutz some very serious problems arise. No matter how much you pay an Arab worker, the feeling will be that the Arab is being exploited.

A Jewish worker, if he wishes, can apply for membership in the kibbutz and, if he is found fit, he will be accepted. But an Arab worker cannot be offered kibbutz membership so freely. After all, the kibbutz idea is a Zionist one. Therefore, though we hope that we will find a way for Jews and Arabs to live together in peace and in co-productivity, we cannot very well, under the present circumstances, ask an Arab to join a society that is dedicated to the upbuilding of a Jewish state.

YOSEF   There have been efforts in the past to incorporate Arabs into kibbutzim as members. One or two of these Arabs were young people who had married Jews. But it did not work out. You can teach an Arab the ideas of socialism and communal living, but, as Saadia has just said, it is a little difficult to ask an Arab to help build a Jewish kibbutz as a member and to assist actively in the upbuilding of a Zionist state. There are other problems, too. An Arab who has been raised in the Moslem faith will find it difficult to celebrate Passover, or any other Jewish holiday, for that matter, along with the rest of the kibbutz. Some kibbutz movements declare that any Arab who wants to join can do so. But Arabs thus far have shown no real interest in joining a kibbutz. The question arises: Should we encourage the Arabs to set up kibbutzim of their own?

SAADIA   I think the kibbutz could do a lot for the Arabs. First of all, it could show them, by its own example, that cooperation can pay off. It was a daring project to take individuals who knew absolutely nothing about agriculture, and very little about technology, organization, or physical work and put them into an utterly barren spot with the hope that they would be able to extract a living from it. The fact that we have succeeded should show the Arabs that if they so choose, it should not be too difficult for them also to use the land and the skills which they have and to organize themselves in such a manner that they will be able to reap a substantial economic yield. Whether or not the Arabs will do this, of course, depends entirely on them. In order to encourage them, one kibbutz movement, the Kibbutz Artzi of HaShomer HaTza'ir, has organized Arab boys and girls into youth groups and trained them in the hope that some of them would be sufficiently motivated to set up kibbutzim of their own. But it would be totally unrealistic to expect the Arabs to help build up a Jewish kibbutz.

Ideologically speaking, Jews and Arabs could get closer together if the kibbutz idea were to become a means of communication between them. The underlying socialism, humanitarianism and equality of the kibbutz will ultimately penetrate to the Arab community and this ideological link will make for a better understanding between the two peoples. I should add here that kibbutz members have been very articulate in expressing their views on the Arab question. This does not apply only to the left wing of our labor movement, which considers the solution of the Arab problem a vital part of its platform. Every kibbutznik gives a great deal of thought to this issue because our kibbutzim are located in rural areas and close to the borders, so that the Arabs are our neighbors in a very real sense.

Let us go back to the question with which we started out: work on the kibbutz. Everybody on the kibbutz works. Everybody does as much as he can for the common welfare. There is no special remuneration for special jobs. Everybody is expected to work wherever he is needed. As a member, you are part of the labor force of the kibbutz. You do guard duty, you do kitchen work, and you may be drafted by any of the various fields of kibbutz activity for seasonal work whenever this is required.

YOSEF

Division of Labor

But ultimately everybody gets a chance at the job he wants. This goes for teachers, engineers, dressmakers, women who like to work with children—you name it. Very often we send people— even those in their fifties—to school for training or retraining because they are interested in doing a certain type of work, or because the kibbutz has a particular position open which needs a person with specialized training.

However, there are certain jobs that nobody wants to do. This caused a problem, but we solved it years ago without too much difficulty. For instance, nobody wants to wash dishes. Nobody wants to work in the kitchen full time, or to wait on tables all his life. But everybody in the kibbutz, regardless of what other work he does here, is expected to take his turn in the kitchen and the dining hall. A youngster who has finished his army service, or a man who has returned from a stint of work outside the kibbutz, is expected to spend two or three months in the kitchen before going back to his own specialty. They may have to do it only once or twice in a lifetime, but during those two or three months they work at it full time—washing the kitchen floors, setting the tables, serving the meals, and getting the dishes done afterwards. However, once they are through with the kitchen they are through for a long time.

We mentioned that many of our *haverim* are spending various periods of time working outside the kibbutz. They are doing this not because they went looking for jobs on the outside but because, for one reason or another, the kibbutz found it necessary to assign them to outside jobs. What are they doing?

There are people employed in the national kibbutz organization at various jobs, such as work in the department of finance, or in the department of education. One of our *haverot* works in the department that deals with problems of difficult children. Chaim, from our own kibbutz, is working three days a week for the national kibbutz movement to which we belong, supervising construction at a new kibbutz. We have a number of *haverim* who are drivers and mechanics in the area cooperative. Others teach at schools in the next city, Kiryat Shmona. One of our members heads the teachers' seminary in Alonim, which trains teachers for the entire kibbutz movement but also takes in students from the cities. Another member is assistant dean of our regional college. One of our engineers is doing research work in the aircraft industry. The current secretary-general of the Histadrut, our national federation of labor, is also a member of a kibbutz—Givat Hayim.

Members of kibbutzim may also be drafted by the government for various jobs. A number of Cabinet ministers and members of the Knesset (our Parliament) belong to kibbutzim. Chuna, a member of our own kibbutz, has held an important job with our Foreign Ministry for a number of years and has just come back from a three-year stay in Washington. He comes home from the city only on weekends. I myself have been sent on engineering missions by the government, mostly in the field of transportation.

Those who work outside the kibbutz usually do so for a number of years and then they return to the kibbutz on a full-time basis. But many of them find themselves ensconced in positions which they would like to keep because they are working in the field for which they think they are best suited. If they do not break their links with the kibbutz, and if the kibbutz does not need them for a specific job, we have no objection to their keeping these positions.

What happens to the wages a kibbutz member earns when he works and lives outside the kibbutz? Except for a small amount which he keeps for his living expenses, all wages and salaries are turned over to the kibbutz. Take my own case. When I spent three years with the regular army on special duty for *Nahal,* the army gave me my monthly officer's pay, but I sent the money directly back to the kibbutz, and drew from the kibbutz the funds I needed to pay for my living expenses. When I was living in Tel Aviv, of course, these expenses were higher; during the period I was stationed at one of the army camps, they were less. In requesting funds for living expenses, the kibbutz expected me to follow my own conscience. I was not supposed to stay at Hilton or Sheraton hotels; I was expected to live on a kibbutz standard even in the city—with reasonable comfort, to be sure, but modestly, as a kibbutznik should.

Why not tell us exactly what you do in the course of one day? SAADIA

As I have just said, I am a professional worker—an engineer. I YOSEF
work in a factory which was set up on our kibbutz where we make plastic household articles. Let me give you an idea of my working day.

I get up, rather reluctantly, at 5:30 A.M. because my working

A Day in the Kibbutz day begins at 6. In the deepest part of the winter, when daylight comes very late, we start at 6:30, but usually it's at 6.

If I wish, I can stop in at the dining hall on my way to work. There's always tea, bread, butter and jam for those who want an early breakfast. However, I have no appetite at that early hour; in fact, it seems few people do. So I go straight to the shop. I am not the first one there. Usually the people in charge of production have already shown up. I go into my office and turn on the radio to get the early news. Then I sit down and start work. The work in the early hours may be just checking through yesterday's mail, or it may be preparing engineering formulas for a construction job we are doing, working out a bid for a job that we want to get, or checking over bills or accounts.

Next, I go into the workshop to see how things are getting along. Until 8 A.M., when we go for breakfast, my time is filled with office work.

At 8 A.M. we all go to the dining hall for breakfast. Those who have already had a bite at 6 call it "second breakfast." In the kibbutz, breakfast is practically the main meal. You can have your choice of eggs almost any way you want them. There is French toast once or twice a week, and we have rolls on Sundays and Thursdays. You can have your choice of two or three kinds of cheese. There is a large bowl of vegetables from which you can make your own salad. There are olives, herring, and *t'hina,* which is made from sesame seed and is a very popular food here. There is coffee or tea and, of course, jam to spread on your bread.

You take as much time for breakfast as you feel you need—usually thirty to forty minutes—and then you go back to work.

I spend most of the morning at the office. I do drafting and also some accounting. There are meetings, conferences with engineers and discussions with the craftsmen who do the jobs. There are salesmen to see, and customers may also come in. The telephone rings all the time. In between, I have to write letters. As a rule, I find that the morning flies by very fast.

At lunch we all meet again in the dining hall. Lunch is the one hot meal of the day. We take from half an hour to one hour for lunch and then we go back to work for the afternoon session, which ends at 3:30. The managers may have to stay another half hour to finish up a job, to supervise the loading or unloading of trucks, or to make out bills of lading. At about 4 P.M. the plant closes down for the day, except during periods when we have two shifts.

My first stop on the way home usually is at the office of the kibbutz secretariat. I may have to talk to the secretary of the kibbutz about one of our workers or about some production problem, or I may request that a certain point be brought up at the meeting of the secretariat or at the general meeting of the kibbutz. If the day is Sunday—the first working day of the week—I then go to the treasurer of the kibbutz and get some money for my weekly expenses.

From there I go to the dining hall where I collect the mail. Often I meet my wife, Ruth, there; she may be picking up some bread, margarine, cheese and vegetables to take home for our afternoon tea. At home, Ruth and I sit down, read the daily paper, and listen to the radio for awhile. The children come in for tea. Afterwards, we take a hot shower. In my place we still have to use a kerosene stove for hot water. It takes about 20 minutes to get enough hot water for one shower. A shower and a shave, and we're all cleaned up by about 5 o'clock. At 5:15 I'm off to visit the rest of my family—we have three generations living here at Kfar Blum. The first one I go to see is my granddaughter; that, of course, is the most delightful part of my day. In the summer I meet everybody—my son and daughter-in-law and my granddaughter, too—at the swimming pool. We spend a pleasant hour at the pool, resting on the lawn, or sitting on the porch reading a paper and listening to the news.

At 6 o'clock we go in to get ready for supper, which is at 6:30. Supper is a light meal—eggs, usually a hot soup, a vegetable salad, herring, and something to drink. After supper, the evening is free, and how I choose to spend my free time is my own business. There is always something going on at night, either on the kibbutz, or nearby. On Thursday evenings there is a series of concerts in the next town. We see a movie at the kibbutz every Tuesday night. There is a choral group, and there is a dramatic society not far away. If I feel like it, I can play a game of tennis; our tennis courts are floodlit at night so we can use them even after dark.

We may go to visit friends, or to our son's place and sit around and talk with his family. Or we can stay home and play chess, bridge or canasta. I can spend the evening reading a book, writing letters, or just sitting by my radio or record player and taking a snooze. If I want to be active in community affairs I can attend meetings of the many committees which we have here at the kibbutz and which are always looking for active members.

We have a club room where I can go for a cup of coffee, read those daily papers to which I do not subscribe, look at a magazine, or talk with other people. I can go into the reading room and watch a television program if I feel so inclined. Or, if it has been a long and hard day, I can just decide that the time has come to go to bed a little early.

SAADIA

As Times Change

So here you have the working day of a kibbutz professional—1973 model. Our views of jobs on the kibbutz are changing all the time. What was once regarded as romantic and exciting may be considered routine today. Take the fish ponds—we used to consider them a very romantic place to work. We would row out in our little boats and sprinkle the feed on the water with shovels. Then we would get out and wade into the center of the pond to see where all the fish were concentrated, check the vegetation, and look to see whether there were any traces of marauders in the area. It was all very romantic.

Today it is so prosaic. You stand at the edge of the pond and you blow the feed into the water by machine. You concentrate the fish at one end into concrete basins. The romance of the fish ponds is all gone. No more getting up in the middle of the night to get the fish into the trucks; the fishing is done in the middle of the day when it is comfortable and sometimes even pleasant. In the summer when you wade into the fish ponds to get out the fish, it is an actual relief to be in the water, even though the ponds are full of all sorts of stuff and not the cleanest compared to our luscious swimming pool. When the temperature reaches 104° in the shade, even the water of our fish ponds feels good!

YOSEF

There have been many changes in our work setup. The

character of our agriculture has changed completely. Sometimes we remember with nostalgia the crops we used to have. We no longer grow potatoes, tomatoes, or grapes. It was a question of economics. Many of the immigrant towns are laid out in such a way that the newcomers have small plots of ground on which to grow crops. It turned out that they could produce a few cratefuls of tomatoes far more cheaply than we could. There was no use for us to compete with these tomatoes on the market. So we only grow those crops for which our farm is suited. We have orchards and cotton fields, and we raise cattle and poultry. We grow a certain amount of corn for our cattle, and we grow flowers for export, but we do not go into large acreages of vegetables unless there is a definite need in the country for it.

Our cow barns are large and mechanized. In the early days we kept cows not because of the milk but because of the manure. (Whether or not they gave milk was of secondary importance. People in Israel do not drink much milk. The American habit of drinking a quart of milk each day has never caught on here.) We needed the manure for fertilizer. Today things have changed. Chemical fertilizers have become so advanced and are so easy to handle that they are cheaper than manure, and certainly more pleasant to work with. The milk, on the other hand, has become important. It is being used for Israel's new, expanding cheese industry. So nowadays we are trying to get as much milk as we can from our cows.

Yet there is a question whether it is worth while for us to keep the cows. For one thing, people usually do not want to work in the stables. Not only is it a messy job, but it also involves difficult hours. We have a number of experts who are working regularly in the stables but, for the most part, they do it reluctantly. It became necessary for us to ask some of the younger people to go into this work at least for a year.

Secondly, while we make money from the sale of the milk—and of the cattle—the investment involved is very great. At a kibbutz near ours, they lost an entire herd of cows overnight from foot-and-mouth disease. The insurance company paid them for the animals but nobody paid them for the cow barns and the milking machines. So the kibbutz decided to cut its losses and stop raising cattle.

At our own kibbutz, the profits which come as a result of the extremely hard work of four or five people do not justify the huge investment. We still have our cattle but we do not know whether we are doing the right thing and whether we will continue doing it.

How are some of our other kibbutz industries organized? Let us take our cotton fields. Our kibbutz has an agricultural committee, which does the planning each year. This committee may decide that, say, 300 acres of our land will be set aside for growing cattle. The committee then proceeds to discuss every detail—the amount of water that will be needed, the number of tractors, the kinds of equipment, and the number of workers.

We may have a nucleus of about five or six individuals who are employed full time at agricultural work. One of them may be an agronomist or a graduate of an agricultural school. This little group of experts will sit down and elect a manager for the cotton department to serve for that year. The newly-elected department head allocates the jobs, and the actual work in the cotton fields begins.

The workers may need several conferences during the cotton season. If the crop at the end of the year is good, everybody is happy. If not, we try to find out what went wrong. Was it the weather, the soil, or poor management? If we see that our manager cannot do the job, we have no compunctions—even halfway through the season—about replacing him and letting him take over an area of lesser responsibility such as planting, watering or spraying. Not everybody has to be good at management.

I have already said that growing numbers of people from kibbutzim with large industrial enterprises are attending special classes held in the cities for farm management and other administrative work. This makes for greater all-around efficiency on the kibbutz.

SAADIA   Speaking of efficiency—looking at things from the viewpoint of cold economics—just how efficient is the kibbutz as an economic unit? How does it plan its economy and how does it put these plans into operation?

YOSEF   The efficiency of a kibbutz must be analyzed in the light of many different factors. For instance, our 1,250 acres could *Job* probably be managed more efficiently by one single non-kibbutz *Efficiency* farmer, with a large family and perhaps a few hired laborers, than on the basis of a kibbutz with several hundred members. From that point of view, the kibbutz is probably not run on an economical basis. On the other hand, if we consider that we have been able to make our 1,250 acres support over 600 people in relative comfort we can say that, in fact, the kibbutz is operating in a very efficient manner.

Whether we can run our fields and our other industrial enterprises efficiently depends upon a number of factors, primarily the availability of the type of machinery we need, the quality of the machinery we can get, and the cost of the machinery. Let me give you a case in point. A number of years ago we received a loan from the United States for the purchase of farm machinery but on condition that we use the money only to buy particular kinds of machinery, from specified companies. It happened that the companies stipulated by our creditor did not have what we considered the best machinery for our purposes. However, since we could not look a gift horse in the mouth, we were forced to buy this second-rate machinery, and it did not do a very good job.

Our production has also been held up at times by machinery which we imported from abroad but which we could not use because it had been made for a certain climate or some other condition that we just do not have in this country. In other instances a machine cannot be used for three or four months because of spare parts that are unobtainable here.

Because of these limitations, we have developed agricultural methods that have placed us among the highest producers in the world. I think we are on a par with the top producers in the world in milk production—both in the quantity of milk per cow and in butterfat content. We are gradually becoming self-sufficient in our production of grain, fodder and seed. We also get a larger cotton yield per acre than any other country. The question, of course, is: What does it cost us to produce that milk and that cotton?

We have just mentioned our problems with dairy farming. In the case of our cotton, we had to invest a large amount of money in a cotton-picking machine because we did not have enough

people to pick it by hand. This machine has turned out to be quite
an expensive piece of equipment because it is used just one month
during each year.

When it comes to buying machinery, or in fact whenever there
is a major decision to be made in our kibbutz industries, we have
to call meetings to talk over the matter. This makes for a lack of
efficiency because, everybody on the kibbutz being equal and
having equal rights, the workers are free to speak out at the
meetings if they disagree with the recommendations made by the
managers of our various enterprises.

Is this efficiency, or a mark of social progress? Here we have the
question: Which is more efficient, democracy or a dictatorship? A
benevolent dictatorship could conceivably be more efficient than
a democracy. However, in the long run, the democratic system
wins out.

While the question of whether or not the kibbutz way makes for
maximum economy or efficiency is subject to debate, we do have
one important asset: the special sense of responsibility that our
workers feel for the branch of agriculture or industry in which
they are engaged. The Israeli army authorities, for one, know that
when they give an order to a kibbutz factory not only will their
order be carried out with dispatch but they will get a fine quality
product. This is a matter of personal pride to every kibbutz
worker, much more so than it would be to many a non-kibbutz
individual who is merely working for his wages.

Our big problem at present is how we should divide our
energies between agriculture and industry. Agriculture has a
certain potential for development but it is not unlimited. There
comes a time for every kibbutz when the painful decision must be
made: Either the kibbutz must take up an industry in addition to
its agricultural work or else it must reduce its standard of living if
it is to be able to absorb additional members.

This, of course, raises many questions that go beyond
economics or efficiency. What happens when a kibbutz becomes
an industrialized community and you begin to have job
distinctions, as between professional people and ordinary
workers? What happens when some members of the kibbutz
become specialists in various areas of technology while others

remain more or less stuck in a menial occupation; when some members have a variety of outside contacts because of their specialized jobs while others are largely confined to the kibbutz in their work? What happens to the kibbutz when some of its people, because of their special skills and training, become so indispensable to us that they can begin to set their own terms for staying with us? Or how may kibbutz life change when some of these experts become so involved in one of their industrial projects that it will be difficult or impossible for them to do the chores at which every member is supposed to take his turn, such as guard duty, or helping in the kitchen and the dining hall? These are issues with which we are now grappling very seriously and for which thus far we have found only partial solutions.

With increasing industrialization, we have the problem of the boss-worker relationship, even between kibbutz members, but it is not really a serious one here. Our "bosses"—the department heads—do not get their positions by inheritance, or by having stepped over their fellow-proletarians. They are either appointed by the kibbutz, or else they are elected by the workers in their department. There is really no feeling that the boss is a figure on a higher level who can exploit the masses.

Of course a great deal depends on the individual. Here and there you will find an overbearing type of person who will give orders as if he were a boss in the old sense, but in such cases it is easy for his fellow-members to remove him. A person of that type usually finds himself working elsewhere as soon as he demonstrates that he is not capable of doing the job.

The conflict between "bosses" and workers on the kibbutz takes a different shape altogether. The people who are responsible for the job are given broad authority, but only within their own departments. Woe to the kibbutz manager who will come into a department for which he is not directly responsible and start giving orders. He will find out soon enough that he is just a plain ordinary *haver* who has nothing to say in any area outside his own department.

On the other hand, the discipline within each department is quite good because whatever arguments there are take place after

SAADIA

working hours. This, of course, does not preclude raised voices on the job from time to time, but everybody knows that it is the person in charge who has the say in the end. Obviously this must be so; otherwise we could not have achieved what we have.

4

THE KIBBUTZ HOUSEHOLD

The ordinary problems of running our farm and our industries SAADIA here on the kibbutz are obvious. But what about our kibbutz household—such housekeeping problems as providing food and preparing meals for a population of several hundred, including old people, infants, children—with all kinds of health problems and personal likes and dislikes? Even the logistics of providing the food, getting it cooked, having it ready three times a day, and supplying various items for people to keep in their living quarters for snacks, are quite complicated.

The women in charge of seeing that all these foods are available *The Kitchen* have a very hard job, every bit as important and complex as *and the* running a major economic activity. The person in charge of the *Dining Hall* kitchen and dining hall is forever battling for more help because naturally the tractor drivers and the farm workers cannot be touched during their season; the engineer must do his engineering, and the professionals must carry on with their professions. So, who is left to take care of the kitchen and serve the meals?

Rotation alone, which Yosef was talking about when we spoke of our concepts of labor, will not produce the proper results. So, in addition to having everybody take his turn at kitchen chores we must have a permanent skeleton staff which understands the work and stays with it month after month, sometimes year after year. There are times when we are desperately short of kitchen and dining room help. If no one wants the job, or there is no one who can really do it, someone will be selected at a general meeting to be trained for the work. This person must accept the assignment. You might say this is coercion, but it is also a matter of understanding the needs of the community and accepting discipline. This is efficient democracy at work. The community must be served, even if sometimes this means that an individual has to do a job he does not like.

83

Kitchen work is quite different from work on the farm or in our factory. To begin with, there are more women here than on the farm. The atmosphere in the kitchen is so different from that, say, at the fish nursery that a visitor would think these must be two different communities. There is greater tension, and considerably more discussion. It is indoor work; hot in the summer and steamy and cold in the winter. And all the time there are crises. Here a member was supposed to show up but suddenly got sick; there, someone began to work and everything was fine until suddenly a big fight broke out over the menu or over the way the food should be prepared. There may be an idyllic situation, with everyone working together, peeling the fruit and singing; then, out of the blue, for no good reason whatsoever, the people are practically pulling each other's hair.

YOSEF   But it is a thousand times better today than it used to be. We have machinery to do things. We have a mixer as big as an ordinary kitchen, a blender and a potato peeler. In the old days it was a thousand times worse because all we had was kitchen knives and even these were in short supply. Today we have steam cookers run by an oil burner and an electric set-up in case the steam does not work. For emergencies when both steam and electricity are not working we have gas, so that we can always prepare some food. From that point of view it is not all that bad. But I would like to mention a few other problems that do arise in our kibbutz household.

For instance, our dairy products supplier may notify us by phone that the truck broke down and there will be no cream and no cheese although our dietician had decided that this was to be the menu for supper or for breakfast. Or it may be just the opposite. The people in our apple orchard notify us that they have an extra ton of low-grade apples and if we do not use them up immediately for applesauce they will have to be thrown out. They say they will bring the apples right over, dump them in the kitchen, and then the peelers will peel the apples and the steam cookers will make the applesauce. All this sounds fine, but it happens that the kitchen people were planning to use the peeler and the cooker for some other purpose. That complicates things just a little bit.

Or you get a problem like this: It is Friday night. You have prepared 600 portions of chicken to feed all the people on the kibbutz. Suddenly, 150 guests turn up. They explain that they were at a nearby kibbutz for a wedding and since they were in the neighborhood and had friends at Kfar Blum, they thought they would drop in—for a bite of supper.

On another Friday, a group of soldiers happens to be in the neighborhood. Well, you know how we Israelis feel about our boys in the army. You can't very well *not* invite them for a meal on Friday night—nor on any other night, for that matter.

And then you have the food problems of individuals right here in the kibbutz. This is not just a question of cranks. God knows we have enough of those, too. But there are people on special diets; one man who cannot eat anything with sugar, and another who is on a salt-free diet. There is a pregnant woman who needs additional protein, and a new mother who needs additional carbohydrates. I may be getting this mixed up, but then I never had a baby, so I don't know.

There are people with ulcers or incipient ulcers, post-operative patients and pre-operative cases. And then there are individuals, like me, for instance, who simply do not like spinach, and you have to be able to give them something else. In addition, there are those, especially among our young and healthy generation, who feel that one helping of anything is just not enough and they want a little more.

Here is another crisis: What do you do when you have 500 loaves of bread to slice and the bread slicer suddenly breaks down? Slicing bread by hand is not an easy job; we do not even have the equipment for it. These and a host of other problems very frequently will drive the kitchen crew crazy.

On top of all this, the woman in charge of household economics, of the kitchen and of the cooking, has an additional problem: The treasurer who comes in to ask for another portion of whatever it is that he happens to like, and at the same time warns her that she is exceeding the daily budget by at least 50 per cent and she has to cut down both on the quantity and the quality of the food that she is preparing. As he finishes his second helping, he says that since he is going into town tomorrow, would she prepare a few extra sandwiches for him to take along?

SAADIA   The trials and tribulations of work in the kitchen are nothing like those of the jobs in the dining hall. The dining hall, which is staffed by anybody you can get, can be the most erratic of all kibbutz institutions.

Sometimes, especially in the winter when the farm work is a bit slow, you can take the farm manager, the grain farmer, individuals who have completed their work in the orchards, the tractor driver who has been laid off because of the rain, and the big shot who has just come back from a government mission abroad, and organize them into a dining hall crew. Then the dining room will be one undiluted pleasure. Every request is met, people are efficient and everything is just wonderful.

But when the summer comes, the farmer returns to his farm work, the tractor driver is back on the tractor and the big shot is out on the road again, saving the world. Meanwhile, back in the kitchen and dining hall, we are left with one harassed person in charge, with a staff of volunteers, perhaps a few children who have just finished school for the summer, and maybe a couple of newcomers who have just arrived at the kibbutz. Nobody knows where the dishes are, where the second helpings are to come from, and what staples are supposed to be on the tables. There may be days when one sits down to eat and finds that the table is set beautifully, but there is no jam, no bread, and no tea.

There are similar problems in any other field of work where you have to resort to the "rotation" method to get the job done. Nobody really enjoys cleaning up bathrooms and public facilities. At one time we had many outhouses and latrines. Today we do not have many of these, but a few are still around and they have to be cleaned. Our public buildings also have to be kept clean.

One week you will find all the bathrooms and toilets spotless, and you can go from the clubhouse to the general meeting hall, to the offices and to the public buildings and find everything spic and span. Then, a few weeks later, you will go to the same places and find them all a mess. It all depends upon the personality and the mood of the individual whose turn it was to clean up on that particular day.

YOSEF   Everybody has to take his turn at *sh'mira,* or guard duty. This may be two weeks in a year or two weeks in two years, or two weeks in six months, depending on the security situation. Nobody wants to be on guard duty permanently because we all have to do enough of that when we are in the army. But there has to be someone who will be around all night carrying a gun and keeping an eye on the kibbutz. Border kibbutzim, of course, need more than just one or two people to do guard duty.

When you are on night patrol during the long, cold and often rainy winter nights you do not wear an army uniform but pile on all the clothes you own. Sometimes, when one of the guards meets one of the other *haverim* on night patrol, his first impulse is to shoot since the individuals are unrecognizable. They wear stocking caps from which only the lower part of the eyes and nose are visible. Of course, for safety's sake, the guards are told that if they want to stop for a minute in the dining room for a cup of coffee or at the clubhouse to have a word with someone they should take the magazine out of the submachine guns they carry. But the people around the kibbutz are not surprised when they see somebody walking around looking as though he were in a commando unit about to go on a full-scale raid. It is just *Haver* Moishe or Baruch who is on *sh'mira* duty.

In the old days, before we became a rich kibbutz and bought alarm clocks for our people, one of the jobs of the *shomer leila*, or night watchman, was to wake up those *haverim* who had to get up at hours different from the regular work schedule. The people who took care of the cows, for instance, had to be awakened earlier for milking. Others had to be awakened at various hours to catch an early bus or a truck. And then there were, of course, truck drivers, tractor drivers and so forth, who had to get up at all hours.

The night watchman would have a list of these individuals and go around waking them up. Very often he did not know exactly which house they lived in and on occasion you would be rudely awakened from a sound sleep at 3 or 4 o'clock in the morning by someone banging at your door, calling out someone else's name, telling you to get up and get your tractor, or catch your bus. Throwing a shoe at him did not help because when he realized that he was at the wrong door he would simply move on to the next house and start all over again.

Work on
Sabbaths
and
Holidays

How do we keep the kibbutz running on the Sabbath? Sabbath or no Sabbath, the animals have to be fed, the cows have to be milked, meals have to be prepared and served, and the dishes have to be washed. There are a thousand and one jobs that have to be done even on *Shabbat* and on the holidays, which are, of course, days of rest throughout the country.

Everybody in the kibbutz works for half a Saturday once each month, in accordance with the principle that if you had a household of your own you would also have some jobs to do on the Sabbath—mow the lawn, or make household repairs, and the mother of the house would have to cook the meals and set the table.[13] Certain members are assigned by kibbutz tradition to work on the same holidays each year. I, for one, always help serve the food at the Passover *seder*. Whether this is a special honor or a special disgrace is hard to tell. But my family knows that at one point or other during the *seder* I have to get up and serve the group—first the soup and later on the coffee. On other holidays, such as Rosh HaShanah—the New Year—I sit back and get served by other *haverim* who do the serving on that particular holiday each year.

SAADIA

The
Clothing
Center

Let us go back to housekeeping details. No job in a kibbutz can compare with work at the *makhsan*—the clothing center —where clothes are laundered, pressed and mended, and where you can also get new clothes—kibbutz-made or factory-made, or bought from retail stores. The *makhsan* is a unique institution, managed by women who are adept at working with clothes. Besides, there are women who are pregnant, who are recuperating from some illness, who are dissatisfied with their own particular job or who have not really decided what they want to do on the kibbutz. Somehow all these women drift into the clothing center.

This means that the clothing center becomes a huge reserve pool for labor. When a big load of fish comes into the kitchen and must be cleaned one-two-three, where do the kitchen people go for help? To the clothing center. If you need extra hands of course

---

[13]At Orthodox (religious) kibbutzim, no heavy chores are done on the Sabbath. Meals are cooked the day before. The only heavy work performed on the Sabbath is that which is essential to the security of the kibbutz and to the health of the kibbutz animals.

you get women from the *makhsan* to help out. If you have a
problem in one of the children's houses or kindergarten—say, one
of the nurses is sick and does not show up—you run to the
clothing center. There you will find unlimited labor reserves.

All this is fine. But how do we get the clothing center work
done?

Here at Kfar Blum, my wife Ruth has been in charge of the   YOSEF
clothing center almost since the beginning of the kibbutz. This
means that very often I am thrown out of my own home when
somebody comes in to be fitted for a dress, a brassiere, or anything
else. I am used to that now. I have also gotten used to hearing my
wife refer to people by numbers. She greets them, "How are you,
113, or 364?" because everyone in the kibbutz has a number
which is sewn, for identification purposes, on every garment he or
she owns. It works very well.

You throw your dirty clothes into the laundry any day during
the week. On Fridays you go to the clothing center to pick up your
clean clothes, all mended, pressed and ready to wear. Of course
there are minor problems. For instance, we had one woman who
tried very hard, but somehow she could not concentrate on her
work. She ran the stocking repair machine. This machine knits
new heels for women's hose. It works very fast. Well, she would
forget for just a minute to watch the machine and it would keep on
knitting the heel, so that the heel got to be about an inch thick and
you could not put the sock on—or if you got it on you could not
get into the shoe. One day this *havera* was asked to look over a
sackful of worn-out socks and make "transplants," that is, to sew
the good toes of one sock onto another that had a toe full of holes,
or the good heel of one sock onto another that had a worn-out
heel. Once I got back a sock and found that she had made a little
mistake. She had attached a toe to where the heel should have
been. So I had a sock which had a sort of tubular thing in the
middle and two toe pieces, one in the front and one in the back!

As contrasted with the early days of the kibbutz, the *haverim*
nowadays do own their clothes. Everyone gets an annual personal
allowance for new clothing and is expected to use it wisely.
People may save up their allowance from one year to another in
order to buy a good winter coat. Theoretically, if you save up long

enough, you could buy yourself a mink coat. You would have to be in the kibbutz for about sixty years to do it, but you can dream! Saadia says, "No, it would take six hundred years." But maybe the price of mink coats will go down.

You can go out and buy new clothes on your own from any store in the city, but you pay less at the kibbutz clothing center because Ruth gets the clothes wholesale from the manufacturers. She brings samples of various garments back to the kibbutz so you can place your order with her.

There are people here who always feel that whatever clothes Ruth brings in must be inferior to anything they can get in the city on their own. One of the men wanted a sweater and looked over the sample Ruth had in the clothing center. He said he wanted that same style but in a different color. Ruth said, "Okay," and placed the order. In a week or so the sweater arrived. The *haver* tried it on and said, "That's not what I wanted. It fits, but I didn't ask for this color. This is junk. I'm going to buy a sweater in the city." My wife, who is used to this type of behavior, said, "Okay, suit yourself. It's your money." And she sent the sweater back. Soon thereafter the man went to a store in town and bought a sweater which he said was exactly what he wanted. He took it to Ruth so she could sew his number in. She reached into the pocket and, sure enough, there was the little slip of paper which she had put into the sweater when she sent it back: "Returned. Wrong color." She had signed the slip and also indicated for whom the sweater had originally been ordered. The only difference was that the man paid fifteen pounds more for the item in the city than he would have if he had bought it through Ruth at the kibbutz.

Ruth gets quite an assortment of people working in the clothing center. Some of the women are extremely capable. There are dressmakers, tailors, and experts in making underwear and work clothes. However, we no longer make a lot of our clothes; we buy most of them ready-made. But we still have a design department and a woman can choose a dress from a copy of *Vogue* or any other fashion magazine and have it made for her by one of our dressmakers.

The sweaters may be knitted right here at Kfar Blum on our electric knitting machine, operated by one of our members. You can choose your own design and we will duplicate it.

Laundry today is less of a problem than it once was because we no longer have to hang our laundry out to dry. We put it in the drier. But when the machinery breaks down, it means that people do not have clean clothes until we can get somebody to make the necessary repairs and this may take a while because we are quite some distance away from the city. The drier must be turned off from time to time because if allowed to run uninterruptedly for too long the motor may burn out. One particular fellow, who is supposed to watch the drier, is a dreamer; very conscientious and well-meaning, but a dreamer. As a result, we have had to replace the motor on that drier six times in one year.

The children's laundry gets first priority. Diapers have to be washed and sterilized. The guest house laundry also must be taken care of promptly. So, when there is trouble, it is the *haverim* who are asked to wait and be patient.

Recently the kibbutzim in our area decided to join forces and set up one laundry for all the kibbutzim in the region. We hope that in the near future we will be able to do away with our own laundry machines, which are obsolete and inadequate. We hope that once there is an area laundry which will serve a dozen kibbutzim we will have more efficiency. At any rate, an area laundry seems to be the only solution to our laundry problems since laundry work is one of the jobs for which we have a hard time getting workers.

In the clothing center itself there is a hodgepodge of the modern and the primitive. There is a modern mangle for pressing sheets, pajamas and things of that sort. On the other hand, a lot of the sewing and mending is done by hand. We have one complaint that is known to people the world over who have their shirts done at a laundry: Instead of sewing on the buttons, the people in the laundry tear the buttons off. Instead of darning or patching a hole, there is a technique of repairing pants pockets by simply stitching the torn edges together, but that process makes the pocket smaller. This is all right if there is just one tiny hole at the very bottom, but if you make that repair three or four times, you eventually have almost no pocket left.

There is a conflict between economy and the desire for individualism. Of course it is more economical to get odd lots of   SAADIA material and sew skirts for all the school girls at one time, but our seamstresses want to do something creative: They want to design clothes catering to the individual tastes of our women and children.

Clothes: Home-Made vs. Ready-Made

There is, of course, the question whether we should have our clothes sewn at the kibbutz at all. Would it be more economical to buy them ready-made on the outside? Here at Kfar Blum we have a shortage of labor and the person who would do the cutting and trimming of material for the clothes could be doing something else that might be much more important for our kibbutz—sorting and cooking the apples, working at the guest house, or even helping out in one of the children's houses.

How this question is answered by the various kibbutzim depends on the size of the kibbutz. In a very large place such as Givat Brenner, with a population of over fifteen hundred, it pays for the kibbutz to mass-produce the clothes for its members and to own the modern machinery that is needed for this work. But in a small kibbutz with only three or four hundred people, or a medium-sized kibbutz like our own, with about six or seven hundred people, it simply does not pay to have all that expensive machinery and, as I have said before, we do not have the time or manpower to make all our clothes by hand. Economically speaking, then, it is certainly better for the smaller kibbutzim to buy their clothes ready-made. But when you consider buying clothes ready-made you have to remember that no matter what bargains you may buy you have to pay not only for the material from which they are made but also for the labor that the manufacturer has put into them.

However, there is something else to consider. There are periods when we have people with nothing else to do; especially on long winter evenings we can sit together and cut and sew. Under those circumstances, we could save money by purchasing the material wholesale and doing the cutting and sewing ourselves. But in our kibbutz the question of economy is only a secondary factor. The essential thing is that many of our women get a lot of satisfaction from their designing and sewing, and we felt that we should really consider the needs of these women. So the dressmaking proceeded with full speed until the next labor crisis arose and we suddenly had to pull the dressmakers out of the clothing center and send them to clean the fish or take care of some other emergency. Then the cry arose, "Let's stop this nonsense of cutting and sewing. Let's buy all our stuff from the outside." Thereupon the women replied, "But don't forget that 50 per cent of our people are women and want their clothes fitted and made by seamstresses. They don't want clothes 'off the rack.'"

But then came the time when our women began to go to the city to buy their clothes. Then the question was, "Well, which is it to be? Do they want to buy their things ready-made or do they want individual designs and styles?" And so on, back and forth. The kibbutz movement as a whole has not solved the problem yet. In some kibbutzim the clothing center only makes repairs; all new clothing is bought ready-made. In other kibbutzim the clothing center has been put on a business-like basis like all the other economic activities of the kibbutz. Kfar Blum has taken the middle road. We buy some of our clothing from the outside, but there are articles that we sew or manufacture ourselves. By making some of our own clothes we provide work for members who for some reason have to stay away from more strenuous activities. What do you do with a woman in the advanced stages of pregnancy, when she really cannot do heavy physical work? Why should she sit around doing nothing when she could be at the clothing center catching up on all the missing buttons and undarned socks which have accumulated that month? Or take a convalescent: Work is often therapy for a person who is recovering from an illness. It is not good just to sit at home all day listening to the radio or reading a book.

We plan to move our clothing center and sewing activities into one central building. Then, instead of being spread out in various wooden huts, all this work will be concentrated in one very large place with modern labor-saving machines and proper storage facilities. We hope that in this way we will be able to make maximum use of our available manpower and solve this problem of homemade versus ready-made.

Since we have been discussing the economics of kibbutz housekeeping, what about the kibbutz budget? Nowadays a   YOSEF kibbutz our age is expected to be self-supporting. Our income has to be sufficient not only to cover all our expenditures but also to yield a profit so that we can pay our income taxes (kibbutzim do pay income taxes to the State like any other economic unit in Israel), pay the interest (and begin to repay the principal) on the loans we have received and make additional investments. This takes a lot of planning, but a well-run kibbutz is usually able to manage.

The Budget   How does the kibbutz set up its budget? Shortly before the end of the fiscal year, each department prepares its own proposed budget for the year to come. To guide the departments in figuring their budgets, the central kibbutz organization sends out sample or suggested budgets showing how other kibbutzim allocate funds for various expenditures. The budget, by the way, must provide not only for the needs of the productive departments but also for the social and cultural needs of the kibbutz. The cultural committee's annual proposed budget will include funds for newspaper subscriptions, books, special exhibits, lectures, musical instruments, and for "family" occasions such as parties and weddings. The committee in charge of soldiers' welfare will request an allocation for the gift packages we send out each month to our youngsters in the armed services. There is also a committee which manages our funds for the support of aged parents who do not live on the kibbutz.

After all the proposed budgets have been received, our economists sit down and figure out what income we can expect that year. We invariably discover that the financial needs of the kibbutz for the coming year are about 75 per cent greater than the income we can expect, so we begin discussing what items we can cut down on. Discussions on this subject may be quite bitter and may go on for months. The woman in charge of the clothing center says that if she does not get the funds she requested nobody will have new bedding that year. The committee in charge of members' welfare protests that if the welfare budget is cut the *haverim* will not be able to afford vacations. The cultural committee people will argue that if they do not receive the amount they want they will not be able to show as many movies or it will not be possible for every member to get his own newspaper.

Then the economic branches are told that they will have to make do with that old tractor for another year; that they will have to cut down on the amount of water they are using, that they will have to postpone buying the machine they wanted to install in the factory, or that the kibbutz cannot afford the new building which had been planned.

Eventually, the financial committee submits the budget to the general meeting with its recommendations. Invariably there are people who do not accept the recommendations of the financial committee and prefer to bring their budget problem up for discussion and ultimate decision by the general meeting. But finally the day comes when we learn what our official budget is. We try very hard to stick to this budget throughout the year. How do we manage to get the money to make ends meet during the year? There are months when there is very little income. How do we get our loans and what are the sources of our capital?

A kibbutz is considered in good financial condition if its income equals its outlay. Kfar Blum at this juncture has investments in excess of IL 10 million; our income is only IL 6 million. If we are to reach an income-investment ratio of one to one, we will have to increase our output and sales quite a lot. A kibbutz does not start with any capital of its own. It is not as though 100 people got together, each one putting in a substantial amount of capital and beginning an operation. In fact, the founders of the kibbutz usually have no money of their own. If a member should come into some money later on, he may put it into the kibbutz treasury—we will discuss that later—but when a kibbutz first starts out, the only way it can go on is with financial support from institutions that have capital to invest.

In the past this function was filled mostly by the Jewish Agency and the Jewish National Fund. In addition, kibbutzim today receive financial assistance through their kibbutz federations, which secure loans for member kibbutzim, through independent loan funds and negotiations with financial institutions or various departments of the Israeli government. Other credits are obtained from the Fruit Growers' Association, the Cotton Growers' Association and other industrial organizations. Loans may be obtained also from private sources, and credits may come from suppliers and marketing agents.

We resort to a great variety of sources for our funds, and to this day it is a complicated job. In fact, Israel's biggest financial wizards learned their economics in the kibbutz movement. The late Levi Eshkol, for one, was treasurer of his kibbutz before he became the Treasurer of the Jewish Agency and eventually Minister of Finance—a job from which he went on to become Prime Minister of the State of Israel.

5

WHAT IS KIBBUTZ EQUALITY?

The kibbutz is founded on certain basic assumptions. One, that YOSEF
there must be no exploitation of one person by another; two,
that we are working together for the common good, and three, that
we are all equal.

Essentially, our equality consists of the fact that the kibbutz
provides us with all our basic requirements—food, clothing,
shelter and medical care.

Housing, furniture and other related items are allocated SAADIA
according to a carefully worked-out budget, which depends not
on the work the member does on the kibbutz but on his
needs—the number of children he has, his seniority on the
kibbutz, his age, and his physical condition.

Medical care, of course, includes doctors, surgery, special YOSEF
treatments—even eyeglasses and false teeth.

Let us make this point clear. If the kibbutz gives me money to SAADIA
get eyeglasses it is not because I have been working so hard or
been here so long but because I need the glasses. A man who has a
better heating system in his house got it not because of what he
has been doing in the orchards or anywhere else on the kibbutz
but because the doctor has decided that he has to have it. Of
course, there are individuals who try to take advantage of their
status as "old-timers" on the kibbutz. If the request does not
exceed what the kibbutz can give, you sympathize and try to help
out. However, in a kibbutz no one can enjoy large-scale material
advantages because there just are no large-scale material
advantages to be had around here. A person may get an extra
piece of chicken in the dining room because he says "I am a

97

vatik[14]" but he will not get a car, because the people in the kibbutz do not own cars; cars are assigned to them only for specific jobs.

YOSEF   As you may have gathered by now, kibbutz members do not receive salaries, but in addition to the basics we have just named there are other benefits to which we think every member is entitled. The kibbutz gives its children a good education; in many cases this includes a higher education or specialized training at schools outside the kibbutz. Adults get annual vacations of a week or two weeks, depending on the age of the individual. We have already mentioned the fact that under certain circumstances the kibbutz will also pay for members' travel expenses, both within the country and abroad. The annual vacation money is not very much; the amount depends on the income of the kibbutz during that particular year. But this is money I can use in whatever way I want. If I decide to spend my week's vacation in Tel Aviv I can do so. Or I can stay home and use the money to buy something I want very much but could not afford otherwise. Or I can simply put the money away and save it.

The kibbutz budget also includes allowances for extraordinary expenses a member may have—special books needed by, say, a technician for his work, or emergency visits to close relatives outside the kibbutz who are ill.

The Kibbutz   Visiting tourists sometimes ask us questions about our
Standard of "standard of living." The standard of living for any one of us here
Living is as high as the total income of the kibbutz permits. You must remember, also, that we are a rural community; we do not have to live by city standards or keep up with the Joneses. We are comfortable and we have the security that comes from the knowledge that nobody here is alone; each and every one of us has the support of a community of souls. Actually I am a very wealthy man. I own approximately 1,250 acres of land, a beautiful farm, a lovely swimming pool, and five tennis courts. There is just one catch: I have several hundred partners in all this wealth. But I do not mind that in the least.

Seriously, though, the kibbutz standard of living has gone up in

14"Old-timer."

recent years. We have refrigerators in our houses, and kibbutzim in the Jordan Valley, where it is very hot, have had air conditioning units installed in the members' houses. Little by little, the standard of living in our kibbutzim is beginning to approach that of a working family in the city. We can never get really rich, but the thing to remember is that we need not worry about our basic needs; all of us have the same degree of security.

Ideologically speaking, of course, the concept of equality lends itself to any number of distortions and misinterpretations. Obviously, if one person gets something like eyeglasses or false teeth while another *haver* does not get them because he does not need them, that is not inequality. But what about smokers and nonsmokers? Smokers get free rations of cigarettes. Is the nonsmoker entitled to a free ration of chocolate instead?

Actually there is no such thing as real equality ever. A man who has five children obviously needs more of the kibbutz income for education than the man who has only two children or no children at all. Someone who is ill needs more medical care than a well person.

To make things even more complex, those who are interested in sports may have certain requirements—whether it be athletic equipment or a ball field or the opportunity to go watch a big game. Others may not care for sports but want to go to a concert instead.

Then there is the matter of taste in decorating our homes. A *haver* who is an artist in his spare time may make a painting for a wall of his house. It may be a very worthwhile picture. Another person who is good with his hands may knit, weave, or work in ceramics to beautify his own living quarters or those of his neighbor.

The man who works in the field where sunflowers are growing will take home some sunflower seeds for his family; the orchard people will bring home apples. It is accepted that the people who work in the kitchen will take some of the leftovers. Everybody, in one way or another, will benefit from his own particular talents or from the department in which he happens to be working. As long as there is no blatant theft it should not and does not make any difference.

Let us carry this a little bit further. A *haver* who works in the city all day long will probably bring some candy for his child when he comes home to the kibbutz for the weekend. A man who works in the fields here on the kibbutz may not be able to do that. The *haver* who works in the city may go to a movie in the evening and sit in a comfortable seat while we who are in the kibbutz all week long have to bring our own chairs for our weekly movie.

We have always had equality problems. In the early days, when a young family in a new kibbutz received a package from a doting mother abroad, that package was turned over to the central canteen. Today that is no longer true. If you get a package, if someone sends you a birthday present—say, a book—it is yours; it no longer becomes common property.

Theoretically, of course, everything I have belongs to the kibbutz. That is the kibbutz ideology. But today my clothes are my own and everything I have in my living quarters belongs to me—my books, my transistor radio, my chess set and my stamp collection.

Equality The equality problem becomes really serious only when there
Problems are gross deviations from basic principles. To some extent we have gone soft, for nowadays, when a child becomes Bar Mitzvah, we permit him to receive gifts from people outside the kibbutz, gifts which may often be more lavish than other children in the kibbutz might get. A child with wealthy relatives may receive a check. He is supposed to put it into the common kitty but no one knows whether this is really done in every instance.

But what if the money involved is more than just a Bar Mitzvah check? What happens if a member of the kibbutz gets a larger gift of money from the outside, or inherits a small fortune? What is he supposed to do with it? Can he keep it or does he have to give it all to the kibbutz?

SAADIA   It depends on how big the amount is. Nowadays, if, for instance, it is no more than $500, you are allowed to keep it or spend it for whatever you want. We did not always handle it that way. In the early days of our kibbutz $500 was a lot of money and you would be required to hand over all of it to the kibbutz treasury. But as time went on, our notion of "absolute equality" was modified by life experience. Today we permit "relative inequality" when it does not involve a significant change in the life style of the member involved. We feel that the things a member could buy with $500 today would not basically alter his way of living or his status in the kibbutz community.

However, if the amount were not $500 but $5,000, that would be a problem for the kibbutz to decide. If the person just took his $5,000 and put it aside, I do not think there would be any objections, except that the kibbutz treasurer might ask him to permit the money to work for the kibbutz until the kibbutz could decide what should be done with it. The problem may then be discussed in a leisurely, relaxed fashion over a period of several months. The final decision may be that the money should stay in the kibbutz treasury but be returned to the member any time he decides to leave the kibbutz, or that—subject to the approval of the appropriate committee—the member may take it if he wants it for a little treat like a trip around the world.

But what if the amount involved is $10,000, $25,000 or even more? Cases like this actually came up when kibbutz members who had left Germany as refugees or had survived Nazi concentration camps received large indemnities from the German government. Such cases presented real problems in a number of kibbutzim because it meant that a member of the kibbutz suddenly came into a large amount of money. In several kibbutzim it was decided that all German restitution payments received by members should be turned over to the kibbutz treasury. As a result, those members who wanted to keep their money left the kibbutz.

In most kibbutzim, however, a compromise was reached. The restitution money received by individual members was not simply put into the kibbutz treasury but was spent for a major project—such as a swimming pool, a library, or a gym—that the kibbutz needed but could not ordinarily have afforded. At the same time, however, it was decided that the individual who had received the money and had agreed to give it to the kibbutz was entitled to keep a limited amount of it to spend for his personal enjoyment—a fine piece of furniture for his living quarters, or perhaps a trip abroad to visit relatives.

But there were people who, after having received a large indemnity from Germany, were not sure whether they wanted to stay on at the kibbutz. In these cases the money was kept in trust by the kibbutz and the individual was given five years—or sometimes as long as ten years—to decide what he wanted to do. If he chose to leave the kibbutz, he could, of course, take his money with him. But of the hundreds of kibbutz people who received such big amounts from Germany, only a few took the opportunity to leave the kibbutz. The rest stayed on, and their money was used for the benefit of the entire community.

YOSEF   There is a story going around in the kibbutz movement of a person who inherited a tremendous amount of money and immediately put every penny of it into the kibbutz treasury. There are other stories about people who belonged to a kibbutz but kept large private bank accounts on the outside. Frankly, I think that both these stories are gross exaggerations.

Individuals who have personal income from outside sources may do with the money as their conscience dictates. There are kibbutzim which have bylaws and regulations about outside personal income received by members. But in the more liberal kibbutzim the attitude is "live and let live." As long as a person does not show up with a new car or with other things which would be conspicuously beyond the reach of the average kibbutznik there is really no point in making a to-do about it. Someone may have a slightly larger radio set, a few more books, or a bigger record collection than the others. In my opinion, this problem takes care of itself as long as people do not make too much of a fuss and are not too touchy about such minor deviations from the rules.

SAADIA   On the subject of equality, there has been a substantial conflict between the members of the kibbutz on the one hand and visitors and observers from the outside on the other. Those who come to visit from the outside in order to see how we live look with horror on the slightest deviation from what they consider to be total and absolute equality. How can we, the great pioneering idealists, dare to deviate ever so slightly from absolute equality?

The answer is, of course, that we live the way we understand it and we follow the dictates of our conscience and experience. Anyone who strives for 100 per cent perfection is unrealistic or perhaps even slightly hypocritical. Attitudes, of course, vary from kibbutz to kibbutz. Some kibbutzim are far more doctrinaire in their approach to the question, and in a certain sense far more mechanically egalitarian.

There are many fine points. Do you remember the stories we used to hear thirty years ago about the aunt who came to visit a kibbutz and brought a box of candy for her favorite niece? Of course not one child touched a single piece until that little toddler had run to her *metapelet*[15], who took the box and then judiciously gave each child no more and no less than his equal share of candy. If the last three candies in the box had to be divided among eight children, she took those three candies, divided them into eight equal parts, and presto, equality!

I do not believe that this story is a deliberate lie or a piece of propaganda. It is conceivable that at one time, somewhere, such a thing really happened. But a real-life situation would be entirely different. If an aunt from the city came to a kibbutz kindergarten with a box of candy the child would immediately tear open the wrapping and the box, grab two, three or four candies and put them in his mouth. Then he would run over to the other children, pass the box around, and by the time the *metapelet* got there she might have one or two candies left for herself, or she might find an empty box. There is nothing basically wrong with that type of approach, because equality does not mean the suppression of normal human behavior. Equality means the recognition of the rights of our peers and the understanding that it is essential to share with them what we have. But it does not mean turning a flesh-and-blood human being into some kind of mythical angel.

We should say here that the kibbutz concept of equality is a YOSEF basic factor in the development of our youngsters. It shows up when our kids go off to do their army service. When my older son went into the army, I was in the army, too. I met him and I asked

---

[15]Nurse or counselor who attends to the small children in the children's house of the kibbutz.

him, "Tell me, how was your first day? What did you do?" He said, "Well, we were told to clean up the tent and get everything organized. There were ten of us. The first thing we did was elect a storekeeper, who went to the sergeant-major and asked him for a box." "A box? Why?" I asked. He answered, "Well, obviously we are all going to bring stuff from home, and we are all going to get food packages from the kibbutz, so we decided that we are not going to have the stuff piling up under everybody's cot but we'll put it all together." This was a typical reaction of a kibbutz youngster in a tent full of youngsters from other kibbutzim who continue to share everything even when they are in the army, away from the kibbutz.

In units where the boys come from towns and cities, the usual thing would be for each soldier to take his own package, offer some of it to his buddies, and hide the rest. But our boys took it for granted that everything had to be shared, although their unit consisted of ten boys from perhaps as many kibbutzim.

SAADIA   When we tell these stories to our visitors from the outside they tell us that all this sounds very nice but that it is hard to believe. One author complained that despite all our talk of equality, women do not have the same rights as the men on the kibbutz. "While the kibbutz may be a great place for children, and for men," he wrote, "the women are miserable; they are dissatisfied because they are restricted to 'service' jobs on the kibbutz." He said that the main reason why couples and families leave the kibbutz is that the wives and mothers are unhappy there. There are tourists who tell us we are not doing enough for our women. They say we ought to be giving them shorter working hours than the men.

YOSEF   Our author probably got his information from a woman who happened to be in a really bad mood at the time. Actually the

The Role   equality of the sexes is basic to kibbutz living. Women have just as

of Women   important a place in kibbutz life as the men. Women on the kibbutz are not "stuck" in "service" jobs. Of course, we have women who work in the clothing center and others who work as hostesses in our guest house, or as secretaries, bookkeepers and teachers. Our librarian is a woman. But women are not forced to accept "service" jobs if they find them uncongenial. Women can take on any job they wish and are capable of doing. Some kibbutz women hold managerial positions; here in Kfar Blum the head of our flower-growing and export department is a woman. Some of our women are psychologists and our kibbutz doctor, too, is a woman. Other women work in the fields. One of our women is a shoemaker.

As for women's working hours, in the old days the women believed that complete equality between the sexes meant the same working hours for both men and women, regardless of age. Those pioneering women had no intention of working fewer hours than their husbands, not even when they got older. Today, when a woman reaches the age of fifty, her working hours are cut since we feel she should take it a little easier, and nobody—man or woman—objects to that any more as a violation of equality. So there is really no reason why any woman should feel particularly unhappy on a kibbutz just because she happens to be a woman.

Sometimes a man who wants to leave the kibbutz will be ashamed to admit that it is his idea and so he puts the blame on his wife. But in reality when a couple, or a family, wants to leave the kibbutz, they may have a thousand reasons for wanting to quit. Of course, it could be the wife who is unhappy on the kibbutz, but it may just as well be the husband who is dissatisfied. Maybe one of the two has been offered a lucrative job outside. Or perhaps there are personality factors. The couple may be ambitious and seek personal advancement, or they may be unable to get along with the other people on the kibbutz. They may be unhappy about the housing, or the school at the kibbutz, or perhaps the climate does not agree with them. But it would be a big mistake to say that the decision to leave is always made because of the wife—or because of the husband, for that matter.

Let us get back to the question of equality between the sexes.   SAADIA
The most important problem is the extent to which it is possible for the sexes to be equal. There is no doubt that in theory the kibbutz intended to have total equality of the sexes. The naiveté of the early kibbutzniks in this respect showed in the ridiculous

lengths to which the women went in order to be "equal." Yosef just mentioned how the early women pioneers felt about the idea of women working fewer hours than men. They had quite strong feelings about equality at work. There are stories from the early pioneering days of women working as road builders and bricklayers. Many a building in our cities was built by gangs of women from the kibbutzim who took construction jobs outside in order to be able to earn extra money for the kibbutz.

In the early stages women felt that it was their right to drive tractors and do all kinds of heavy labor. This was their idea of complete freedom and equality. The roles of men and women were conceived to be so totally identical that the women tended to forget about the normal differences between the sexes. Of course, these efforts at "equality" were rdiculous. First of all, men and women are not all equal in physical stamina. On the other hand, consider this: Women may have unusual staying power. A man may be able to expend a far greater initial output physically, but he might not be so good at maintaining a steady effort. A woman can work at her kibbutz chores outside the home for eight, nine or ten hours and then go back to her house, clean the room, do some sewing and then wash up and look as fresh for the evening as though she had done no work at all. A man comes back to the house after eight hours of work and just collapses. Of course, there are women who are so frail they find any physical work difficult. But there are also men whose physical capacity is quite limited.

This business of physical differences between men and women is extremely complicated and varied. It is therefore altogether stupid simply to declare that all people can do the same jobs, regardless of sex. On the other hand, you cannot say that there are some jobs which only men can do, and other jobs for which only women are suited; not every man can do every "male" job and not every woman can do every kind of "female" work.

There are certain personal work preferences which are largely dependent not on sex but on temperament. One person will get satisfaction from a job which may give little pleasure to another. In the course of time these personal preferences will assert themselves, but the issue involved here is not equality between the sexes in terms of physical ability; rather, it entails a recognition of equality between the sexes in terms of personality. It took the kibbutz movement many decades to achieve this concept of equality.

In the early days the women and men felt so completely "equal" that even the formalities of marriage were considered improper. It was decided that any time a man and a woman began to live together they simply reported to the housing committee that they wanted to share a room. They were then regarded by all as a couple. The many stories of free love, of interchangeable husbands and wives, and generally loose life in the kibbutzim date from that very brief early period when the kibbutz was searching for complete equality and experimented with the issue also on the sex level. But we will leave that for later discussion.

YOSEF

A little more about "women's work." A woman may be a good tractor driver until she gets pregnant with her first baby. Then she stops driving a tractor because it is bad for her, bad for the baby, and ultimately bad for the tractor, too. Little by little, as women began going into their niche and started to raise families, it became apparent that they were going to take on certain "female" jobs. To be sure, the men had no objection to working in the kitchen or perhaps even to taking care of the children but it was the natural thing for the woman to take care of her children, especially because she is not required to work during the nursing period—the first six weeks after the baby is born. After that she works part-time, about four or five hours each day, for six months to two years, so that she can take care of her child.

Here and there at some kibbutzim you will find a woman who does heavy farm work or a man who is working in the kitchen all the time. Women usually take care of the laundry; perhaps they will not do the difficult physical job of repairing the laundry machines but certainly they will do the ironing, the mending, and the sewing. There are some men who are tailors but generally the men have come to take on jobs which require more strenuous physical work. So, in time, driving tractors came to be considered a man's job and it was generally agreed that child care should be left to the women.

6

CHILD REARING AND EDUCATION

We have just discussed women on the kibbutz and we mentioned their place in child care. This, I think, naturally leads us into the subject of child rearing and education on the kibbutz. Though I am the father of two, and have two grandchildren, I am not much of an authority in this area. Far more capable people—after seven weeks at a kibbutz—have written authoritative tomes on the subject of kibbutz children. They are great experts although they do not even know Hebrew; I can boast of only thirty years' experience with our youth. Excuse my acerbity. Just now we are somewhat upset about a book which has recently been published by an expert on the subject of kibbutz education.

YOSEF

Our children are the pride and joy of the kibbutz. First of all, a word about their names. There was a period when classic Biblical names were chosen—Avraham, Moshe, Yitzhak and Yaakov. Later we became more modern and there was a string of names such as Uri and Uzi and Udi. Then came more complicated names: Amitai, Avital, Amihai, Amikam.[16] There are annual fashions in names. When I went into the army a few years ago, I met the class of 1940; all the girls were named Nina, Nitza and Nera. The next year, the class of 1941, showed up with girls called

---

[16]These changes in name "fashions" may be of interest to the student of the history and sociology of the kibbutz, and of Israel in general. The names Avraham (Abraham), Moshe (Moses), Yitzhak (Isaac) and Yaakov (Jacob) are those of the early patriarchs and religious leaders of the Jewish people. A more militant note is reflected by the names Uzi ("My Strength," after Uzziah, King of Judah; note the suffix *yah* in the original name, i.e., "The-Lord-is-my-Strength"), and Udi ("My Firebrand"; see Zach. 3:2: "Is this not a firebrand plucked from the fire?"). The names Amitai ("My Truth"), Avital ("Father-of-Dew"), Amichai ("My-People-Lives") and Amikam ("My-People-Arose") are associated with the prophetic era and the rebirth of the Jewish people; Amitai was the father of the prophet Jonah, and Avital and Amikam are the names of two new villages (*moshavim*) in Israel.

Anna, Aviela and Arela.[17] This goes on to this day. The names chosen nowadays are very short, like Gai, Shai, Chai. People have forgotten about Sarah and Rivkah, but these names will probably be back a few years from now.

The Children's House Usually, kibbutz children are born in a hospital near the kibbutz. For the first six weeks, the infants live with their parents. During that period—as I have already pointed out—the mother has no kibbutz chores so she can devote full time to the care of her baby. The child care experts in the kibbutz—women trained in child rearing—are available at all times to give the young mother any help she may need.

When the child is six weeks old, he is transferred to the babies' house where a *metapelet* is in charge.[18] The mother then goes back to work for a few hours each day, but wherever she works, she takes off time to nurse her baby and spend a pleasant hour with him. The father, who is usually told to keep his clumsy hands away from the infant, stops by the babies' house three or four times a day to visit his child. Of course, the kibbutz photographers are always extremely busy then.

SAADIA   Stop here for a minute, Yosef. We have just said that kibbutz infants live with their parents only until they are six weeks old. From that time on, the children do not live with their parents but in children's houses with other boys and girls of their age. Some of our visitors find this disturbing. Just the other day a tourist asked me: "No offense meant—but how do the parents in the kibbutz even know whose children belong to whom?"

YOSEF   I think that the children on a kibbutz are more closely attached to their parents than many children elsewhere. In the kibbutz the parents do not keep their children at home but they have more free time to spend with them, undisturbed by other problems, than many parents outside.

---

[17]Nitza means "bud." Anna is derived from Hannah, mother of the prophet Samuel; Aviela is the feminine of Aviel ("God-is-my-Father") whom Sam. I (9:1) names as the grandfather of King Saul.

[18]Our new generation is trying out a new idea—having the babies stay with their parents until they are seven, when they move to the "children's house."

Let me explain this. Back in America, when I was a child, I would play out in the street in front of my house after school until my mother called me in. I saw my father for perhaps an hour each day. He came home from work about 6 o'clock, very tired. We seldom ate supper together. After supper my father read the paper or napped for a while. In the meantime, I would do my homework and then go to bed. My father rarely had time for me. My mother was a very busy woman. She cooked, cleaned the house, and was active in a Zionist organization. Mother made a nice home for us, and she saw to it that I was well fed and well dressed, but I doubt that she and I ever conversed more than fifteen or twenty minutes a day.

Now compare that with what happens on a kibbutz. As we said, while the child is very young the mother goes to visit him at the babies' house every single day. The children's house—and the schools here at Kfar Blum—are only about fifty yards away from the adults' living area. Even the fathers drop by the children's house after breakfast or at odd times during the working day to say hello. It is quite usual to see a father wheeling a baby carriage after work or carrying a child on his shoulders, or going with the children to visit the cows or sit on a tractor.

Since we start work very early in the morning we are also through quite early—3 or 3:30 in the afternoon. By that time, the mother, too, is free. When she comes home from her kibbutz chores she does not have to prepare supper because the cooking for the entire kibbutz is done in the communal kitchen and we have our meals in the kibbutz dining hall. This leaves both parents free to devote all their attention to their children after work.

The children have supper with their parents in the dining hall. After supper, each little family goes off to the house of the father and mother. There is a corner in the parents' room where the children keep their favorite books and toys. The children stay with their parents until their bedtime. In most kibbutzim, the parents themselves help the *metaplot* (counselors) put the children to bed in the children's house. Parents take turns telling bedtime stories to the whole group.

On the Sabbath the parents have all day with the children.

Parents and children go to the pool for a swim, on hikes, or maybe they just spend the day together on the lawn or at the parents' house. So I would say that parents on the kibbutz have much more time to enjoy their children than do parents elsewhere, and this, of course, makes for a special closeness between the parents and children at the kibbutz.

Now, back to the children's house. What happens there during the day, while the parents are out working? When the child reaches the age of three or four, his kindergarten days begin. We have here at Kfar Blum what we call a mixed kindergarten; this is a very interesting setup. One class consists of two age levels—five-year-olds and three-year-olds. In this way the weakling among the five-year-olds can find a younger child with whom he can compete, while the bully among the three-year-olds will always meet some five-year-old who is bigger and stronger. But do not ask me what happens to the five-year-old bully or the three-year-old weakling! They need special attention, of course.

School Days When they are six, the children start getting instruction in reading, writing and a little arithmetic. To ease the transition from the completely free environment of the kindergarten playroom to the more rigid environment of the school, six-year-olds who are not yet ready to accept the discipline of school for even an hour a day are allowed to play outside with the younger children.

The younger children, on the other hand, look with awe at their older brothers and sisters who already have the privilege of going to school and learning how to read and write. So they start imitating them and look forward to the day when they, too, will have the same privilege.

When they are seven, the children graduate from kindergarten and enter elementary school. Starting with the second grade, elementary school classes are more or less formalized. The children follow a set curriculum, and the second, third, fourth and fifth grades each live together in a house of their own where they eat, sleep and study. Everything in the house, in the classroom and playroom is built to the children's scale. Even the showers are low so that the child learns how to keep himself clean without having to stretch to reach the faucet. The children remain in this house with a teacher and a house mother until they reach the sixth grade. At that point, for the first time in their lives, they have their dormitory separate from their school. They go to a regular schoolhouse where, instead of a house mother and only one teacher, they have different teachers for each subject in the curriculum. In addition, every class has an "educator" who is responsible for organizing the group, not just for formal studies but for hikes and other out-of-school activities as well. He also takes care of the children's problems. He makes sure that any child who needs help gets it.

If we are talking about children who need help, we should SAADIA mention that there are thousands of parents all over who would like to send us their problem children. You know the sort of thing: "I have a son who has a wonderful mind; he just needs a little strict discipline, which I am sure he could get in a kibbutz." Or, "A friend of mine has a marvelous child but he is every so slightly retarded. Would you accept that child at your kibbutz? His parents would be willing to pay."

The answer, unfortunately, is that the kibbutz cannot be a YOSEF shelter for problem children. Later on we will talk about the Youth Aliyah children whom we took into our kibbutz. Some of them did have problems but these were children we rescued from war and persecution. Today when we do accept nonkibbutz children into our school system, these are normal children and we do it only when we feel that it is good for our kibbutz. If one of our classes or age groups is too small, we may agree to take in other children. Or we may take in children from the outside to give our own youngsters a chance to meet boys and girls their age who do not live on a kibbutz. In this way they get to hear what is going on in the rest of the world.

We start training our children at a very early age for their role as workers on the kibbutz. When they are in elementary school, they are expected to do a certain amount of work on the children's farm, which has its own animals. They begin to learn the fundamentals of responsibility in the management of a farm. They may want to play, but when the time comes to feed the ducks, then somebody—it is usually done by rotation—will have to go and do it. Furthermore, we feel that it is all right, if necessary, to close our school for a few days so the children can help the grownups when the apples or the potatoes have to be picked, or if the rainy season is imminent and certain jobs have to be done before the rains come. When we do this, all the children participate and perform whatever chores they are physically capable of doing. During the potato-picking season the first or second grade children may work only an hour a day, but that hour is a very important one for them. They get up early in the morning, put on their work-clothes and go out with their teachers to do their hour of work. When they are through, they shower and change their clothes. Then they sing songs and have a class discussion about potatoes. It is a special week for them: Everything centers around the work of harvesting the potatoes and the necessity for doing the job. When the children are in the third grade, they may work two hours each day, and gradually increase their working hours as they move up through the grades. By the time they have finished elementary school, these youngsters can take over many adult chores.

Secondary   When they enter high school, the kibbutz boys and girls have to
Education   go to the district high school. In our case, the district high school happens to be right here in Kfar Blum. The children now begin an intensive study program. If we consider that children in Israel go to school six days a week[19] we find that over a period of twelve years they actually get two more years of formal education than many children abroad. Along with their classroom work, high school students are expected to put in additional hours of work per week on the kibbutz. During the early part of their high school career, the students are assigned to work in various branches of kibbutz activity. Usually they spend two or three months in each department so that, say, a boy may have a chance to work with the cows, in the machine shop, or as a carpenter or tractor driver. Only during the last two years of high school do we permit the boys and girls to choose a field in which they would like to specialize and work on a permanent basis.

This system has worked out very well. During the Six-Day War, when the men of the kibbutz were away in the army, the

[19]There is no school on the Sabbath and on national and religious holidays.

youngsters under military age took over all the work that had to be done in the fields. While the women continued caring for the small children, the high school students, and even younger boys and girls, did everything from milking the cows and taking care of the chickens to seeing that the fields were irrigated and properly cared for.

Our children have a fairly informal relationship with their teachers, and call them by their first names. If they need help in the evening with their homework, or if they have any other problem, they can simply to go the teacher's house and say, "Look, this is bothering me." It is taken for granted that the teacher will give them all the help they need. (The children, by the way, have this same informal relationship with all the other adults on the kibbutz. It is not unusual for some little three- or four-year-old to walk into the nearest house and ask the grownups inside for a piece of candy, a piece of gum, or a glass of water.)

The school year includes an annual hike. The little ones go on short hikes, sometimes staying overnight on another kibbutz. As they grow older they go further and further away from home and stay away for longer periods of time. By the time they reach high school age, they may go on trips to Jerusalem for three or four days, or as far south as Eilat and Sharm El Sheik. On these trips they not only spend time with their own class but also meet children from the schools of other kibbutzim, so that there may be three or four hundred children in one age group traveling together. In this way our youngsters begin to get out of their somewhat provincial environment.

The reason I do not like many—I might say most—of the studies
that have been published about kibbutz education is that none of
them seem to take into account the fact that while our educational
system has certain constants, it is continually evolving. Statements made in Spiro's study[20] are not necessarily true today, and
studies made a year from now will certainly not reflect the early
days of kibbutz education.

SAADIA

Our educational system began as a product of the particular
conditions that existed at the time. Before their children came, the

[20]Melford E. Spiro, *Kibbutz: Venture in Utopia.* New, augmented edition. New York, Schocken Books, 1971.

young pioneers gave no more thought to child rearing and education than they did to hosts of other problems. They started to develop their educational system only when the problem became immediate.

Of course there always were philosophical discussions about educational philosophy and what the child of the future would be like. But these were just interesting theoretical discussions—very much like the big debates on idealism versus materialism, or Marxism versus Utopianism. And then the first woman in our group become pregnant. Suddenly there was the problem of what to do with the baby about to be born. Where do we house the child? Where do we house the new mother? Should mother and child live together, or separately? In a relatively short period of time, the young people discovered that if six mothers, with one child apiece, were each to take care of her own child, this would take six people out of the kibbutz labor force. It took no great mathematical genius to see that if just one woman would be given the job of caring for these six children, the other five would be left free for other work on the kibbutz. Then there was the security situation. If you had all the children in one place, all the time, you could watch them more closely in times of danger. Finally, we could not send all six mothers out to study hygiene, child training and pedagogic methods. So, for all these practical reasons, we devised a system of collective education.

Once we had decided on collective education, there were endless variations from which to choose. Jews tend to rationalize their activities and turn necessity into a philosophy. Being good Jews, we kibbutzniks, too, began to rationalize. We decided that collective education was the only way of creating true socialists. I remember seriously asserting one night that we were going to develop the new "cooperative man." One psychologist cited Freudian theories in defense of collective education. I think an analysis of Freud might prove just the opposite, but this was quite irrelevant. Freud was the rage and collective education was our need, so we fused the two.

One of our people who had studied at New York University came back quite an expert on collective education. He demonstrated conclusively that there was only one thing to do with a child: take him away from the erotic atmosphere of the closed-in conjugal circle and put him in the free and stimulating environment of his peer group. Have the babies stay with the babies, and the kindergarten children with the kindergarteners. Naturally there was to be no differentiation between the sexes; boys and girls would stay together to get away from decadent capitalist attitudes toward sex. At a certain stage it was not unusual to see teenage boys and girls, just before adulthood—at the age of seventeen or so—taking showers together. There you had Moshe's towel hanging in the shower right next to Rina's, and Benjamin's next to Dahlia's. This was considered wholesome education, approved by psychiatrists as the only proper sex education, free from the smut which accompanied the capitalist system.

Later on, we discovered that instead of developing wholesome attitudes toward sex these children became asexual; they simply lost all interest in sex and it took many years before their sexual development took place. There were also certain questionable side effects. In the end, this notion of complete co-education at all stages up to the age of eighteen was abandoned.

Today the sexes are separated, not by any arbitrary rule beginning with a given age but whenever sexual or presexual stirrings first appear. This may be as early as the age of eight, or perhaps at eleven but usually it comes before the onset of puberty. When the girls begin to be a little shy, and to giggle, when the boys start to do a little more peeking, we quite naturally separate the boys from the girls. As a matter of fact, there seems to be a new trend coming up. I've heard that some of the young mothers want even the babies grouped according to sex—the girls separately and boys separately—and so on back to the Middle Ages!

Of course, the educational system varies from time to time and from kibbutz to kibbutz. When an anthropologist or a psychologist comes along at a given moment and says, "This is kibbutz education," he is completely wrong. He has to say, "This is what it was. That is how it evolved. This is how it is to date. And this is how it may, or may not, develop in the future."

When my older son was a baby, there was a theory that   YOSEF mattresses caused weak backs. So during the first three or four years of his life the poor kid had to sleep on a plywood board covered with just a thin blanket. Buy my younger son was allowed to sleep on a mattress which was reasonably firm and comfortable. Today he says, "If I'd had to sleep on a plywood board I would have gone crazy." I look at both boys; I do not see any difference between their backs. Neither of them suffers from a weak back. So I really do not know what is good.

I also remember that when our first son was born the practice was to let the child suckle as long as he wished. The mother would sit and the baby would work away for an hour or two until he was satisfied. But by the time our second one was born, there had been a change. We were told that a child got all his nourishment during the first five minutes of the feeding; accordingly, one should train a baby from his earliest days to be disciplined and to get the job done quickly. So the baby was given the breast at stipulated times for five minutes and that was it. He could yell his head off but he got nothing more. Now that my granddaughter is here, they are back to theory number one: Do not feed at stipulated hours but only when the baby wants to be fed. Theories come and theories go.

SAADIA   And we ought to add that the child survives them all. Anyway, all our babies are beautiful.

YOSEF   Our children are brought up together in classes. All babies born during the same six or seven-month period will be together in one group, which retains its identity as its members grow up. When they enter school, they choose a class name. It may be *S'nunit* ("Swallow"), *D'ror* ("Sparrow"), or perhaps they will choose the name of a plant or fruit, like *Shaked* ("Almond"). These class names remain almost forever. Even after they are married and have children of their own the members of the class refer to each other as *"Sh'kedim"* or *"D'rorim."*

The   Because they develop this class identity, they have a sibling
Group   attitude towards each other. It is very rare for a boy to marry a girl
Spirit   from his own class. He may marry a girl from the class above or the class below, but within the class there is a brother-sister relationship, and so marriages between classmates are very few.

Traces of this intimacy remain even when the young people go into the army. The idea of comradeship, of taking care of any member of your class, makes itself felt in every platoon or section. The tradition in the Israeli army never to abandon the wounded or the dead has probably derived from this mutual devotion that every kibbutz child learns from earliest youth. The soldiers know that they are responsible for one another, just as, back on the kibbutz, the problem of any one member of the class was the problem of the class as a whole.

Within a class you may have one or two children who are especially talented in some field. On the other hand, there may also be a child who is retarded or who has learning difficulties. Of course, such exceptional children receive whatever help they can get from psychologists and special teachers. But there is no substitute for the wonderful support they get from their classmates. The class will do everything it can to help a backward child and to include him in all the class activities, even if on occasion this individual may hold back the entire class.

At one kibbutz, in the Emek, there was a boy who was mentally deficient. He was carried along by his class until high school. While the others studied, he would just sit in the classroom, drawing pictures or doodling, but he remained within the group. Of course, once the group got to high school the situation became untenable. But every day, after school, the others drew the boy into their social and sports activities. Today he is a worthy member of the kibbutz community. He does his chores and very often he will be asked to do some special job. Before a holiday, for instance, when a lawn has to be raked, he will be given the rake and told that he must save the day for the kibbutz. Everybody understands his problems and, with the help of his group, he has become a useful member of the kibbutz. In the kibbutz, you do not have the struggle for personal success or the idea of "the survival of the fittest." In the kibbutz group, the weak also survive. We know several cases of physically handicapped people who have been carried along by the group from childhood on, all through the years—at work, at play, in sports. In short, they are helped to participate in all the experiences of the group.

So you can see that collective education, as it evolved in the kibbutz, has certain basic ingredients which make for healthy development. No child can fail to respond to the inordinate amount of love, attention and concern shown him by the adult community of the kibbutz. The child is considered a very important person, because the children represent a sort of guarantee that the kibbutz has firm roots and will continue to exist and grow. The very fact that the child gets all this attention probably does more for his ego development than the kind of training his *metapelet* had or the courses his mother may have taken from the experts of the day. Personal attention is unquestionably an important aspect of the kibbutz educational system. The children do not have to fight a big battle for their rights. It is taken for granted that every child has certain needs because he is a developing human being. The job of the adult community is to anticipate these needs and to provide for them.

Another positive factor in kibbutz education is the physical environment. The kibbutz children are born on a farm, where the child learns to live with nature. He lives outdoors and this has a significant effect on him.

In any case, the results of our collective education were very good, even in the days before we had professional educators. The role of the parents has been differently assessed at various stages. At one time the parent was considered no more than incidental to the educational process. Nowadays in almost every kibbutz we have discovered that the parent has such a vital role in the development of the child that, except in those rare cases where a parent is really unfit, there can be no adequate substitute for parents. When a child has no parents, the kibbutz community has to help find a parent substitute.

The question whether kibbutz education tends to supplant the parent by replacing him with a substitute who is better trained for the job may have had some relevance many years ago, but today it is not asked very often except by visitors who are still thinking of the olden days.

YOSEF   We should add here, I think, that there were years in which entire kibbutzim had to serve as parent substitutes for the children of Youth Aliyah. Youth Aliyah was originally set up by Henrietta Szold during the 1930's to rescue children from Germany and

Nazi-occupied countries and bring them to Palestine. When they
arrived here—without their parents—these boys and girls were
cared for and educated at kibbutzim. *Youth Aliyah*

The first group of Youth Aliyah children which we received
here at Kfar Blum came from Austria and Czechoslovakia. After
the war, Youth Aliyah brought in children who had survived the
Nazi holocaust and the concentration camps in Europe; most of
these children were orphans. Later, Youth Aliyah brought to
Israel children from North Africa, Iran, and the Arab countries.

Many of these children were suffering from emotional
problems. I worked as a director of Youth Aliyah groups for quite
a while, so I ought to know. I remember one little girl who was
afraid to go out or to take a bus because she was afraid that her
husband would turn up and take her back! Before she had left
home—one of the North African countries—her father had
married her off to a man thirty years her senior. Her father was
afraid that if she came to Israel with Youth Aliyah as an
unmarried girl she might end up marrying a man who was not
religious, or perhaps even a non-Jew.

Youth Aliyah did not provide the case histories of these
children and perhaps wisely so, because they did not want me to
be influenced by their records. Some of the children placed into
my care went through experiences which might well have broken
a strong adult. We had one little girl from an Arab country who
had been abducted by an Arab. This man had misused her
sexually. Youth Aliyah literally ransomed her but her parents
would have nothing to do with her because she had been
"shamed." One little boy had spent four years in jail for acting as a
lookout for a group of marijuana smugglers. Since the North
African country where he was born had no penal institutions for
young children, he spent four years of his childhood—from about
age seven to eleven—in a regular prison where he was the
plaything of several hundred adult criminals. Another little boy
had come to Israel with his parents, but one fine day his parents
told him that they had decided to go back to where they had come
from. They gave him half a pound and the address of Youth
Aliyah and left him on his own. He, too, eventually landed in Kfar
Blum.

How we solved these problems is a story all its own. It took many years. We could not get much help from textboks. All of the forty children—twenty-four boys and sixteen girls—who came to us through Youth Aliyah grew up, went into the army and became useful citizens. Three of them eventually went to America because they married American girls. One of them went to France. But the rest remained in Israel. Some of them have become members of our kibbutz—by now, they are regular "old-timers"—and some have joined other kibbutzim. Others have become career officers in the army and the police. None has ever been in jail or at an institution for the mentally disturbed.

The care of these youngsters cost the kibbutz a great deal of time and money. We had to house them and to feed them. Youth Aliyah contributed to their support, but it could never compensate our kibbutz for the tremendous amount of manpower and working time which the kibbutz had to devote to the health and happiness of the children.

Five adults were assigned to live with the group. Also, the children were "adopted" by various members of the kibbutz who took them into their houses for visits so they would get a feeling of family life. Little by little, the children became accustomed to kibbutz living. It was very hard work, but over the years they adjusted and today there are Youth Aliyah graduates not only in our kibbutz but in practically every kibbutz in the country. Some of Israel's better-known army officers and government officials were once Youth Aliyah children.

SAADIA   At this point we ought to stop and look at the kind of education kibbutzniks get after they finish high school. As we have already said, the kibbutz takes care of all the needs of its members and their children. This includes education—elementary school, high school, and in many cases college, university or other specialized training outside the kibbutz.

YOSEF   College and university—this brings up an interesting point. The original kibbutzniks did not think it was in the kibbutz spirit for individuals to go out and get an advanced formal education. It smacked too much of personal ambition. Today we are eager to have our young people get a higher education. But some people from the outside tell us we are not going far enough: We ought to insist that all our young people go to college. Let us take a look at this question. Should we require everyone to go to college straight from high school?

As I have pointed out earlier, twelve years of school from Grade 1 to Grade 12 in Israel is really equivalent to fourteen years in America because our school day is longer than the American school day and the children go to school six days a week. So the Israeli boy or girl who completes Grade Twelve here already has the equivalent of what would be two years of college, or a junior college diploma, in the United States—in other words, a sound basic education even if he does not go on to an institution of higher learning.

Another element to consider in the college question is the fact that when a youngster graduates high school (that is age eighteen) he—or she—has to do three full years of service in the army. This is regrettable but there is nothing we can do about it.

When the young people are through with their army service, they are already twenty-one years old. But if you are a kibbutznik, this is not the end of it, because once you are finished with the army you are expected to give an additional year to what we call "national kibbutz service," either working for the youth groups of our political party in the cities or towns, or going out to help a new kibbutz get started. This means that by the time you are free even to consider higher education you are already twenty-two. At that point many of the youngsters feel that with their twelve years of formal schooling, their two years in the army, and their year in the city, they have had enough education. They want to settle down on the kibbutz, get married and start a family.

But what about those who do want to go back to school? We have fine universities right here in this little country of ours—the Hebrew University, the Haifa Technion, Tel Aviv University, the Negev Institute for Higher Education in Beersheba, Bar Ilan University, the Weizmann Institute, and several other good institutions of higher learning.

So we do have opportunities for higher education close at hand. But what are the criteria by which a kibbutz decides whether or not we should send a young man or woman to an institution of higher education?

First of all, we would want to be sure that the person involved really wants to go to college. We cannot force a person to go if he is unwilling, not even if we think it might be good for the kibbutz if he got the additional training.

Next, we take into consideration whether the training the person wants to get would be useful for the kibbutz. Assuming that we would need a biology teacher for our high school, an engineer for our factory, an agronomist for our farms, or perhaps an economist and a cost accountant, and we have young people who would like to train for these professions, then these young people are happy and so is the kibbutz.

The third consideration is a financial one since, after all, the kibbutz does have to pay the student's tuition fees and other expenses. The kibbutz could not afford to send too many people at a time in any one year. Fortunately, so far, in our own kibbutz the number of people who wanted to go, and whom we considered fit to go, has never exceeded our financial ability to send them. But let us assume that during one year twenty-five people would tell us that they want to study at the Hebrew University. That would mean a huge outlay of money all at one time. In that case we would have to set up a system of priorities because we would not be able to send all twenty-five at the same time.

What if a young man or woman wants to study a subject such as comparative ancient religions, not in order to teach or for some other practical purpose but simply because he or she wants to know more about it? In that case we would have to consider several additional factors, such as whether the person really showed capacity for scholarship in the past and whether he or she has made enough of an effort. If the youngster never used to give a damn for study and could not wait to get out of high school, we would probably say: "Take it easy. Spend a year or two here at home on the kibbutz. Maybe you can take a correspondence course. Show us that you are really prepared to study hard, because if our community is going to lay out such a large amount of money for you we will not do it simply because you happen to think just now that it would be a good idea to go off to school and get out of a few years' work on the kibbutz."

Formerly there were kibbutzim which allowed no more than a specified number of young men and women to go away to college during any given year but this turned out to be a serious mistake. Within the last few years our own kibbutz has decided not to set up such arbitrary quotas but to send all those who meet our standards. This has also been set down as a general rule by the central kibbutz organization of our movement.

At first we thought we would be swamped with applicants but by the time a young person is through with the army and with his year of kibbutz service, he usually wants to settle down and start a family. Unlike many people in the cities, kibbutzniks do not feel that they must have completed all their higher education by the time they are, say, twenty-six years old. Many of our people get married, start their families, work at the kibbutz for several years, and then, when they are in their thirties, apply to us for permission to go back to school. Usually we accept their applications. We sent one of our members to study business administration and economics when he was in his fifties.

Let us put it this way. Our people do not go to college just so they can say they are college graduates. A degree is not the *sine qua non* of an educated person. We send people to college when they want to go, and when we think they should go. But I can say that we have become increasingly aware of the need for higher education because we see how much specialized training is required nowadays to run this kibbutz—and the country as a whole.

In recent years there has been a new development: "regional colleges" in rural areas where people from surrounding villages and kibbutzim can take informal evening courses in any number of subjects. There is such a place at Tel Hai;[21] it serves the entire Upper Galilee and many of our *haverim* from Kfar Blum go there. Interestingly enough, the Tel Hai "regional college" began quite innocently as an outlet for the artistic talents of people living in our area. Some men and women got together, formed a class in ceramics, and before long they had developed great skill in working with clay. Others started out playing with ordinary *shmattahs*—just plain rags—and ended up making sophisticated

---

[21]The classes at Tel Hai use the facilities of a youth hostel. The "regional colleges" are run by "regional councils," governing bodies consisting of representatives from villages and kibbutzim of the area.

batik cloth. Fiddlers, trombonists, piccolo players and drummers with vague memories of instruments have picked them up again and formed miniature orchestras, so that music now abounds in the hills and valleys of the Upper Galilee.

Culture and the Kibbutz
From such beginnings, the classes have branched out into regular lecture courses in a variety of subjects. Many older people who had no chance to finish high school attend these courses. Recently, the Tel Hai College has started a working relationship with Tel Aviv University with a view to getting formal academic recognition.

Here on the kibbutz, too, we have people learning Hebrew, or English, or Bible, and of course we have a cultural committee that plans holiday celebrations, lectures, and concerts. We read books and we like to listen to good music. Those who come here to speak or perform are invariably impressed by the reception they get in the kibbutz.

A number of years ago a noted pianist who was visiting Israel came to our kibbutz and was asked to give a concert. We have a grand piano in our dining hall and that evening he gave us a concert. At the end of the first half of the program he was greeted with thunderous applause. Our people were thrilled that this famous artist should have agreed to come and play for us. During the intermission the pianist left the hall. When he returned for the second half of the program, he had changed from his informal clothes into full concert regalia—white tie, tails, everything. "There is no reason," he explained apologetically, "why I should show less respect for an audience like this than I would for an audience in some concert hall in the city." He sat down at the piano, resplendent in full dress, just as if he had been performing at the Mann Auditorium in Tel Aviv.

There are a number of painters and other artists on our kibbutzim and efforts are made to encourage them. Our central kibbutz organization has a committee of experts who come around to the kibbutzim to look at the work of potential artists. In some cases they say: "We recommend that this boy, or this girl, should get a chance to go to art school. We will give him—or her—a scholarship." Or they may suggest that the budding artist should be permitted to take off three days a week from his regular kibbutz work so he can devote his time to his artistic pursuits.

I do not know whether there is any other society or community that arranges it so that a youngster, or a man with a family—in some cases a father of two children—can go on for years working only three days a week and spending the other three days painting. Of course, you could starve in a garret and have the entire week for painting but we on the kibbutz try to find a fair compromise between working to support yourself (or rather, to pull your weight as part of the kibbutz) and expressing your artistic inclinations.

Education, culture, art, music—all these combine to provide a   SAADIA
varied and satisfying life. Self-expression is a basic human need. Here on the kibbutz we reached the conclusion long ago that only if we permit the individual to express himself, to find satisfaction not merely in his work but also in his life after working hours, will we achieve the purpose for which the kibbutz was organized.

7

KIBBUTZ RITUALS

Let us begin this chapter with a discussion of some very personal relationships on the kibbutz. Take this business of "free love" on the kibbutz that everybody wants to know about. It is an attractive idea, I must admit, but it is a difficult thing to practice in a small, closed commune. A small group invariably acts as a control of morals because people always know what everybody else is doing. This is not necessarily a virtue; it just happens to be a fact that in a small community you know which families are getting along well; you also know who is playing around and who is sleeping around.

As a result, there is very little free love or promiscuity in the kibbutz. A person may not pay too much attention to the formalities of marriage but he or she certainly decides that "this is the person with whom I want to spend the rest of my life." This is how families are started. The incidence of divorce in the kibbutzim is far lower than in the cities. I should also say that the number of illegitimate children born in kibbutzim is probably smaller than in other communities of similar size.

YOSEF

Marriage and Social Relationships

The question of sex relationships is a very intriguing one because so far no solution totally satisfactory to all concerned has been found. Many young people today believe in the absolute freedom advocated by the sexual revolution. However, they will be disappointed to hear that the kibbutz at one stage had this sex revolution but did not find it really satisfactory. In the early days—thirty or forty years ago—there was greater freedom. Many kibbutzim started out with the idea of a new society which liberated everyone from all his complexes and inhibitions. The taboo of being restricted to one person, one man to one woman, was considered so old-fashioned as not to be applicable to this modern age. To those kibbutzniks, this was not a matter for

SAADIA

experimentation but one of conviction. Marriage was viewed as a kind of enslavement of one partner by the other. How, they asked, can one person be bound to another for such a long period of time by the mechanism of a marriage contract? Of course, we should bear in mind that the people involved were in their late teens and early twenties.

One must remember that these relationships were never promiscuous; these kibbutzniks did not just go to one person one night and to another the next. They considered their attachments to be "permanent" while they lasted—a week, a month, a year, five years or ten years—but they did not commit themselves to a definition of permanence. However, no Don Juan complex, of being all things to all men or all women, was acceptable. Couples got together and as long as each partner remained interested in the other, the arrangement worked, both in practice and in theory. The problems began when one of the partners remained attached to the other, while the other had already lost interest in the relationship. Would it be fair for one partner to hurt the other? Would it be right for the one who had tired of the relationship simply to pick up and go off to another partner?

A much more serious problem arose when children began to come. It was no solution to say that the children would be taken care of in the children's houses of the kibbutz, whatever befell. No matter how qualified the *metaplot* and the teachers, a child had to know who his father and mother were. If his father was no longer living with his mother but with someone else on the kibbutz, the child would be confused. Responsible parents were upset by the adverse effect this would have on the children.

The "free love" which existed for a very brief time in a very few places proved just as unsatisfactory a solution to sexual problems as other arrangements. The kibbutz experience can be instructive in this respect because at various stages every conceivable form of relationship existed in the kibbutzim.

It may be significant to note that over the years the kibbutz has come to be increasingly conservative and in many ways conformist in matters of marriage. Today practically no kibbutz marriage takes place without a rabbi performing the ceremony. There is also rather strict adherence to monogamy; divorces, of course, being a component part of monogamy as conceived in the twentieth century.

The kibbutz society is so close that if there is a split in a family, then that split must result in formal action—which means either divorce or formal separation. It is not possible to carry on and pretend that all is well with the marriage.

Actually, the kibbutz movement has not come to accept the idea   YOSEF
of a religious wedding ceremony, but this is the only legal way of getting married in Israel today. A number of kibbutzim have tried to have civil marriages. Couples have flown to Cyprus to have their marriages performed by a justice of the peace. There have even been efforts by kibbutz members to introduce civil marriage into Israel. This issue is still being debated—it is part of the larger question of the relationship between religion and the State.

But be that as it may, there does not seem to be too much objection any more to formal wedding ceremonies. Brides want to be married in a bridal gown. Only fifteen or twenty years ago, young couples wondered why the wife should have to take her husband's last name and not vice versa, but now that question is no longer discussed. On the other hand, it is not ususual here—perhaps to a much greater extent than in America—to see a pregnant bride. The young couple may have been living together for quite a long time before they decided to get married. Here again, what Saadia said before is quite correct. There is no promiscuity, not even among the younger generation. If the girl becomes pregnant, she is not "in trouble." Although abortion is not free and easy in Israel, it can be managed. But abortion is rarely sought as the solution to the problem. What usually happens in our kibbutz is that when there is a baby on the way the couple decides to get married. We have a big party, despite the fact that the bride may be a little heavy on her feet by that time.

There is no stigma attached to illegitimacy, whether a child is born just shortly after the wedding, or out of wedlock altogether. But the child would be unhappy if he did not have a father as well as a mother. This problem has been discussed many times in educational circles. When he sees the other children with two parents who come to the children's house and who take turns putting the children to bed and telling stories, the child without two acknowledged parents feels bereft.

The young people in our kibbutz receive sex education. Their behavior, on the whole, is fairly circumspect, but what complicates matters is the fact that quite a large number of volunteer workers who come to us from other countries for the summer are not always so understanding, nor do they have the same approach to sex and to family responsibility as our own kids. Kibbutz children are frequently somewhat bewildered by the attitude of the people who come to us from abroad. The new "freedom movement," the hippies and the beatniks of a few years ago have sent their representatives to us, and many of them were quite attractive and persuasive.

The idea of a person coming to a kibbutz as a "volunteer" always led to the question of what he was volunteering for. Some of our volunteers seemed to be "volunteering" for everything. That made it a little difficult so far as our own circles were concerned. Let me say, however, that many of the volunteers have been a positive factor. Here again, on the whole, the problem seems to have solved itself. Many of the volunteers who have come just for the purpose of studying Hebrew or learning what a kibbutz is like have married our young people and have set up families either in the kibbutz or elsewhere in this country.

We are singularly fortunate in Kfar Blum in that many of these young couples have settled down on the kibbutz—even mixed couples, in which case the newcomer was expected to convert to Judaism.

I should say that the kibbutz—at any age level—is probably a more moral institution than any similar society of this size, not just because there is gossip in small communities like ours but because people here do not place an exaggerated stress on premarital or any other sexual relationships. We have a more normal and healthy approach, I should say, than the one you see in cities, and perhaps in the Western world.

SAADIA   The reason for the change in attitude toward marriage is best understood in the context of the ideology of the early kibbutzniks. Many of them were true atheists; they were convinced that there was no God, and that religion in any form was an opiate which had to be eliminated from the cultural and social life of the community.

Being atheists, they of course considered it pointless to have a religious ceremony when two people wanted to get married. Such ceremony as they had was improvised without any trace of religion; the "bride" and "groom" simply informed the housing committee or the secretary of the kibbutz that they considered themselves husband and wife and therefore wanted to live together in a room of their own. The government as such was not involved because in those days, when Palestine was still a British mandate, the kibbutz was a self-contained community and what we did among ourselves was nobody else's business. Inheritance and property rights certainly were no problem in a kibbutz. As soon as a child was born, the community would take care of him. So why be bothered with a ceremony or any kind of formal recognition of the fact that two people wanted to live together?

The women were the first to insist shyly but firmly that something ought to be done to mark the day of their union with the mate of their choice. And so, almost shamefacedly, people began to give official recognition to the wedding day. Thereafter, it occurred to many people that the question of marriage was not only one of religion but of tradition. For generations Jewish mothers had led their daughters to the *huppah*[22] where couples were joined in the religious ceremony which has distinguished Jewish marriage throughout all these years.

After the establishment of the State of Israel, all Jewish marriages performed in the country had to be solemnized by a rabbi in order to receive legal recognition. (Non-Jews had to be married by clergymen of their own faith.) As a result, the kibbutzim, one by one, accepted the law of the land and even came to find it interesting and satisfying in many ways. It is not unusual today to come to a kibbutz and find a very elaborate wedding with all the trappings—*huppah*, rabbi, *minyan*,[23] the Seven Blessings[24] and all—in good, traditional style.

---

[22]Bridal canopy used in Jewish marriage ceremonies.
[23]Quorum of 10 adult males required for Jewish religious services.
[24]These are recited as part of the traditional marriage ceremony.

A Drift   The same gradual drift toward tradition has taken place also in
Toward   many other aspects of cultural life in the kibbutz. When the
Tradition   kibbutz pioneer first came to establish a new society, he was going
to rid himself of all diaspora superstitions. The holidays he
observed would be given content that would be meaningful to
every child; they would be relevant to the new society and
significant to the future of the new nation. Thus, Passover would
not signify the departure of the Jews from Egypt thousands of
years ago; it would not be celebrated with a Haggadah[25] which
discussed the intricacies of Rabbinic lore. Passover was to mean
the rebirth of the Jewish people and the rejuvenation of Israel. It
was to be a festival symbolizing the triumph of mind and spirit
over the dark forces of capitalism and feudalism. Very little
thought was given to the fact that the dates of the traditional and
the new celebrations were identical and that there was a certain
contradiction in the new rational approach. The contradictions
were hidden by incorporating the poetry of Bialik and passages
from great world literature into the new Haggadot that were put
out by various secularist kibbutzim—complete with modern
music instead of the traditional chants.

This attitude persisted for several decades. But as the years
passed more and more of the traditional Passover customs were
re-introduced. Whereas the early atheists ate bread[26] on Passover
as a matter of principle, today practically no bread can be seen in
kibbutzim during the Passover week. There seems to be no need
any more to demonstrate that we are emancipated, and there
seems to be nobody to revolt against. Nowadays it is perfectly
legitimate to have matzot on Passover. Those few individuals who
must have bread for health reasons, or who still insist on strict
secularism on the kibbutz, do get bread, but it involves an effort.

YOSEF   Back in Buffalo, in the United States, I had a friend who decided
to show his atheism by going to school on Yom Kippur.[27] This did

---

[25]Special prayer book containing the ritual for the *seder*, the home ceremony
performed on the first two nights of Passover.

[26]According to Jewish religious law, only unleavened bread (*matzot*) may be eaten
during Passover week.

[27]The Day of Atonement, the most solemn holiday of the Jewish year, which is
marked by fasting and by all-day services in the synagogue.

not make any sort of impression on anybody because lots of other people—all the non-Jews for instance—also went to school on Yom Kippur. So, in order to make people understand that he was going to school on Yom Kippur as a matter of principle, he used to skip school the day before and the day after.

The early kibbutz atheists really had a tough time. They had to explain that the day of rest, the *Shabbat,* was Saturday instead of Sunday because that happened to be the day of rest for everybody in the country, but that it had nothing to do with the Sabbath of traditional religion. They also had to explain that we speak Hebrew not because Hebrew is a holy tongue, the language of the Torah, but because it happens to be the tongue of the revived Jewish nationalist movement.

SAADIA

A more serious problem was the teaching of the Bible. Since Palestine and Israel were so closely interlinked with the Bible, it was impossible to think of the country's life cycle without the Bible. The schools of the country had the Bible in their daily curriculum, place names were derived from the Bible, the first names of many kibbutz members were of Biblical origin, and so on. Even the Hebrew that was spoken throughout the land recalled the Bible at every turn. In every corner and at every step the kibbutznik found that the Bible was with him. So the kibbutz atheist had to explain to himself and to others that in Israel the Bible was part of the cultural, national renaissance and had nothing to do with religion.

The Kibbutz and the Bible

When the atheist teacher explained to his class the meaning of such statements as "And God said unto Abraham," or "God said unto Moses," his usual formula was that "God" was a theoretical concept and that there were people who believed in a personal God. So, by adding the phrase "there are people who believe," the teacher was able to discourse on all the commentaries of the Torah from the early days through the Middle Ages, the Hasidic tales of God and His wondrous work, the Jewish traditional concepts of God and the thousands of martyrs who died "for the sanctification of God"—all without doing violence to the atheism for which the kibbutz stood.

But nowadays that ludicrous anomaly, the kibbutz atheist, has almost passed from the scene. There still are atheists around but

*The
Vanishing
Kibbutz
Atheist*
the average kibbutz member today is a traditionalist without any rigid doctrines. He is a Jew in every sense of the word. He is a clear opponent of the "Canaanite" philosophy which was briefly in vogue some fifteen years ago—the idea of developing a new Hebrew nation which would have few links with the Jews in the rest of the world but turn instead to the indigenous population of the Middle East. The "Canaanites" considered themselves "Hebrews" rather than "Jews." Very few kibbutzniks still follow that kind of nonsense today. They are Jews; they are Israelis; they are traditionalists. They speak Hebrew because it is their native tongue and they observe the Jewish holidays. Some have even adopted traditions which have clearly religious connotations.

It is no accident that many young kibbutz fathers today observe the Bar Mitzvah of their sons by taking them to the synagogue and having them read from the Torah. In several kibbutzim synagogues were built at the request of the elderly parents of the members, but with the complete consent and understanding of the members themselves. At Kfar Blum at holiday time you often see the old, the young and the very young attending services together. Mothers bring their children to the synagogue to hear the prayers. Young men look in and, quite frequently, they stay. As a matter of fact, people from the neighboring kibbutzim come to our synagogue. The same thing is happening in other kibbutzim where synagogues have been established. But the big surprise is the new synagogue at En Harod, which was built by the kibbutz after many decades without traditional observances. In many ways there is a closer fusion between the old and new than existed ten or fifteen years ago.

Funerals
There is one aspect of kibbutz life for which no satisfactory ritual has yet been found: that of death and mourning. Funerals in any society are moments of great difficulty. However, strictly religious societies do find some solace in following a very strict and rigid ritual. Somehow, the acting out of what is considered proper at that moment gives solace to the bereaved, to close friends and to the community as a whole. But in kibbutzim where the whole life pattern is not Orthodox it is quite impossible to revert to an Orthodox burial ceremony. In the early days kibbutz funerals were marked by the strangest behavior of all. People

simply came to the burial ground, the body would be lowered into the grave and the grave would be covered, all in absolute silence. Then the mourners simply walked away. The harshness of this kind of farewell to the dead was painful to many. Before long, people began to look for a new way. First of all, the *Kaddish*[28] was re-introduced at many funerals and a few prayers were recited. Then impromptu eulogies were delivered at the cemetery. But no really satisfactory ceremony has evolved thus far. We have had funerals of young people who died of some illness and of old people who departed when their time came, but the most tragic and the most difficult of all have been the funerals of young people who were brought back from the battlefields. On those occasions the pain was complicated by an inability to respond in a way that could bring solace—assuming that solace is possible in such circumstances.

I do not quite agree with Saadia. I cannot see where there is a   YOSEF
problem. I have very often felt that at somber moments such as a funeral anything you could say is superfluous. I do not quite agree with the idea of saying the *Kaddish,* especially over the grave of a person who was never religious in his life and expressed no strong traditionalist belief. It would not do him any good or give his family any comfort. I would say that I accept this very simple principle: Do whatever the person would have wanted or whatever his family wants. If the person has left some sort of will to the effect that he does not want any eulogies over his grave, that's it. Occasionally the family says, "We would like to have some of his friends say a few words." In that case, that is what we do.

There is one thing at a Kfar Blum funeral which is perhaps typical of other places as well. When the coffin is lowered into the grave, all the men present take turns filling up the open grave. As the shovels are passed from hand to hand, everyone feels that this is his way of saying goodbye to someone who was very close.

Thirty days after a death, the kibbutz has a short ceremony in the dining hall which is usually attended by the friends of the

---

[28]Prayer glorifying God recited by mourners at the funeral of a close relative and subsequently during the year of mourning and on each anniversary of the death.

deceased, with some appropriate reading or musical selection, and perhaps some of the people who knew the person well will say a few words about him.

Bar Mitzvah But let us go on to happier occasions. As I have said before, the kibbutz is a family. Our sorrows are not the sorrows of an individual but of the family as a whole. When sorrow comes to one member, the entire kibbutz grieves. By the same token, when we have a celebration, everybody is happy. A birth, a Bar Mitzvah, or a wedding does not concern only the people directly involved. There is a holiday atmosphere in the entire kibbutz. When there is a Bar Mitzvah—and it is usually a group observance for three or four children, or occasionally even half of a class or an entire class at one time, depending on the number of children—you can feel a change in the air a week before. You know that there will not be a general meeting on that Saturday night.

The guests begin to arrive. People come over to each other's houses to borrow chairs and ask whether you could put up guests at your house for the celebration. The women begin to bake cakes, and the dining room is a hustle and bustle as they make all sorts of preparations. The cultural committee is working furiously, setting up a stage. Decorations are put up and the photographers polish the lenses of their cameras. In the dining room you can feel the tenseness when the kitchen crew tells you, "Look, don't bother us now because we have to get ready for the Bar Mitzvah." This goes on until you reach a point where you feel it is your own personal Bar Mitzvah because the entire kibbutz is involved.

The ceremony itself is only a culmination of a long period of preparation. The Bar Mitzvah ceremony we have today is the result of many years of experimentation. I would not like to say that our present way of celebrating this great event will remain for all time. I will try to explain.

We have come to several basic conclusions. One is that the Bar Mitzvah marks a transition between childhood and the beginning of maturity. Secondly, at this moment the child must prove himself by carrying out a number of tasks, by assuming certain responsibilities. He must also be prepared to leave, even if only for a short while, the world of play and involve himself in more serious matters.

Perhaps I ought to mention here that we do not differentiate between boys and girls in our Bar Mitzvah ceremony. We do not accept the diaspora way of having boys become Bar Mitzvah at the age of thirteen and girls Bat Mitzvah at twelve. We have a celebration at age thirteen for boys and for girls, and both are considered equally important.

About three months before the Bar Mitzvah, the children are usually awakened with some ceremony in the middle of the night and told that the time has come for them to think about their Bar Mitzvah. They are offered a list of twenty-five or thirty *mitzvot*, good deeds, to perform, of which they have to choose thirteen. Two or three of the *mitzvot* are compulsory, such as an essay on a Biblical theme of their choice. A boy or girl may choose to spend a day working on our kibbutz, on a moshav,[29] in the city, or at a kibbutz of a different political persuasion, or perhaps at a religious kibbutz. Then the youngster has to write up his experiences. A rich variety of physical and intellectual tasks is open to him.

The week preceding the Bar Mitzvah is a busy one for the children and for their parents. A few days before the Friday night when the Bar Mitzvah ceremony is held, the children are formally inducted into the HaNo'ar Ha'Oved V'HaLomed (Movement of Working Youth and Students). This is a very solemn ceremony, conducted around a huge bonfire. The children are dressed in blue shirts, like those worn by all the members of the movement. Their parents are there. A district representative from the movement usually comes and gives the youngsters the oath of allegiance to which they respond: "I will fulfill my duties to the working class of which I am a member; I will never exploit anyone and will do my best to be a friend to my fellow man."

After the boys and girls have given the pledge of allegiance to the youth movement and to the working class, the bonfires are lit and the youngsters finish out the evening by sitting around the bonfire with their parents, telling stories, singing songs, and probably eating some goodies or roasting corn on the cob.

---

[29]Cooperative agricultural settlement differing from the kibbutz in that each member has his own home and a plot of land worked by himself and his family. However, some of the farm machinery is owned by the moshav as a whole, and the moshav produce is marketed and supplies and equipment are purchased through cooperative institutions.

On another day of their Bar Mitzvah week the boys and girls are expected to demonstrate their proficiency with the rifle. This is usually not done in the evening but sometime during the afternoon. They go out with their fathers and show that they can handle a rifle—take it apart, clean it, and fire it at a target with reasonably good results.

The formal and informal Bar Mitzvah ceremonies have become a major holiday in the kibbutz.

SAADIA   The Bar Mitzvah celebration and ceremonies seem so obvious as to be a natural part of Jewish life. Yet in the kibbutzim they represent a departure from the past. In some kibbutzim there were many very furious debates. Why have a Bar Mitzvah at all? What does age thirteen mean? Is it puberty? If it is puberty, then it should be celebrated for one child at the age of eleven, for another child at eleven and a half and for another at fourteen. Why stick to that archaic idea of thirteen? Does a child become a man all of a sudden? Nonsense; he does not suddenly become a man at the age of thirteen.

Very serious ideological debates took place with reference to the whole issue of Bar Mitzvah and Bas Mitzvah. Especially in the very Marxist-oriented kubbitzim the celebration, as a matter of principle, would take place not on the 13th birthday but sometime before or sometime after. But this, too, has become a thing of the past. The kibbutz movement today, in one way or another, celebrates Bar Mitzvah and Bas Mitzvah in a good, old Jewish traditional fashion.

A Kibbutz   The next important ceremony in the life of the young
Wedding   kibbutznik is his—or her—wedding. In young kibbutzim the wedding ceremony takes place in two parts. First, one pays one's due to the State. The rabbi is invited, the marriage contract is signed, and the ceremony is performed. But then comes the real wedding celebration which very often takes place in the evening as follows: A mock *huppah* is held aloft by two boys with rifles and two with pitchforks. In one wedding here at Kfar Blum, just before the Six-Day War, the boys were all at the battlefront so the girls did the honors. They held the rifles and pitchforks for the *huppah* and served the refreshments.

But this was an exceptional situation. Generally the boys do the heavy work and the girls just add the color; they wear flowing gowns, arrange the flowers and join with the boys for the glorious entertainment that follows. In the summer we occasionally have the ceremony outdoors. When my son got married, three weddings were celebrated together on the big lawn. At a signal, following the ceremony under the *huppah*, the three brides reappeared, sitting on a tractor-drawn wagon, looking beautiful and carrying huge bouquets. From the other direction came a second tractor pulling a wagon on which the three sheepish grooms were seated. As the two wagons met, the tractors roared away and with a blast of smoke the couples met, officially, for the first time as far as the kibbutz was concerned.

Not too long ago, when the State was first set up and bridegrooms were absent on military service, there were quite a few "proxy" weddings. If Moshe happened to be away in the army when the rabbi came to the kibbutz to perform his wedding, Moshe's place at the religious ceremony might be taken by one of his friends—Uri or Uzi or whoever—and the rabbi wouldn't know the difference.

Today we at the kibbutz have become hidebound and conventional. Weddings here are performed more or less in the same way as they are in the cities. I do not think we have reached the stage as yet where the girls go to the *mikvah*[30] but if the brides in town are wearing mini bridal gowns, the girls at the kibbutz also wear mini bridal gowns. If the city girls wear maxi bridal gowns, our girls wear the same. A wedding is a great occasion and we all enjoy it.

How does the kibbutz celebrate the national holidays which are observed all over the country? There is the First of May. This used to be a big holiday, especially on the kibbutz. As part of the international workers' community and the socialist world, the kibbutz demonstrated its solidarity with all toilers and downtrodden people. But it became less and less possible to develop enthusiasm for the First of May after the German holocaust, when the Nazis perpetrated their atrocities while the rest of the world

National Holidays

---

[30]Bath where observant women perform ritual ablutions before the wedding and after menstruation.

pulled its punches and dozens of nations subtly or overtly participated in those crimes. The marvelous behavior of the Danes and the Scandinavians, some of the British and some of the other democracies, was not enough to change the feeling of many kibbutzniks. The international community had watched with indifference, or at best with mild concern, while an entire people was being destroyed. Hence the First of May has become much less meaningful even for those kibbutzim which still feel that the international labor community ought to be a constant factor in their ideological lives. The First of May celebration was a beautiful thought. It still is a beautiful thought. Would that we could really have one day on which we could truthfully proclaim the internationalism of man; would that we could find all workers, all of humanity concentrated on a common goal. Regrettably, such is not the case, and there is no point in pretending.

One of the reasons why the First of May lost its position of YOSEF pre-eminence in the kibbutz calendar, and in the calendar of our country, was the fact that during the same month, roughly a couple of weeks before or after May First, we celebrate a double holiday: Remembrance Day or Memorial Day, followed immediately by Independence Day, which is probably the major holiday of the State.

The day preceding Independence Day is dedicated to the memory of the soldiers who fell in battle. There are ceremonies in the military cemeteries, and the radio stops playing light music. All places of entertainment are closed. The country is solemn and remembers its dead. In the kibbutz, as in every other place, it is a day of *yizkor*, a day of remembrance. It usually starts the evening before. All the members of our kibbutz, wearing white shirts, assemble in a little grove where there are huge boulders engraved with the names of our soldiers who did not come back. There is a brief reading of appropriate selections. An eternal flame is lit. Also, symbolically, there is an upturned army helmet in which a candlewick is burning. A group of our own soldiers, in civilian—not military—dress, take up positions on the roof of the dining hall and fire three shots into the air. This is how Memorial Day begins.

The next day, Independence Day, is a tremendous thing. In the city, people dance in the streets all day and all night. We do that, too. We love a party, a picnic with good food and a pageant in which everybody participates. People who are in the army wear their various combat ribbons, and we invite a company of soldiers, if there is one in the neighborhood, to enjoy the day with us.

There are races and competitions—how fast you can lay a pipe, or how fast you can change the wheel of a tractor, or climb a tree, and so forth. There are games of chance. We call it a circus, or a "fun fair." There are booths where you can test the steadiness of your hand or test your strength by banging down on a weight with a hammer to see whether you can make the weight go up high enough to ring the bell.

Later on, usually beginning at midnight, there is a *kumsitz*.[31] The *kumsitz* is a unique Israeli institution which consists mainly of barbecuing a lamb or a sheep. Everybody puts on his work clothes. We go out into the fields, have a huge barbecue and sit around with a drink. We serve cups of black Turkish coffee. The day is usually a very happy one for everybody concerned.

By comparison with these national holidays, the First of May has become weaker and weaker. I do not know whether it will continue, or whether it is doomed to be filed away on the list of holidays that once were, but are no longer, part of our calendar.

In general, the kibbutzim have been looking for new ways of observing our traditional Jewish holidays. For some of the holidays we have gone back to the fundamentals and ask ourselves, "What does it mean? Was Passover only a religious holiday or a historical commemoration of the Exodus from Egypt? Or is it also the festival of spring?" In our own observance we have combined all these elements.

Religious Holidays

Hanukkah is the time when we hold aloft the light of freedom. To symbolize the Hanukkah holiday, we light bonfires all over, and we pass a torch from one to another, as they did in the old days in the relay from Modin to Jerusalem to celebrate victory in battle, the beginning of the revolt of the Maccabees. At our own kibbutz the children have a spectacular torchlight procession.

---

[31]From the Yiddish: *Kumm sitz*, "come and sit (around the fire)."

Candles are distributed to every family. In the first and second grades, the *hanukkiyah* (candle-holder) may consist of just a branch from a tree with eight knobs for the eight lights and an extra one for the ninth light, the *shamash*, with which the other lights are kindled. As the children grow up, they make very elaborate and sometimes very, very beautiful *hanukkiyot*.

On Purim we have a masquerade. Usually we have people dressed up as beatniks or hippies, and replicas of historic characters like Nasser and Ben-Gurion. There may be famous characters from fairy tales but Queen Esther has almost disappeared.

During the Sukkoth[32] holiday, every child practically lives in a *sukkah*. Every class builds its own *sukkah* and there are some very elaborate specimens. Children have parties in their sukkoth to which they invite their parents and some of the other classes. Holidays such as Tu BiSh'vat[33] or Shavuot[34] are celebrated primarily as agricultural holidays. We have farm games that are played out on the field, and we have revived such ceremonies as the bringing in of the sheaves, which comes during Passover.

I sometimes find it difficult to explain to my younger friends why a set format for the holiday is necessary. They ask, "Why do the same thing over and over again, year after year?" They would like to see every holiday celebrated in a different manner each year.

Most of our cultural activities, then, center around the celebration of holidays, around the young people who combine learning how to behave as human beings with learning how to live and enjoy life.

There is one day which has been set aside for a sort of general stocktaking—*Yom Kippur.* There was a time when the atheists and the anti-religious refused to give any consideration to Yom Kippur and Rosh HaShanah in the kibbutz calendar and Yom Kippur was just another working day. They claimed that these

---

[32]Feast of Tabernacles, a fall holiday celebrated in a *sukkah* or booth made of wood or canvas and thatched with leaves and branches.

[33]Jewish Arbor Day.

[34]Pentecost, which comes late in May or sometime in June.

holidays[35] were so obviously religious that it would have been a travesty on socialism to observe them.

With the changes in attitude towards Jewish tradition and towards the Jewish past that came after the Nazi holocaust, even strictly religious holidays have come to be seen as significant. But it would by hypocritical for a person who is not really observant suddenly to go to the synagogue and pray. Prayer, after all, signifies a response to a personal God, or to a deity of a non-personal nature, but certainly to a deity to whom prayer could be addressed. Many rationalists found this impossible to accept. But then the need to consider the meaning of the lives which we were leading began to assert itself. We felt the need for a moment to pause, to get together, not in order to speak of anything practical but to think for a while, aware that at this moment every single Jew throughout this world was thinking of exactly the same thing—his association with the entire Jewish people.

Because of this need, the kibbutz as a whole has sought a way of commemorating this association through Yom Kippur. In many kibbutzim special assemblies are held on that day. On Yom Kippur Eve, after the *Kol Nidre*[36] has been heard on the radio, after the special meal for those who will fast has been served—and those who do not fast have had their regular supper—and after services have been held for the older generation, people get together in the dining hall as a community to discuss the year that has passed, the state of the kibbutz, the state of the nation, the state of the Jewish people, the significance of the holiday, the meaning of their Jewish roots, and all related subjects which have nothing to do with either economics or work or daily schedules.

To sum it up, maybe we have become conservative. Or perhaps we have become a little more—ourselves.

---

[35]The High Holiday season, beginning with the solemn celebration of Rosh HaShanah, the Jewish New Year, and culminating in Yom Kippur, the day of Atonement.

[36]Opening chant of the Yom Kippur service.

8

SOME KIBBUTZ TYPES

What are we really like? The kibbutznik is indistinguishable from any other animal that walks on two feet. Consequently, you cannot tell a kibbutznik just by looking at him. However, there are certain types that you will find in practically every kibbutz. Let me describe some of them.

SAADIA

There is the Eternal Revolutionary. He is always on the lookout for new ideas, ready to jump on the barricades and fight for the revolution. He will come to any meeting, any discussion, ready to accept new challenges. He is so dedicated that the community could not survive without him. The outstanding example of this type is Benny Marshak, who was the cultural director of Palmach, our Palestine commando corps during World War II. Benny is now past sixty but he is still fired with the same enthusiasm today as he was forty years ago. He was the first to volunteer for any mission, to organize recruiting units, and to join any group that went out as pioneers. He is a remarkable individual whose zeal has never cooled.

The Eternal Revolutionary

Closely related to the Eternal Revolutionary is the Pioneer. He will make fewer speeches than the Revolutionary about the tasks that lie ahead, but he will always be on the spot when there is work to be done. When a truck has to be unloaded in the middle of the night because it must start on the return trip early the next morning, he is ready to do the unloading. When the security situation is tense he is there, ready with his shovel even before the order has been given to dig trenches. He volunteers to clear the tables in the dining hall whether or not his name appears on the work schedule for the job that day or week. Whenever there is an emergency, or a problem, or just a person in need of help, you will find the Pioneer right in there pitching.

The Pioneer

The exact opposite of the Pioneer is the Cynic. He will do what he is told, but no more. When his name is put on the work

The Cynic

147

schedule to clear the dining hall tables, he will do the job. But if his name is not listed—or he misses it because it is misspelled or perhaps not written out clearly—he will not put himself out. When a new branch of activity is started on the kibbutz, the Cynic is positive that it is going to fail. Whenever a new educational method is suggested, he knows that it has failed elsewhere and therefore will certainly fail with us also. He watches the foibles of his *haverim* and smiles benignly as problems arise because he knew all along that it would happen that way.

The Big-Time Operator
As contrasted with the Cynic there is the Big-Time Operator. When we discuss growing an experimental crop of avocados on five acres of ground, he will say, "What do you mean, five acres? If we are going to do it, let's do it right. Let's start with fifty acres right away." When we talked about starting our electrical workshop with a crew of five, the fellow I am thinking of looked at us as if we had been born in the Dark Ages. "Five people, you say? How can you start any project on such a small scale? If we are going to have an electrical workshop, start with at least fifty, fifty-five or sixty. Not with five people." When we spoke of starting our guest house with six rooms, he was aghast. "What do you mean, six rooms? Every textbook on hotel-keeping says you have to have at least a hundred rooms as a viable economic proposition. How can we be so ridiculous as to talk of six rooms?"

The Gossip
The Gossip may be pleasanter to have around but he does not exactly command a position of great respect on the kibbutz. He knows all the news long in advance of everyone else. He quickly spreads the word about who is going with whom, who used to go with whom, who is divorcing whom, who is about to get married—or who has had an accident on the road. He listens to BBC news before the Voice of Israel comes on, or vice versa, so that he can report to the others what is going to happen before anybody else knows. He is constantly giving out information, some of which may even be true.

The Don Juan
Every kibbutz has a Don Juan. His hair is sleek when sleek hair is in style. Nowadays his hair is likely to be quite long, and he is likely to sport well-groomed sideburns, very far down his cheeks. He watches every person who comes and he knows exactly who of the fairer sex is in the kibbutz at any given moment—when she

came, how long she will stay and what she will do. Sometimes he even makes it a point to find out whose husband is away on business and at what time it would be nice to drop in on the wife for a late cup of tea. The people in the kibbutz know all about him and the girls will spread the word: "Watch out. One hour after you get to the kibbutz this fellow is going to see you, and these are the questions he is going to ask you." Sometimes you really feel sorry for him. He tries so hard, but his occasional successes hardly justify the endless efforts he must exert in order to maintain his status.

The female counterpart of the Don Juan is the widow who was very beautiful—many years ago—and has never forgotten it. Poor thing, she has lost her husband and she craves male attention. We tolerate her flirting and her kittenish ways because we understand her. She is still living in the past. Why should we disillusion her?

Then there is the Know-It-All. He knows all the statistics on any subject. He also knows exactly what is happening in the government and what the policy of the State of Israel is going to be. He can tell you in advance that it is going to rain—or that it is not going to rain—or whether we are going to make a profit or take a loss. Just name the subject—he knows all about it. *The Know-It-All*

Next comes the Culture Commando. He cannot understand how it is possible, after all the effort and money we spent on their education, that our children still do not understand that classical music is the highest form of music. Why is it, he demands, that we do not have more lectures, or more serious discussions, the way we used to do? *The Culture Commando*

The Culture Commando will sit through a movie—an American comedy or a musical—laughing all the time and enjoying every bit of the hour and a half, or two hours, of the show. But when he comes out and you ask him, "Well, how did you like it?" he will answer, "Oh, it was terrible. It has no social content." YOSEF

Then we have the Shirker, who somehow never shows up when he is assigned to do a job. When he is called to task, he will say, "Oh, yes; I quite forgot." In a group of people doing a job together somehow he always manages to be the last in line. When suitcases SAADIA *The Shirker* have to be loaded for a trip, he arrives on the scene only after all the luggage is already on the truck. He never fails to arrange things so that he can get away with doing the bare minimum and no more.

The Ideologist   Now let us look at the Ideologist, who views every problem, no matter what it is, in terms of party ideology. When a group of us has to decide whether to spend our annual vacation in the mountains or at the seashore, he opts for the seashore because it is near party headquarters and thus we could benefit from lectures by the national leaders of our party even while we are on vacation. When we discuss the educational program of our children, he never tires of reminding the committee in charge that we must not neglect the ideological training of our boys and girls.

The Philosopher   Unlike the Ideologist, the Philosopher does not relate our day-to-day problems to the labor movement or to the party philosophy of our kibbutz, but views them all in terms of larger concepts such as good and evil, humanity in general, and the ultimate significance of every act we perform in our lives.

The Orator   Now for the Orator. The Orator is the fellow who will tell you with great eloquence at lunchtime that since the hour of the day is now twelve, it is only fitting that we should repair to the dining hall and engage in the culinary ritual of the noonday meal. The young people, particularly, find the Orator exasperating, and they show it. No matter how often we try to remind them to watch their manners because the fellow is an older person and means well, our young folks will not put up with the Orator. They prefer the Realist.

The Realist   The Realist cuts right through to the heart of any matter; he analyzes every problem without fear, checks all the relevant facts and figures, and always comes down on the side of facts and figures when they conflict with the philosophical approach to the question at hand. His motto is: "Let's face the facts. Let's be realistic. Let life experience decide."

The Born Teacher   The opposite of the Realist is the Born Teacher who sees everything in terms of morality and educational impact. He constantly urges us to remember that the younger generation watches everything we do and will copy our behavior and our actions. There are many Born Teachers in the kibbutzim; some of them put their talent to good use in our schools, teaching our children. But there are some who do not get satisfaction from teaching schoolchildren and prefer to go around lecturing the grown-ups.

Another type is the Self-Centered Person who can calculate at lightning speed the effect of any development, decision or activity in his kibbutz on his personal well-being. When we take up the question of whether or not to accept a new member, he will quickly determine whether it would be "good" or "bad" for him if the kibbutz accepted the candidate. Would it give him a higher seniority for housing? On the other hand, the candidate might have the same occupation as he himself. Would the new member pose a threat to him or his job? Only hours or even days later will it dawn upon us that this man's vote on the candidate was not determined by altruistic considerations but by thoughts of his own welfare.

The Self-Centered Person

It takes much ingenuity to detect the motivations of the Politician. If the Politician holds forth very volubly on, say, the construction of an amphitheatre in our area, it usually is obvious that he has already asked to be the representative of our kibbutz on the regional council, or that he is already negotiating for a place on the building committee or the arrangements committee. At any rate, you can be sure that he is already deeply involved in the amphitheatre project. Just because his approach is so devious, only the most naive will take his words at face value. As soon as he starts to talk, everyone will ask, "What is he really after?" The Politician does not fare very well in the kibbutz.

The Politician

The Lobbyist generally does better in the kibbutz than the Politician because he is lobbying not for his personal gain but for things which, in the final analysis, will be for the good of the entire community. If he wants to get the kibbutz to appropriate more funds for his particular branch of work, the Lobbyist will find a way of demonstrating how much our community will stand to gain if it invests the funds, how much it will lose if it does not, and that a decision must be made at once because things cannot go on as they are. Usually, it is all a matter of timing. If it is a project such as new storage space for clothes, everybody will agree it is necessary and it will be done sooner or later. Some

The Lobbyist

projects may be advanced by a year—or perhaps two years —through effective lobbying. In any event, the Lobbyist is generally accepted by his *haverim* on the kibbutz because everyone knows he is not out for selfish gain.

The
Miser
The Miser is considered a slightly ludicrous figure because the small savings he effects are not worth the effort he expends in the process. During the austerity period when soap was rationed he would manage to accumulate a reserve of ten bars of soap when the ration was two bars per month. He did this by skimping and by walking long distances to a public washroom where he did not have to use his own soap. Today there is no austerity but he still goes on saving newspapers and bits of string.

Nudnik
vs. Plain
Bore
We have two types who do a lot of talking: the Delightful Nudnik and the Plain Bore. It can be quite pleasant to sit next to the D.N. when you wait for a meal because he always has stories to tell you. You may have heard the same stories five or six times before but you do not mind because he is a nice chap. There is a difference between him and the Plain Bore. The P.B. will collar you at every opportunity and tell you about his aches, pains and other troubles. He will ask you to help him resolve his personal, family and job problems. He is always out to bend your ear about something or other. The Nudnik you do not mind, but nobody can stand the Bore.

The
Semi-
Invalid
Next comes the Semi-Invalid, who manages to exploit to the full whatever health problem he may have. There are those who are really ill but who fight their invalidism to the point where they will outdo any healthy individual on the kibbutz. But we always have some who enjoy poor health and use it as a means of getting special privileges.

Special-
Diet-
Cranks
Then there are the Special-Diet-Cranks. We have on our kibbutz people who really need special diets because of health problems —salt-free, fat-free, protein-free. However, there are others who are perfectly healthy but who, no matter what is served, always want something else instead. When chopped meat is served they will ask for chicken; when chicken is served they will want chopped meat. We have found a simple way of handling these characters. Give them anything "special," anything different from what the others get, and they will be perfectly satisfied.

We had one fellow—he is no longer with us—who insisted that   YOSEF
he could only eat white bread. This was at a time when everybody
ate black bread or rye bread and white bread was very expensive.
Every day the baker would bring black bread and rye bread for
everyone else, plus one or two loaves of white bread for several
invalids and for this one character who insisted upon eating
nothing but white bread. Eventually it was found that white bread
was actually no more costly than rye bread or black bread;
besides, it did not get stale as quickly as the black bread. As a
result, the entire kibbutz eventually switched to white bread. But
then this "white-bread" friend of ours reversed himself and
insisted he had to have rye bread. And so, every day the baker's
truck would come loaded with white bread for everybody else,
plus two loaves of rye for our "privileged character."

Now let us turn to a type who is a curiosity in the kibbutz but   SAADIA
who enjoys universal respect—the dish-washing Knesset member. As we have pointed out elsewhere, many government   ***The V.I.P.***
officials, from ordinary members of the Knesset up to the Deputy
Prime Minister of Israel, are members of kibbutzim. They have
private apartments or residences in Jerusalem, but when they
come to the kibbutz they are expected to do chores like all the
other *haverim*. I know of one member of the Knesset who always
gets the job of doing the dishes when he is on his home kibbutz.
The other *haverim* make a point of nodding to him as they pass
by—they get a kick out of watching this V.I.P. at work washing
dishes. To give you just one instance, the dishwasher at Kibbutz
Ginossar—when he is there—is Yigal Allon, who happens to be
our Deputy Prime Minister.
There you are, this is the way we see ourselves.

Could you recognize a kibbutznik if you saw him on the street?   YOSEF

At one time, you could. The city person wore city clothes; the   SAADIA
kibbutznik wore khakis. Even in the early days when Israel was
poor and Israelis did not have woolen pants, woolen skirts, and   ***The Typical***
dressier clothes, you could tell the kibbutznik from the others   ***Kibbutznik***
because he dressed more modestly, so much so that some people

thought all kibbutzim were ascetic. But this was an erroneous impression. There is no doubt, of course, that some ascetics were drawn to the kibbutz movement. Some kibbutz people enjoyed poverty and the visible marks of an austere standard of living as a form of self-expression, but the kibbutz movement never had asceticism as part of their ideology.

Today, with the exception of the necktie (which is taboo for any kibbutznik of the older generation except when he is attending a formal function, say, in the government) there is practically no way of distinguishing the kibbutznik from city folk. The younger kibbutzniks wear blazers, psychedelic colors, mini-skirts or long skirts—whatever happens to be the vogue in the world outside.

YOSEF   That is not entirely true. The kibbutzniks may dress up when they go into the city, but at home they usually dress with a complete lack of formality except on Friday nights, holidays, or for parties. It simply is not practical to walk around the kibbutz in long skirts. Girls wear shorts because it is more comfortable, and boys wear shorts because when you sit on a tractor, anything else is liable to get in your way. Usually the girls do not bother with heavy makeup, and the boys do not bother too much with fashion. Everything is very informal.

SAADIA   When I first came to Kfar Blum back in 1947, the people here wore all kinds of colors, and I saw nothing unusual about that. But after getting settled at Kfar Blum I wanted to see some other places in the area. I visited Kfar Giladi, the oldest kibbutz in the region—big, solid and respectable. I was not quite sure then what it was, but I felt there was something strange about that place. Not until much later did it dawn on me that all the people at Kfar Giladi wore gray. There was not a drop of color in that whole community.

I began to ask questions about this and got a number of explanations. One was the "Jewish" explanation. In the old country, colorful clothes had been associated with the peasants— not very nice. The respectable Jew in the *shtetl*[37] wore black,

---

[37]Literally, "little town." Small-town or village communities of Jews in pre-1939 Eastern Europe.

maybe gray, but certainly not fancy colors. As for even a hint of color in women's clothing—that was considered a sign of levity or worse, and therefore not to be tolerated.

Still another explanation lay in the kibbutz notion of total equality. If one person wears one color and the next another, the one who has a better esthetic sense and expresses it through brighter colors in his or her clothing might appear superior. But whatever the reason, the kibbutznik fashions of the early days were rather somber.

When we who came here from the United States in the early 1940's first brought in a light touch, we were accused of being really irresponsible. Of course, if you go to a kibbutz today you can see kibbutzniks of all ages sporting every color of the rainbow. **YOSEF**

When I first came to Kfar Blum—about four years before Saadia arrived—I walked into the dining room wearing a T-shirt. One of the members who had already been in the kibbutz six months—the whole kibbutz was then just about six months old[38]—said to me, "*Haver*, we do not allow anyone in the dining room in his underwear." I tried to explain that a T-shirt was not considered underwear, but a regular and proper piece of clothing. It did not do any good. I had to change my shirt.

Coming back to the somber clothes they wore at our kibbutz in its very early years, before Saadia ever got here—I rebelled against them at an early stage. I did not like everybody wearing the same color. So, I went out and bought myself a deep orange shirt made of some heavy material. I was not yet a member of the kibbutz but I knew I was going to join, and I wanted to bring one or two of my own things with me. One of the first places where I was sent to work happened to be out in the fields, not far from a prison. Only when the police began to run after me did I discover that orange shirts like the one I was wearing were made especially for prison inmates. They came in this bright color so that an escaped convict could be easily identified. I had a hard time convincing the police that I was not an escaped convict but just a kibbutznik.

You might think that by now we would have solved the **SAADIA**

---

[38]Kibbutz Kfar Blum was founded in 1943.

problem of what is proper to wear. But even today when you come to the kibbutz in the summer, you should see the eyes of the good, solid, modern, progressive kibbutzniks when volunteer workers or visiting youngsters show up. Only a few months ago one of the grandmothers came to me and said, "Will you explain to that girl over there that we don't walk around here naked? This is our home." The girl was wearing a mini-skirt and a brief halter topped by a blouse. She was certainly not naked.

Progress may be expressed in many ways. Today, long hair and shabby clothes seem to be the latest in fashion, but apparently some of us have lost our revolutionary spirit because we do not always find it easy to tolerate hair which obviously has not been washed for weeks. In fact, it seems strange to us to equate such things with ideology. Perhaps this is one good indication of how conservative we, the former revolutionaries, have become. Does one naturally become more conservative with age? Does every change represent a revolutionary departure? Or do externals mean anything at all?

Be that as it may, dress alone no longer shows who is or who is not a kibbutznik.

YOSEF   In the early days you could definitely tell a kibbutznik from the others. First of all, as we have already said, you could tell him by his clothes. Many of the kibbutzniks who came from Europe, for instance, wore what was then the accepted "going-out uniform." The boys wore shirts and pants; the girls, blouses and jumpers. The girls never wore makeup. The boys had their hair neatly combed—and short.

There was something else about kibbutzniks which distinguished them from city people: their general attitude towards life in the city. They were hicks. If they were not literally chewing on a straw you could visualize them doing it. If you saw somebody standing on a street corner obviously wondering how he was going to get across—there were no traffic lights in those days—you knew it was a kibbutznik.

Also, the first thing the kibbutzniks used to do when they came to town would be to buy something good to eat. The kibbutzim, in the early days, had very little good food—for a number of reasons.

One was that they did not have the money. I recall there was a saying, "When a kibbutznik eats chicken either the chicken is sick or the kibbutznik is sick." We would have meat perhaps once a month, and chicken for the holidays: Passover, and maybe for Rosh HaShanah, although that was not always guaranteed either. The food was extremely dull and monotonous, and sometimes there just was not enough. There was heavy black bread. There was no sugar; you could get hard candy to suck with your tea instead. Our menus depended largely on the crops we grew.

I remember a time when we had a surplus of tomatoes. We had tomato soup, tomato salad, and tomato jelly to spread on our bread. We had fried tomatoes, baked tomatoes, stewed tomatoes —tomatoes in every conceivable style, until they were coming out of our ears.

It is a lot different today; the food in the kibbutz is fairly good.

In many ways the kibbutz bears the stamp of the Russian SAADIA intellectual. There was genuine appreciation for classical music, literature, and any form of art. Today, if you want a pop concert, you might find one anywhere in Israel, including the kibbutz.

Each person sees us from his own point of view and in terms of **As** what he has been taught to believe. To the psychologist we are **Others** very interesting types. It is a challenge to him to find out why each **See Us** one of us is here on the kibbutz. To the psychoanalyst, we are escapists from life. To the anthropologist, the kibbutz represents a retrogression to a primitive form of society, one of those periodic backslides from civilization. The sociologist sees us as a group of individuals who huddle together for security because none of them could stand on their feet alone. It does not occur to him that if he were to examine us closely he would find that there are perhaps more individualists per square yard in the kibbutz than in any other form of society. But he has made his judgment; we are huddling together for security and that is it.

Newspaper reporters, being the most practical people of all, love the kibbutz because it always makes good copy. If there is a little conflict in the kibbutz, that is good copy. If there is nothing going on, that is still good copy because the kibbutz is a strange society. To the politician the kibbutz is essential for his campaigning. A flying visit to a kibbutz is good for a whole speech about how the politico has studied the kibbutz carefully and how in his opinion the kibbutz is unquestionably here to stay as part of the new Israeli society.

To the tourist, a kibbutz is one of the sights he has to see. It is inconceivable to come to Israel and not have seen a kibbutz—even though sometimes this does not mean much more than stopping in for a quick lunch, hearing a brief talk by a kibbutznik, seeing some slides at the guest house or whizzing by on a bus, with the guide saying: "See, that is a border kibbutz over there."

To many clergymen the kibbutz represents true religion. Kibbutzniks may be non-religious or even atheists, but the clergyman is convinced that the kibbutz is the one place where true religion may be found.

The Marxists, the "scientific" socialists, know that the kibbutz misses the point. It is kid stuff—totally irrelevant from the viewpoint of Marx and the scientific socialist analysis and the basic forces, the class struggle, and all that. To the democratic socialists, on the other hand, kibbutz life is the only right way. It is the cooperative commonwealth, the new society of the future.

Our Arab neighbors say that the socialism of the kibbutz is all just a big sham, another Zionist trick to gull the world into sympathy for the Zionist State.

To visitors from the developing countries in Africa, the kibbutz is a model to emulate. The Burmese used the kibbutz as a pattern for their border outposts to repel the Communists who were infiltrating their country from Red China. To the Communists, of course, the kibbutz is anathema because unlike them we have succeeded in our effort to set up a genuine communal way of life.

So there you are—the kibbutz is all things to all people. But it is only the observers from the outside who are the real experts on the subject of the kibbutz. The kibbutzniks themselves are never the experts; they are too busy living and working to analyze themselves.

9

OUR YOUNGER GENERATION

SAADIA

We are happy that although the pioneers who started our kibbutz were a homogeneous group in their teens we have learned to bridge the gap between the various age groups in our population—young, middle-aged and older. Believing as we do in the principles of democracy, we have found that by giving each generation freedom of expression we have obviated the need for rebellion and we have been able to work together on activities and projects that benefit all age groups.

The Generation Gap

This does not mean that there are no conflicts, but they are constructive, not destructive. The older generation has come to recognize that it is only a matter of time before the new generation takes over. In many an older kibbutz thirty-year-olds are directing a community in which most of the members are considerably older, and the older members accept the direction of the younger members without hesitation. Be it said to the credit of the thirty-year-olds that they give their directives in a friendly, matter-of-fact tone rather than in an arbitrary or otherwise offensive manner.

One of the reasons for the absence of a generation gap on the kibbutz is that both physically and psychologically the younger generation has always had room in which to move around. The wide open spaces in which we live have also made for freedom of expression and whatever friction occurs is usually with peers rather than with the older generation. Our children have few inhibitions about expressing themselves. A six-year-old has no compunction about telling his kindergarten teacher, "You are wrong."

We have been thrown together, for better or worse, all kinds of people, of all ages, in close proximity, and in time we have all learned how to live with one another.

By now, of course, there is a third generation, but the largest grouping on the kibbutz is the second generation. What motivates that second generation? They did not come to the kibbutz voluntarily to build a new society. They are there simply because they were born there. To them the kibbutz is home, their natural way of life, so that the ideological struggle and the mental anguish which marked the youth of their parents are totally absent. Some people are telling us that, in fact, the kibbutz is becoming too affluent, too comfortable and too complacent for its own good. Flabby, you know—the beginning of the end.

YOSEF   As far as being "too affluent" is concerned, let us not generalize. We here at Kfar Blum have been around for thirty years. But some of the younger kibbutzim, Moram HaGolan or G'rofit, are still quite far from affluent. Their members are no more than twenty-five or twenty-six years old, on the average. They have only a few buildings and they have set themselves up in a completely uncultivated and unpopulated area quite a distance away from the nearest city. They are going through the same process of development that we went through thirty years ago. They need more workers, there is not enough money and there is constant turnover—new people join, others leave. They still do not know how to organize their kibbutz. However, the remarkable thing about these new places is that none of them falls apart. It may take ten years or more before they really get on their feet, but the kibbutz is a strong and healthy plant—it does not shrivel up and die.

As we have pointed out all through our talks, the kibbutz is still an important factor in Israeli life today—above and beyond the fact that many of our top government, army and labor people come from kibbutzim. You might not feel the kibbutz influence so much in Tel Aviv, Jerusalem or Haifa, because kibbutzim are not being created in the urban areas on the Mediterranean coastal plain—those are well-settled areas. But if you go to the Galilee, or the Jordan Valley, or the Negev, you can sense the aura of the kibbutz. In those regions you will find areas that are completely settled by kibbutzim—no towns or villages. In the Upper Galilee alone there are twenty-five kibbutzim within a radius of fifteen miles.

As for the idea that our kibbutzim are getting too complacent for our own good—you ought to attend some of the hundreds of meetings that are called each year to deal with problems that many of our kibbutzim have in common: what to do about our aging members, whether or not to set up a kibbutz university, or the question of whether, and how, to employ outside labor. There is a tremendous amount of cooperation among the kibbutzim; in many areas they function together as one group. So, you see, the kibbutz is still a powerful force, far beyond its numerical place in the total population of Israel.

How many of the second generation have actually remained on the kibbutz? Statistics vary from kibbutz to kibbutz but the overall number is between sixty and seventy per cent. Whether this should be interpreted as a positive sign or as a negative development depends on the viewpoint from which you evaluate these figures. Considering the trend all over the world to leave the countryside and move to the city—in industrialized societies the trend from the farm to the city is sometimes as much as eighty per cent—you would think that even if just thirty per cent of the young people were to remain on the kibbutz it would be a good sign. SAADIA

There are many reasons why young people leave the kibbutz. They may marry somebody from outside the kibbutz, they may have gotten into some kind of squabble, or they may just want to try a different way of life. The important point is that there has been no mass exodus from the kibbutz. In fact, the total number of people joining kibbutzim today is larger than the total number of people leaving.

I would like to point out that of the thirty or forty per cent of the new generation who do leave, a large number do not go to the city but to another kibbutz. Some of them start new kibbutzim of their own. They go out to some remote outpost, into the Negev or into the Sinai desert, with a group of other young people to set up a YOSEF new kibbutz, or perhaps a *meshek shitufi*[39] or other new pioneering enterprise. By the way, many who leave the kibbutz return several years later.

SAADIA   There has been much discussion about the emotional makeup of the kibbutz *sabra*. These studies are for the most part inconclusive and many of them seem to reflect the prejudices of their authors. According to one study, the kibbutz sabra's emotional reactions are flat—no great ups or downs but somehow dulled. Another study cites extraordinary acts of heroism

The performed by kibbutzniks in the army and says that the
Kibbutz second-generation kibbutznik is close to Superman. A third study
Sabra comes along and tells us that our kibbutz children are really neurotics who have found very interesting ways of covering it up. Another study has demonstrated that there are no substantial differences between the sabra of the kibbutz or the sabra who lives in cities like Tel Aviv or Haifa. Differences between children, we are told, reflect family background rather than specific kibbutz-versus-city environmental factors. There was one thing, however, that we thought we had learned from our own experience: The second generation of the kibbutz, and of Israeli youth in general, has less of an intellectual bent, is less prone to delve into its own emotions, and more practical than youth elsewhere. But then, shortly after the Six-Day War of 1967, a series of dialogues, entitled *The Seventh Day*,[40] appeared and demonstrated that our kibbutz kids are just as soul-searching as their parents were, except that they express themselves more naturally and are more forthright and incisive in self-analysis than the earlier generation.

YOSEF   That is true. People think the younger generation has less *Weltschmerz*, probably because outwardly our youngsters are

[39]Also known as *moshav shitufi* (cooperative moshav), a form of settlement combining certain features of the kibbutz and the moshav, or cooperative smallholders' village. In a *moshav shitufi* all the land and industrial installations are collectively owned and operated, as in the kibbutz, but each family has its own household, does its own cooking, and cares for its own children, as in the moshav.
[40]*The Seventh Day: Soldiers Talk About the Six-Day War.* Recorded and edited by a group of young Kibbutz members. Abraham Shapira, principal ed. English version published in New York by Charles Scribner's Sons, 1970. The original Hebrew book, *Siakh Lohamim*, was published in Israel in 1967.

more reticent. Displays of emotion are considered inappropriate. When they have a reunion with someone of whom they are very fond, they say "Hiya" or "Hello," and that is it. On the other hand, tragedy will leave them stony-faced. Only when they begin to express themselves in free discussion, or in writing, do we realize that they are not too different from what we ourselves were like when we were their age, and that the problems of the world which affected us concern them also. The difference is that rather than walk around with a worried look they are accustomed to translating their feelings into action.

I have a sneaking suspicion that they are far more activist than we were, because they are not afraid to carry out their ideas, whereas we used to do a lot of yackety-yacking before we actually did anything concrete.

There is no doubt that both the second and the third SAADIA generation—all our children in general—are far better workers than we were. Physical work represents no special effort to them because even the games they played in early childhood had a work component. As we have already said, at the age of five our children start going out to help pick potatoes, even if their total effort consists of nothing more than walking for twenty minutes to the field, picking up one potato and taking it back to the adult in charge. Helping the adults in that way, and working on the children's farm, becomes automatic to them. It is part of their daily childhood routine; so, unlike their elders, they do not wait till adulthood to learn how to work.

At the same time, our younger generation, as distinct from the older pioneers, knows how to relax and play. When they bandy about the soccer ball or go to the movies, they are completely relaxed. When they get together for a sing, they forget about the problems of tomorrow. During the months and years of border fighting I have seen many a youngster return from the battlefront for a weekend furlough. During that weekend those soldiers of ours played and sang and even worked at kibbutz chores with complete abandon. Then, the next morning, they would put on their uniforms and go back to their posts to face the greatest of dangers. Our young people certainly know how to enjoy life.

YOSEF Another thing about these youngsters is that they have a real contempt for material things. They are happy if they have one shirt, one pair of slacks and one pair of shoes. They like nice clothes on occasion, but they refuse to be burdened with a lot of luggage when they travel. They want what they need, but they need an absolute minimum. As a result, the motivation of personal gain and of accumulating a roomful of stuff which they *Personal* may or may not use is totally foreign to them. They borrow and *Property* lend their things freely and are not interested in keeping up with the Joneses.

What they do want out of life is adventure; they want to travel and see the world. But they do not care about traveling first class. They like to eat well, but they are not what we would call gourmets—they like a lot of anything, provided it is well cooked. Their desires, to a great extent, are much simpler than ours were when we were their age.

In the last analysis I would say this: Our children are neither greedy nor money-mad, and they do not covet their neighbors. They want the simple things of life, and their intellectual stimulation comes from books, movies, discussions, TV (which is just beginning to appear in this country) and contacts with others.

SAADIA It is easy to understand why a sabra born in the kibbutz will not have the same attitude as the young nonkibbutznik towards private property or the acquisition of personal property. He was born in a society in which all his needs were met. If a person knows that when his shirt is torn he can just go to the clothing center of the kibbutz and get a new shirt free of charge he does not have to worry about accumulating two dozen shirts.

Since he is accustomed to having all his needs supplied in that way, the kibbutznik sometimes gets into trouble when he enters the army. In the army, when a soldier loses an article of army clothing—a cap, a shoe or other military gear—it is practically a court-martial offense because the Israeli army has so little of everything. So, the woman in charge of the clothing center here at the kibbutz occasionally visits army stores to lay in a supply of army clothing, and when a kibbutznik soldier comes home and says he lost his cap, or his army shirt, or his army belt, all he needs to do is go to the clothing center and get another one—free, of course. The sergeant back at the camp does not have to know.

Let me tell you a story to show the attitude of kibbutz youngsters towards personal property: Several years ago a platoon of kibbutz soldiers had gone out on a 100-kilometer[41] march as part of their training. The hiking did not bother them but they got very hungry, the way youngsters that age do. They came upon a flock of sheep with a couple of stragglers. They took a lamb from the lot. That night they had themselves a *kumsitz*—a barbecue—with roast lamb. But trouble was not long in coming. The shepherd, a small Arab boy, had hidden when he first saw the soldiers because he was afraid of them. But when he saw them take one of his lambs he ran to the nearest police station to report what the soldiers had done.

The police traced the culprits very easily because the boys had made no effort to cover their tracks. The police realized that they were dealing with a kibbutz group because the boys looked at them wide-eyed. "Theft? Stealing?" they said. "Why, we wouldn't dream of such a thing. All we did was take a lamb."

The police turned the problem over to the army. At the time, I was an army officer, and since this was obviously an army-cum-kibbutz affair, the army very wisely decided to ask me, a kibbutz soldier, to handle it. I assembled the platoon and for 20 minutes I lectured them on how ashamed I was of them and how they had stained the good name of the entire kibbutz movement.

Their reaction was as follows: "We're terribly sorry. We'll make full restitution. We'll pay for one lamb. We'll even pay for three lambs. We'll give the Arab boy anything he wants. We'll go to the Arab who owns the flock and tell him the boy wasn't to blame. But why do you call us thieves? We'd never dream of stealing anything. All we did was take some food because we were hungry."

These boys had been brought up on a kibbutz where, if you are hungry, you simply walk into the kitchen and grab some food. Somebody might yell at you and say, "Hey, don't take that! That is supposed to be for supper!" But nobody would ever call you a thief. They might say that you are a pig, but not a thief.

---

[41]About 60 miles.

Anyway, I made the soldiers understand that outside the kibbutz there was such a thing as private property. They went to the Arab shepherd boy and begged him to forgive them. Then they went to the owner of the flock to apologize, and they paid for the lamb. But what upset them most of all was what I had told them: that they had done wrong by the entire kibbutz movement.

When any member of the group gets into trouble, he can count on the support of his *haverim* through thick and thin. I remember the case of a girl in another kibbutz who was involved in a very complicated and unhappy love affair. It was the only case of rape in a kibbutz that I know of, a real tragedy. Everybody in the kibbutz knew the story—except the parents of the girl. The girl's group knew every single detail, but did not tell what they knew. They carried the girl through this most trying situation, and helped her survive and overcome her tragedy.

Only years later, when the girl had long been happily married to someone else, did the story come out into the open. The man involved in the case was still around and there was a debate as to whether he should be expelled from the kibbutz. By that time it was a theoretical question, but there were some members who felt that in the name of abstract justice the man should be asked to leave. On the other hand, there were those who said that he had acted in a moment of weakness; he had behaved well ever since, and it would be ridiculous to expel him now for a crime he committed so long ago. In the end the man took care of the problem himself. He could not stand the stares he got from the members; he could not bear even the forgiveness of the girl's parents, and so he left of his own accord.

YOSEF   How does the younger generation see the kibbutz? This is a question not only in my mind but in their minds as well. Undoubtedly they are going to introduce a great many changes. In our own kibbutz, for instance, they have changed the arrangement whereby the children slept in children's houses from earliest infancy. Our younger generation wanted to try out another way—have the babies stay with their parents until the age of seven. This necessitated making adjustments in existing buildings in accordance with the new requirements.

Comes the question: Is change heresy? I think the only possible **Is** approach is one of pragmatism. The kibbutz is not only a **Change** revolutionary idea but also an evolving one. If the kibbutz is to **Heresy?** continue to exist for the new generation a great many changes can, and must, be made.

In our own kibbutz, the young people have introduced certain innovations. For instance, they want every young couple, and every youngster after completing his or her army service, to go abroad for a few months to see the world and broaden their horizons. They feel strongly that after twelve years of kibbutz schooling everybody should have the opportunity to get a higher education if he wants it, even if the subject he wants to study is not of immediate practical value to the kibbutz. Thus, the kibbutz may agree to send a youngster to school to study philosophy or history even if he does not intend to be a teacher. Another new idea is that every member may have the use of a car for a specified number of miles per year. He can take the car for a day or two to see the sights in the big city or visit friends, or he can just go for a ride.

At one stage in the history of the kibbutz all these things would have been considered wrong. But just because something was once done in a certain way does not mean that it has to be that way forever. The younger generation is building a kibbutz the way they think it should be built. People like myself recognize the necessity for letting things evolve as time and the understanding of the younger generation dictate. I do not personally believe I have a right to say that things should be rigidly defined. I think that the kibbutz is an amorphous society and as a living and dynamic group it has the right to keep looking for new ways of expressing its basic ideology. And the younger generation is the instrument which is going to translate these new ways into action.

We ought to point out, I think, one basic difference between the   SAADIA second and the third generations on the kibbutz. The third generation has a better sense of history and continuity than the second. The second generation bore a certain resentment against the first. Practically from babyhood they were continually told, "We started this and we achieved that; now it's up to you to

The
Third
Generation

continue." So they sometimes asked, "Why do we have to continue? You started because you wanted to. We don't have to."

The third generation does not feel this resentment. They accept their role naturally. They also have, as I have just said, a greater sense of historic continuity than their parents. They have lived through events that had a profound effect on Jews the world over. The Eichmann trial and the impact of the knowledge that a world stood by while the Holocaust took place gave them the sense of a sweep of events in which their own tiny selves and their own little efforts merged into something big and continuous. In the third generation there has been much less questioning about Jewishness and Jewish values than there was in the second generation. It is all taken as a matter of course today. But neither generation can understand how six million Jews could have been led to slaughter. "How could you have let such a thing happen? Where was the Resistance movement?" they ask. Although we have tried to explain to these youngsters the psychology of the people who were led to their death, and given them background material for understanding Buchenwald and Auschwitz, they view our explanations as nothing but feeble excuses. "You are weaklings," they say. "You allowed the war to happen. You allowed Hitler to rise to power, and when he did rise to power you permitted six million of our people to be slaughtered. This will not happen to us, and we do not want to hear about it any more. Why should we have to remind ourselves of this tragedy of ours, which isn't just our tragedy but definitely our shame?" So they prefer not to talk about the Holocaust. They would be prepared to listen to a detailed description of a military defeat. This could happen. They could understand that. But a defeat without a battle—this they cannot accept. That is the way they interpret it.

The attitudes of our young people are very much affected by the problems that bother all of mankind today. The threat of "the bomb" hovers over them no less than over people anywhere else in the world. But in a way, our children are not bothered so much by the possibility of an ultimate atomic holocaust because we here in Israel are faced with immediate dangers that are with us every day. As a result, the attitude of our young people toward the nuclear threat is more mature. They know it is there, but they are not driven to total despair by thoughts of the remote future as are so many of their contemporaries in the Western world. Is a sense of utter helplessness one of the explanations for the New Left? Does a person reject society because he thinks it is all hopeless anyhow? Some of the very sophisticated New Left slogans may just be forms of escapism.

In any case, our young people here in Israel are not seriously upset by the New Left one way or the other. They accept much of the new "youth culture" in the form of music. They enjoy the new rhythms, but they do not accept filth, personal neglect, or the drug culture. A few have tried drugs; only recently four youngsters in our own high school were caught trying hashish. They were given a stern warning that hashish would not be tolerated at our high school.

The same rule applies at the Hebrew University in Jerusalem. Hashish, marijuana, "speed" and other drugs are forbidden, because we have seen what happens to drug users. One of our youngsters who decided to experiment deteriorated within a very short period of time. Within less than four years his health had been gravely impaired; he became pale, withdrawn from society, and stopped functioning as a kibbutznik. Philosophically, this may be acceptable. Maybe a human being is just as good if he does not function, but then he becomes a parasite and the kibbutz cannot afford parasitism. Perhaps very wealthy industrial countries can afford a large class of parasites, but a growing society under siege cannot. We have found evidence that the Arabs have been sending large quantities of hashish into Israel and that they have been trying desperately to introduce it into our army.

Nobody has as much experience with drugs, particularly hashish, as our immediate neighbors. The Egyptians have been smoking hashish for generations, and we can see the results. We see what the Egyptian soldier and the Egyptian farmer are like. Hashish has drained them of energy. In a world of pure philosophy, where you sit under your tree and meditate, perhaps somehow manna will drop from the roof or from the sky so that you can be fed and taken care of while you smoke away. But in a world where everyone has to earn his own living, in a country still faced with problems of survival and development, hashish is a real danger.

YOSEF   Let me tell you a little about the hippies who come to the kibbutz. We get them in all sizes and shapes, from all countries. Some come with love beads, long hair, batik blouses, brocaded pants, wide belts and free and easy manners. At one time our kibbutz seriously considered not accepting them, until we realized that the worst thing to do was just to say "no" to anybody whose hair was a little longer than we thought proper, especially after some of our own children began to let their hair grow longer.

Young   Some of these hippies come here out of sheer curiosity. Some
New-   are looking for a cheap way of spending time. Others are
comers   intellectually interested in the nature of the kibbutz. Within a few days you can tell whether or not they are going to stay, because then they are expected to work. Nobody, regardless of his dress, who is capable of working a full day and who maintains a minimum norm of cleanliness will be thrown out of the kibbutz. But if he comes with the idea of just being a freeloader in the dining hall, then in a day or two he is made to feel that he is *persona non grata*. If we insist that he put in a hard day's work, this sort of individual leaves on his own.

As for those who decide to stay, something happens to them. Many think that they are going to maintain their hippie dress and attitude even though they are going to be good workers and part of the kibbutz. But little by little they begin to discover that long hair interferes with work; a headband is not enough to keep it out of their eyes. If they are working in the fields and there is a lot of dust, it is a bother to have to wash your hair fifteen times a week, and so they cut it a little bit shorter. Then they find out that batik shirts and brocaded pants have a way of getting caked with mud and dirt. Besides, shorts are much more practical in the summer, so they start wearing ordinary work clothes. Sandals are not really very good for walking in the fields or even on a gravel path; stones hurt your feet. So they begin wearing work shoes. A wide belt does not fit ordinary pants, so they change to a regular belt. Dangling love beads can get caught in a plow or a lathe, or some other piece of machinery. As a result, after a few months you find that the hippie who is a good worker suddenly begins to look like any Israeli boy or girl; they begin wearing the clothes that our young people wear. They also begin enjoying the things our young people enjoy—the music, the swimming pool and the intellectual discussions. The next stage—and this has happened so many times that you can almost foresee it—is that many of them say they would like to stay on in the kibbutz for another six months, or another year, or maybe stay on permanently. At this point we begin to look back at the year or six months they have spent on the kibbutz and decide whether or not we will accept them. If they have been good workers and fit into the society, there is no reason why they should not stay.

Little by little, proximity has its effects. The marriages that take place every year between our youngsters and those who have come from abroad make a steady contribution to the kibbutz population. I should say that in the past few years at least twenty-five such newcomers have married our children and, in most cases, they have remained on the kibbutz.

Some of the results are even funny. There was a hippie girl who came to us in extremely exotic clothes, with earrings hanging down practically to her elbows—the most appalling costume I have ever seen. She decided to stay. Now that she is married and has two children, she has become one of the most conservative people in the kibbutz and is completely intolerant of anyone who does not conform. I would say she is a *gute yiddishe tochter*[42], if she had started out Jewish. As a matter of fact, she became a convert to Judaism on joining the kibbutz. This has happened in many such cases. I should say that the kibbutz as an educational form has affected the hippies to a greater extent than the hippies have affected the kibbutz.

In the final analysis our own younger generation, being a healthy generation, has prevailed. The people who come here because they are rebelling against the establishment find that in the kibbutz the "establishment" is sufficiently "far out" for them not to have to rebel against it. On the kibbutz, they can find self-expression in a normal life and in normal activities with other

---

[42]"Good Jewish daughter (girl)."

people of their age. Israel in general is a happy hunting ground for young people who come to try new ways of life. The kibbutz is, of course, one of the most interesting forms of this new life and consequently an attraction for many of the present generation.

SAADIA   Which, then, is the best generation? I would be hard put to answer. There is no "best generation." There are different generations. What will be the end? That is for the historians to say.

10

WAS IT WORTH WHILE?
REFLECTIONS OF TWO OLD-TIMERS

" A re you happy here on the kibbutz?" Since we come from so many different backgrounds and live here for so many different reasons, this seems an intriguing question. Happiness is really an individual matter. Kibbutz life is no different from any other way of life. Is everyone's life happy? What is happiness? People are not all alike and living in a kibbutz does not change one's personality. Happy people will be happy in a kibbutz. People who tend to be miserable will also be miserable in a kibbutz.

SAADIA

Self-fulfillment or economic security have nothing to do with inner states of mind. Some day, perhaps, a study will be made comparing happiness in a collective society to happiness in an individualistic one. In a psychological sense, happiness might be defined as adjustment to one's environment. Is true adjustment possible for any human being? Who is happier? Is it the rich man who strives for more and more wealth, or is it the idealist? These are all complicated problems. One thing is certain: People who have chosen a certain way of life have various reasons for their choice. When you visit a kibbutz and want to find out whether or not a person there is happy, there is only one way to do it: Stay there a while and find out for yourself.

Let us ask ourselves: Has it all been worth while for us as individuals—myself, my wife and my children? What have we been able to accomplish as individuals and as a community? What satisfactions have we derived from life and work at the kibbutz?

YOSEF

The Kibbutz and the State of Israel

To begin with, what have we, as a kibbutz, been able to do for the welfare and prosperity of our country?

173

The kibbutz is not a very big movement in relation to the State of Israel as a whole. The people living on kibbutzim make up just about 4 per cent of Israel's total population. But what has this 4 per cent meant to the history of our country?

There are people who say that we kibbutzniks are not a part of the real world. In answer to this, I can only repeat what we have already said in many different ways in our previous discussions: The kibbutznik is a citizen of the State of Israel like any other Israeli. Whatever affects the State affects us also. When there is a war or a national emergency, the kibbutzim are the first to feel it from every point of view. Because so many kibbutzim are in border areas, they are the first to be attacked and their members are the first to be called into the army. During defense emergencies the kibbutz is stripped of its active and healthy men and left in the care of women (I mean those women who are not subject to the draft themselves)[43] and the children.

The kibbutz is also vitally affected by Israel's economic realities. Some people are surprised to learn that kibbutzim pay taxes to the State. Why shouldn't they? The kibbutz is not a charitable institution that it should be tax-exempt. With regard to taxes, the kibbutz is no different from any capitalist business enterprise, or any trade cooperative, in this country: It is an economic unit within the State of Israel and therefore subject to taxation. We pay not just the indirect taxes that are part of any purchase anybody makes in this country; we also pay quite a sizable income tax to the treasury.

When the economy of the nation is in trouble, the kibbutz also feels it immediately. All building activities will come to a stop, although there is a constant housing shortage in our kibbutzim. Fuel prices will go up. The kibbutz will have difficulty marketing its produce because people will not buy the more expensive items. But there are certain expenses on which the kibbutz cannot cut down. Even if the price of fodder goes up, you cannot let the cattle starve. So you have to readjust your budget by reducing the benefits usually provided for the members. The members will get less vacation time; they will have to forego the trips abroad for

---

[43]The draft age for women in Israel is from 18 to 38. Married women, and some with religious objections to women serving in the army, are exempt.

which they have been due, and less money will be spent for food and clothing. So, you see, the kibbutz is not a place to go if you want to run away from the world and the realities of life.

There was a time before the Six-Day War when the State of Israel suffered from long, zigzag borders which were most difficult to defend. Here the "border kibbutz" came to play a very important role. Wherever there was a frontier kibbutz, there the border was clearly defined and secured. In border areas where there were no kibbutzim, there was Arab infiltration.

Could not the same thing have been accomplished in some other way—without kibbutzim? Yes, of course. You can take soldiers from somewhere else, move them to the border area and tell them to defend it. But you would need a great many soldiers to make up for one important lack which is common to all armies—the soldier forms no close attachment to places where, after all, he is stationed only on a temporary basis. No soldier really cares about any one particular camp. If you tell him he is going to be transferred from Camp 26 to Camp 426, or any other new base, his only concern, most likely, will be whether or not the new place is any closer, or farther away, from his home than the old base. On the other hand, if you set up on the border not merely an army base but a kibbutz, each man who lives on that kibbutz will know he is defending not just a piece of Israel, but his own home, where he lives with his family; he is guarding the school which he has set up for his children and the trees he planted with his own hands.

During the War of Independence, the Egyptian army, with all its men and tanks and planes, was incapable of overrunning such small outposts as Kibbutz Negba and Kibbutz Yad Mordekhai, or other kibbutzim which held out against incredible odds, because the people who lived in these communities felt that these were their homes and were determined that they would not be driven away by the enemy. In the end, the enemy forces decided to by-pass these strongholds and come back only after they had conquered the rest of the country. But of course things never came to that point.

The pioneers who set up the original border kibbutzim had a variety of motivations for choosing those border areas to settle in.

Many of them went despite dire warnings that they could not possibly go there. Our own group, the pioneers who set up Kfar Blum[44], were warned against this area because of the mosquitoes and the malaria. It was not just the British government, but also the Palestine Jewish settlement authorities who told us to wait until the swamps could be drained. But we did not want to wait.

The Kibbutz-nik as Pioneer, Builder and Defender

Who knows—perhaps if we had not settled in this area at that time there might have been another Arab enclave in the upper Galilee, and if we and the other kibbutzim around here had not kept the area safe for Israel maybe the Arabs might have taken over the entire upper Galilee in one war or another.

Nothing can replace the dedicated worker. I recall a project that was set up somewhere in South America. The Ford Motor Company decided to start a rubber plantation and invested millions into putting up a company town for the workers to live in. They cleared the jungle and built a shopping center—in short, a real city. But then, during World War II, these people all left the company town. When they came back, they found that the jungle had taken over completely; it was hard to believe that there had ever been a town there. What would happen if we were to set up "company towns," if we simply sent hired workers to the Negev to clear the land and build roads? If no one wanted to settle permanently in the Negev, if there were no places like, say, Kibbutz G'rofit[45], I doubt that the desert sand would have enough Zionist spirit to stay away from these spots. If it were not for these settlements, it is very likely that these green and lovely spots, these oases in the middle of the vast desert, would again be covered by sand within a year or two.

Hired labor can build a place, but only people who actually choose to make it their home can keep it going. Soldiers can fend off an attack, but only people who live in a place permanently can be responsible for its defense at all times. We hear mentioned in the news such kibbutzim and moshavim as Yardena, Gesher, and Kfar Vitkin—these places have all been under fire for two or three

---

[44]The Lebanese border is less than 10 miles to the north and to the west of Kfar Blum; the Golan Heights, which until 1967 were part of Syria, are less than 10 miles to the east.

[45]Kibbutz G'rofit, founded in 1963, is located in the southern Negev near the Beersheba highway.

years now from the Jordanian side, and there was Nahal Oz, which used to be under attack from Egyptian infiltrators. During the Six-Day War the kibbutzim near the Golan Heights withstood Syrian shelling until our regular army moved in to silence the Syrian guns for good. These outposts, incidentally, are not merely places where people live; they have been very definitely a part of Israel's defense operations. The kibbutz, then, has been responsible for keeping the borders of the country intact. Had we had another sixty kibbutzim on our borders at the time of the 1948 War of Independence, it is just possible that we would not have had the problem of the "Little Triangle"[46] or of the West Bank that we have today. People occasionally forget that the lands which Jordan now demands were not in Jordanian hands back in 1947 when Palestine was partitioned.

Prior to partition, the kibbutz proved to be a training ground for the State. Many of the democratic institutions of the State of Israel today were patterned upon the communal life of the kibbutz. During the British Mandate era the kibbutz was the only place where one could speak with complete freedom, without fear of spies, informers, or British officials listening in. That is why, during the years immediately preceding the establishment of the State of Israel, the leaders of Palestine's Jewish community would meet at kibbutzim whenever they had important decisions to discuss.

The Kibbutz as a Builder of the State

You might say that the kibbutz was literally the Jewish State in the making. Men and women from the kibbutzim helped build up the Jewish underground defense organizations. Indeed, the vast majority of the Haganah, the official Jewish defense organization, was recruited from the kibbutzim. During World War II the kibbutzim supplied men and women who volunteered to serve as parachutists in the British Army.[47] Among these were such heroic figures as Hannah Senesh and Enzo Sereni, who became legends

---

[46]This narrow strip extending from the Jezreel Valley to Kafr Qasim is an Arab enclave with some 30,000 Arabs.

[47]These Palestine Jewish parachutists—twenty-nine men and three women—were recruited by the Jewish Agency and dropped by the British over Nazi-dominated Europe to make contact with underground resistance groups and help Allied prisoners of war to escape. In addition, they helped organize Jewish rescue and resistance activities. Of the thirty-two, twelve, including Sereni and Miss Senesh (Szenes) were captured by the Nazis. Of those captured, only five survived.

in their own lifetime. Also, during the war, and immediately
thereafter, kibbutzniks turned up in Europe as emissaries to
organize the illegal immigration of Jews who had survived the
war in ghettos and concentration camps.

*The
Kibbutz-
nik in
the Army*   Let me tell you a little about the role the individual kibbutznik
plays in the present-day Israeli army. As I have said before, the
kibbutz people represent only 3 per cent of the total population of
Israel. But when we look at the casualty figures of the Six-Day
War, we see that almost 25 per cent of those killed and more than
25 per cent of the wounded, came from kibbutzim.

In many commando or paratroop units the majority of the men
are from kibbutzim. In some very heavy fighting on the islands in
the Gulf of Suez, a couple of years ago, we had six casualties. Of
these, five were members of kibbutzim.

The majority of our air force—and we owe a lot to the Israeli Air
Force—are members of kibbutzim. So are many junior officers of
our Defense Forces. We are well represented also in the senior
ranks; the present commander of the armored forces in the south
belongs to a kibbutz. We have had kibbutzniks in the army high
command ever since the State was established.

Yigal Allon, now Deputy Prime Minister and Minister of
Education, who was once the commander of Palmach[48], belongs
to a kibbutz. Incidentally, some 80 or 90 per cent of our
Palmachniks also came from the kibbutzim.

Did we in the kibbutzim raise our youngsters to be soldiers? No.
We taught them to respect the Arabs as neighbors and to hope that
ultimately we would find a way of living in peace with them. In
The Seventh Day several kibbutz youngsters who had fought in
the Six-Day War were asked how they felt about the war. Did they
hate the Arabs? To everyone's great surprise the elation which we
had felt after the war was overshadowed by the fact that these
boys looked back upon the war with sorrow because they had had
to fight and to kill, because some of their own friends had been
killed, and because there was so much hatred. I should say that
the boys in Israel's army are the most atypical army you have ever

---

[48]*P'lugot Mahatz.* Commando units of the Haganah, Palestine Jewry's defense
force prior to the establishment of the State of Israel, and subsequently the shock
battalions of the Israeli Defense Forces.

seen. They want to do the job, and do it well, so that they can get it over with as quickly as possible and return to their task of building the country and helping it to prosper.

I might mention that when kibbutzniks go to the army for their stint of service they are "allocated" to the various units just as you would judiciously allocate precious tanks and heavy artillery. An army commander might tell headquarters: "I am having a morale problem in my outfit" (or "I need some experts in such-and-such a job"); "let me have five or ten kibbutzniks." The reply from headquarters will probably be, "We can give you three kibbutzniks, but no more." That shows you how greatly our army values its kibbutzniks.

Of course, the kibbutzniks are concerned not only with national defense but also with "peacetime" problems that affect the entire country. You can find a kibbutznik in every field of national interest. He is vitally interested in the advancement of agriculture; he is just as deeply concerned about education and social problems. Kibbutzniks are appointed to many control commissions and other public bodies. The kibbutznik in the popular mind is one who is very devoted to his cause but who at the same time has a deep-seated sense of fairness. Therefore, when a committee or other public body requires a panel that is truly impartial, the choice usually falls on a judge, a scientist—and a kibbutznik.

So, the kibbutz is closely interrelated with politics. Each kibbutz as such is a unit of local government, and along with other local government units in the area it is part of a regional council. As a rule, kibbutzniks are very active in their regional councils. (There, they were instrumental in the setting up of the "regional colleges" we mentioned in our discussion of education.) Kibbutzniks have also begun to participate unofficially in the local councils of our development towns. Thus, members of Kibbutz Tel Yosef have been prominently active in the Beth Shan regional council, while people from Kfar Giladi and our own Kfar Blum have been prominent in the affairs of Kiryat Shmona. In the local council of Ofakim, members of Kibbutz Urim became involved beyond the unofficial basis and were elected to office.

The political involvement of the kibbutz in the Histadrut—Israel's general federation of labor—is expressed primarily through the Agricultural Center. We all belong to the Union of Agricultural Workers which comprises about half the total membership of Israel's trade union movement. Our trade unions, of course, deal not only with strictly trade union matters but also with technical, cultural and political problems. Histadrut encompasses the whole life of the individual, not only in terms of personal health and welfare (we all belong to Kupat Holim, Histadrut's national health insurance plan) but also in terms of representing the individual member as a bearer of the ideals of our State and as a citizen of the larger world.

When a person becomes a member of Histadrut he automatically has the right to vote on all political, educational and cultural questions discussed by the organization. He also automatically becomes a member of the holding company which controls all of Histadrut's economic enterprises. So it is possible for kibbutzniks to exercise considerable political influence in all the policy-making bodies of Israel's labor movement.

We kibbutzim do all our marketing cooperatively through T'nuva, the agency which markets the farm produce of the kibbutzim. There is always a kibbutz member in the administration of T'nuva—as a matter of fact, the present director-general of T'nuva is a kibbutznik. So is the present director-general of HaMashbir HaMerkazi, the principal purchasing agency of the kibbutzim affiliated with Histadrut. Today HaMashbir deals with goods in the value of hundreds of millions of pounds each year. T'nuva and HaMashbir together represent an annual turnover of nearly a billion pounds. Consequently, they are an important factor in Israel's economy, and hence in the country's politics. Through them, therefore, the kibbutz can exercise a considerable amount of political muscle.

Kibbutzim are prominently represented also in the direction of Solel Boneh, the building and contracting organization of the Histadrut. The present general manager of Solel Boneh is a kibbutz member, and the late Nahum Cohen, of Kfar Blum, served as its treasurer for a number of years.

SAADIA   So the kibbutz is good at defense and good in politics, but its real contribution lies in what it has done for the social fabric and the ethical underpinning of the new Israeli society. By stressing such values as democracy, social and sexual equality, education and constant service, the kibbutz has laid the groundwork for the new Israeli society which will represent Israel as it should really be. Through the kibbutz, men and women have learned to become workers and to develop habits which stress the dignity of labor. The basic kibbutz philosophy of equality and of the importance of labor has helped the State as a whole to absorb and integrate newcomers from many lands. The kibbutz concepts of mutual assistance, and communal care of the sick, the aged and the handicapped has given an impetus to the State as a whole in its search for new and better ways of coping with its social problems.

As I have already said, I believe, in our discussion of the kibbutz concept of labor, the kibbutz in a very real sense provides the guidelines for our future cooperation with the Arabs. The concept of a cooperative society will in the long run hold the key to peace between Jews and Arabs and, indeed, to the prosperity of the entire area.

YOSEF
*Can
Non-Jews
Join?*

We have said quite a bit about the kibbutz and Arab-Jewish relations. But we have not talked about the application of kibbutz concepts to Israel's relations with Christians, or with Blacks. Can a person become a member of a kibbutz if he is a Christian? Can a Black from Tennessee be accepted as a member at Kfar Blum?

SAADIA

The answer to the question whether a non-Jew or a Black can join a kibbutz depends on why that individual wants to come. Let me say at the outset, though, that considerations of race or color as such play no role whatsoever in this question. We have had blacks, browns and yellows, and every conceivable pigmentation in many of our kibbutzim. Comparatively speaking, Israel is probably the freest community on the face of this earth. We have Egyptian Jews who are dark, Moroccan Jews, some of whom are quite black, and Jews from Cochin in India who are pitch black. We have them right here in our own area. The fellow who works at the bakery in Kiryat Shmona and delivers bread to our kibbutz is the blackest individual I have seen in a long time. There is absolutely no racial discrimination in Israel. There was something of a color problem during the period immediately following the establishment of the State but it is gradually disappearing.

There is complete freedom of choice. On the one hand, there is a great deal of intermarriage between members of the "Oriental" and "Western" Jewish communities; on the other hand, those individuals who wish to retain their ethnic identity within the larger community of Israel are free to do so. This freedom of choice holds good also for the kibbutz. If a person wants to come to a kibbutz and he is colored, fine. If he is black, fine. If he is yellow, also fine.

The question of whether a Christian—black, white or yellow— can become a member of a kibbutz is a little more complicated. The purpose of the kibbutz was to establish a Jewish national home, and one may wonder why a person who is not Jewish should take such an absorbing interest in establishing a national home for the Jews. There have been Christians who wanted to participate in this work for religious reasons. About a hundred such people have come to Israel and joined kibbutzim. They remain Christians but they consider their work for the Jewish people as part of their religious life. However, most of the Christians who have applied for membership in kibbutzim have not been motivated by religious sentiment but by socialist ideals. They see the kibbutz as the embodiment of their concept of socialism.

Of course, Christians with such religious or idealistic motivations were accepted. But once they are in the kibbutz, problems do arise. Not every Christian is able to adjust to being in the minority in a close-knit community where the culture, the calendar, and the holidays, are completely Jewish.

We do know of one Christian family that has managed very well. The kibbutz in which they live makes it possible for them to go to church on Sundays and to have special religious instruction for their children. But they are the exception. Many of the Christians who join a kibbutz find their minority status difficult to live with. Some of them eventually convert to Judaism because their children become Jewish by osmosis. Others decide to leave and settle in a part of Israel where they can be near a Christian community. And there are, of course, those who are determined to stay on because they feel capable of coping with the situation.

But all these are exceptional cases. It is unusual for a Christian to want to join a kibbutz, because the development of a kibbutz is the result of certain historic and cultural forces representing a specific culture and a specific set of people.

It is, of course, conceivable that Jews and non-Jews might get together and set up a cooperative based purely upon socialism. But it would certainly be much more normal for, say, the Moslems to want to establish kibbutzim in their own countries rather than in Israel. By and large the kibbutz is an extended family, and an extended family requires a certain amount of homogeneity.

This problem of homogeneity exists even when everybody on the kibbutz is Jewish. There is always the question of "how Jewish" a kibbutz is. Orthodox Jews would find it very hard to live together with non-observant Jews in so closely-knit a community as a kibbutz. This is the reason why we have "religious" or "Orthodox" kibbutzim in Israel. It is only in a very large kibbutz, over a period of many years, that variations of religious observance can develop and coexist. In the early stages, certainly, there must be homogeneity. A person will not feel comfortable if every single day he meets someone whose behavior rubs him the wrong way. An Orthodox Jew would be upset every Sabbath if he saw people smoking all around him. If a free-thinking Jew, on the other hand, somehow got into a kibbutz run according to strict religious law, he would find that a constant irritant.

So here you have a long answer to what started out as a simple question. Theory is one thing—practice is almost always another.

Kibbutz Ideology: Past, Present and Future

What does the future hold for the kibbutz? Now that the State is here to stay, has the kibbutz accomplished its job as part of Israeli society, or has it outlived its purpose? We still have not achieved peace, but let us assume that peace will come in another year, or in another five years. When peace comes, will Israel be able to get along without the kibbutz? Conversely, could the kibbutz continue to exist as a contented enclave while poverty exists anywhere else in the country?

YOSEF

No one can give pat answers to such questions. No one can predict the future. But we know that those who have foretold the speedy demise of the kibbutz have been proven wrong time and again. It is true that there is a gap between hopes and ideals on the one hand and actual performance on the other. There is always a difference between theory and reality. But thus far the kibbutz has shown a remarkable resilience. The kibbutz has changed some of its forms and approaches, but it continues as a very distinct form of social organization despite the fact that even many of our own old-timers on the kibbutz prophesied doom and lamented that we are going to the dogs because we are abandoning some of the old ways. But all these dire predictions, both from without and within, have not materialized.

Of course, we do not have the answers to everything. But we do know that no one here thinks of throwing in the towel or believes that our way of life is a vestige from the past. When you attend a convention of any one of the national kibbutz organizations, you will hear hundreds of young people having lively discussions of specific issues—but never the question of whether the kibbutz has a future. That item may be on the minds of others but it is not on our agenda.

You see, it all depends on what you want from the kibbutz—what you think a kibbutz should be. In order to be a true kibbutz, must a kibbutz have a communal dining hall, or a children's house where the children live separately from their parents? Or is a kibbutz a kibbutz only if it has communal showers? At one time, if you asked such questions, the answer would have been "yes."

I recall reading an article by one of the founders of the kibbutz movement, Yitzhak Tabenkin, in which he said that your room in the kibbutz should consist of four walls, a floor, a ceiling, and a bed on which to lay your head. Your room was just a place to sleep. Everything else, you were supposed to do as a community. You ate in the communal dining hall, and you used communal showers. You were not supposed to lock yourself up in your own room.

Today, however, your living quarters in the kibbutz will include a kitchenette. At one time it was considered a terrible thing for a kibbutznik to want to do any cooking in his private living quarters, but today many people do prepare and eat light meals in their own rooms. At 4 o'clock each day the kibbutz kitchen provides coffee and cake which one can eat in his own room, as an afternoon snack.

Also, it is no longer considered a heinous crime for a kibbutznik to want to spend the evening alone or with his family or friends in his own living quarters, listening to his radio or playing some records.

The original kibbutzniks tended to feel that one should seek neither privacy nor too much education. I have already said that a few years ago it was considered anti-kibbutz behavior for a youngster, when he finished high school, to want an official matriculation certificate as confirmation of his personal achievement. You had to have a high school education, but if you had a matriculation certificate you could apply for admission to a university outside, and this was not in the kibbutz spirit. But in recent years our kibbutz movement has come to the decision that it is all right for a kibbutz youngster to want to attend university after high school, and so our high school graduates receive these certificates just like the children in the city. *Personal Advancement and Kibbutz Values*

The way I see the kibbutz, these matters are all just details, and our attitude towards them may change as we go along in our great experiment. In my opinion, questions such as whether or not to allow individual *haverim* to have private amenities, or for some *haverim* to get a higher formal education than others, are not basic to the survival of the kibbutz.

There are, of course, two fundamental concepts which are accepted by all of us in the kibbutz and which are basic to kibbutz ideology. *Unchanging Kibbutz Ideals*

First of all, there is the idea that you are working to support not only yourself or your immediate family but also all your *haverim*. This is in accordance with the classic socialist principle: From each according to his ability; to each according to his need. No one exploits anybody else. All live together as one family, working for the common good.

Secondly, we are all dedicated to the Zionist cause. We are working together to rebuild the Jewish homeland. We are not afraid of settling as pioneers on swampland, on desert soil, or in border areas. As a matter of fact, in many instances young people from the older kibbutzim will forego the comparative comforts of the kibbutz in which they were raised and go out to set up new kibbutzim in areas that pose a challenge to pioneering skills.

For the rest, our own kibbutz, Kfar Blum, has few "immutable" tenets or principles. One man who used to be a member of another kibbutz told us that while the intellectual level at that kibbutz was much higher than at ours he found it hard to live there. He said it had so much culture and punctiliousness, so many principles, that the total weight was crushing. He felt that Kfar Blum, with its empirical way of solving problems, and its flexibility, was a much more pleasant place to live in.

Attitudes
Toward the
Kibbutz

So much for that one *haver*. But how do Israelis in general feel about the kibbutz? As we have already mentioned, probably one-third of the total population of Israel today has lived on a kibbutz at one time or another. Some went as youngsters, as part of their training within their youth movements. Children who came to Israel as refugees with Youth Aliyah were assigned to kibbutzim, where they were educated and grew to adulthood. Many older newcomers went straight to a kibbutz because they had heard so much about kibbutz life and wanted to give it a try. There were refugees who worked on a kibbutz until they got adjusted to Israel and could decide what they would do and where they would like to live on a permanent basis. There are people also who spent various periods of time at kibbutzim as hired "outside" workers, or as volunteers to help with the crops. Soldiers stationed near kibbutzim who also came over to help get to know a kibbutz at first hand.

Some of these visitors are so much impressed by kibbutz life that they are overawed by what they see. They say: "A kibbutz is a wonderful place, and a great idea. But it is not for me." Most Israelis, even those who feel that they themselves could never live on a kibbutz, have tremendous respect and affection for the kibbutzniks. I can feel this very often and it makes me very proud. When I come to the city on an official mission for the government or to lecture on some phase of engineering I make sure I am introduced as a member of a kibbutz rather than in terms of my academic qualifications. I think the audiences are surprised—and duly impressed—when they see that an expert in some special field has chosen to be a member of a kibbutz. "This fellow," their reasoning goes, "could be earning a good living, working in his profession in private industry. So, if a man like that chooses to live on a kibbutz, his kibbutz must be a good place to live in."

Of course there are people who are opposed to the whole idea of the kibbutz. They may feel that socialism as a system should not be encouraged, or that the kibbutz is an outworn pattern and should be replaced by new ways of living, or perhaps they just do not like the kibbutz idea because they personally cannot see themselves living on a kibbutz and feel somewhat guilty about it. But these people are often in a quandary when they meet with visitors from abroad, because Israel has discovered that the kibbutz is a very good export item and tourist attraction. A book on kibbutz life will sell (as witness the book we are doing right now), a movie about a kibbutz will draw large audiences, and a kibbutznik is an intriguing figure. Visitors who come to Israel often want to visit a kibbutz, even if their visit is no more than a stopover at some kibbutz guest house for lunch. When they get home they have to be able to report that they saw a kibbutz, and talked to a real kibbutznik, or at least with some child who was raised on a kibbutz.

When a kibbutznik misbehaves, it is hard for the people in Israel to believe it. When a member of a kibbutz gets into trouble with the law or is found to have done something that is not of the highest ethical or moral order, the news creates a real shock throughout the country. We, the people of the kibbutzim, are expected to be leaders and paragons of virtue.

SAADIA

But let us get back to the question we started out with. Are we, as individuals, happy with the way of life we have chosen? Did I, personally, make a sacrifice by coming to a kibbutz? I was born and raised in the United States in a middle-class family where I never knew real economic hardship—not even during the Depression period. There was a time when we could not afford to trade in our old car for a newer model, or to buy modern furniture for our apartment, and my mother may not have been able to get herself a fur coat. But we always had enough to eat and I always had a good, warm winter coat. I could go to the movies with my

YOSEF

Are We Happy?

friends, and I had a pair of skates for the winter and a bicycle for the summer. Compared to kibbutz life, this was great wealth.

Yet, when people ask me—as they often do—whether I ever feel I made a sacrifice by coming to the kibbutz, I tell them that frankly I do not think so. Even the richer members of our kibbutz, meaning those old-timers who are given more and better things because of their seniority, have no more than 35 square yards of living space. I have no kitchen of my own; we do not even have an oven. If my wife Ruthie wants to do some baking she has to use a little kerosene stove. If we want some hot water, we have to heat our water in a kerosene boiler—we call it Sputnik because of the noise it makes—and it takes quite a while till we can get our hot shower. But you get used to all that.

Besides, how important are all these material things? When I think of what I do have here at Kfar Blum I think it is worth much more than anything I may be lacking. First of all, I have security. I know that if for any reason I am unable to work, if I am sick or if anything happens to me, not only will I be properly taken care of but my family, too, will not suffer. Furthermore, in addition to the deep feeling of satisfaction we have talked about, there are the emotional and spiritual rewards. I have the opportunity of working at a job which I like, but if I should ever get really sick and tired of that job I have a chance of changing it. I have my family near me, so I have more time to spend with them and to enjoy them. Also, our children have a better life on the kibbutz than they would in the city. We educate them without the tension and without the competition for high marks that they have in the city. You simply study for the sake of study. And my wife and I have a lot of friends.

So I don't have luxuries. If I want to have a bottle of liquor in the house, that is a real financial strain because liquor is expensive in Israel and a kibbutznik does not have that kind of money. I may not smoke the best brand of cigarettes or use the best brand of razor blades. But I have the basic comforts and a maximum of security. I really do not miss anything. I have everything I need.

One day I had a visitor, a very nice man, very intelligent, who   SAADI
asked me: "Why are you kibbutz people so narrow-minded? Why

all this emphasis on being Jewish? Why not be a little broadminded and think of how you can serve all of mankind? What about the revolution? What about the ideals of universalism? Why aren't you honest with me?"

I had several possible defenses against this verbal onslaught. One would have been to throw him out bodily. The other would have been to just look at him, smile and go on about my business. I tried a third way—to explain things to him. But it was hopeless. There is no way of answering a person who has made up his mind in advance that we are narrow and chauvinistic and limit ourselves to the really unimportant Jewish problem when there is all of mankind to serve.

In order to understand what the kibbutz is all about, you have to understand the traditional Jewish view that every individual is a world unto himself. The kibbutz did not set out, in theory or in practice, to cure the ills of the entire world. The kibbutz seeks first of all to serve the people who actually live on it. Beyond that, it tries to carry on its way of life in such a manner as to influence others, not by preaching or acting as missionaries, but simply by being open to all who want to see how we live.

You have just been given an inspiring picture of the kibbutz as part of Israel and its society. Or, even if it is not exactly inspiring, at least it is a true picture of the kibbutz as it is now and of the way in which it is most likely to develop. **YOSEF**

I would like to add one or two items which have not been covered in our talks so far. We have come a long way. Anyone who visits Kfar Blum today will be struck by the sight of a huge antenna on the roof. It belongs to our very modern and efficient ham radio station. Every evening you will find young people and old trying to make contact with other radio stations the world over. We have had contacts with ham operators in Russia, America, and even places as far away as Japan. **What Was It Like in the Early Days?**

As an old-timer here at the kibbutz, I can allow myself the luxury of reminiscing about what it was like when we first came here to set up our kibbutz. We were all alone in this little sector of the Huleh Valley. We had no buses, no telephones. Our only means of communication with the world outside was the heliograph by day and flashlight signals by night. The heliograph, I think, dates back to the Middle Ages. It is a device for sending messages by reflecting the sun's rays from a mirror. We sent our signals in Morse code. We would send heliograph messages to Kfar Giladi, a much older kibbutz some 15 miles away in the mountains. "Do you have a doctor available?" Or, "Our washing machine has broken down. Could you take our laundry?" Or, "Could you let us have twenty-five loaves of bread?" And Kfar Giladi would flash back its reply. At night we would send flashlight signals from the roof of the silo to tell Kfar Giladi about any suspicious movements in the area and to let them know if we needed anything in the way of food for the next day. Today we use a complicated set of electronic devices to get in touch with the outside. Also, there are buses three or four times a day, and the mail comes every day, too. There is a mobile post office which supplies such services as postal banking. And then, of course, we have the telephones, which work most of the time.

Those were the days! Nowadays, when we walk around on a warm evening, we wear shorts and thin shirts or blouses and are very comfortable. But there was a time when we could not walk around like that, not even on hot summer nights, because of the swarms of mosquitoes that came from the swamp each night. If you went outdoors in the evening, no matter how hot it was, you wore slacks and rolled down your sleeves. If you were on night patrol you also wore a hat, a veil and gloves. Despite these precautions, everybody had malaria in those days. To protect our children from the mosquitoes, we made them go to the children's houses at 5 o'clock every afternoon and did not let them out of doors again until the next morning. One or two adults stayed with them. The children's houses were sprayed with insecticide and the doors were kept tightly closed during the evening and throughout the night. There were screens on every window and the children slept under mosquito netting. That is how we tried to keep our children from getting malaria.

It was hard, but somehow we got along. We put our cows on the south side of the kibbutz because this is where the swamps were. In this way, we figured, the mosquitoes zeroing in on us would hit the cows first. We did not wish our cows any ill, but, we felt, better them than us! Today, of course, the swamp is gone, so we have no more mosquitoes and no more malaria.

The cold, rainy winters at the kibbutz used to be quite an experience! Going to the communal dining hall for breakfast or lunch was not too bad because you were out working, anyway. Going to supper, however, meant that after finishing the day's work, going home, showering and changing your clothes you had to go out again into the pouring rain and plow your way through the mud to the dining hall. But you could get around that problem. You could take some food out of the dining hall, say, at lunch, and eat it in your living quarters for supper. You could fry an egg, or heat up some water for coffee or tea, over a kerosene stove in your own room. But what if you wanted to take a shower, or, worse, if you had to go to the toilet during a winter night? In those days we had no bathrooms, only outhouses. I still remember how miserable it was to have to get out of a warm bed in the middle of the night, put on a pair of cold and clammy hip boots and a raincoat over your pajamas and walk out into the pouring rain, splashing through puddles and plodding through the mud to get to a very wet and somewhat lopsided outhouse.

Ah, those were the days! Today, things are pretty good. Today, everybody here has reasonably good housing. However, I ought to explain that just now we do have a shortage of housing here at Kfar Blum. We do not have tents any more, but we still have some wooden shacks. When they come home, many of our soldiers stay in those shacks, which have no bathrooms, so even today they have to use the nearest outhouse. Our people have become accustomed to these problems—even those who have come to the kibbutz from the developed countries of the West, and our professionals, who were used to better facilities elsewhere.

Speaking of the professional people on our kibbutz, what are they doing? After a period of drifting from one branch of kibbutz activity to another, many of them have gone back to their original professions. One of our members, a mathematician, worked at various jobs for some time but now is back in his original field, teaching mathematics at our high school. Another *haver*, an economist, worked at agriculture for a while. Or take me; I am an engineer. During my early years on the kibbutz I worked as a

**Profes-
sionals
on the
Kibbutz**

tractor driver, in the machine shop, and at a number of other jobs. Now I am an engineer again. But some of our professionals have developed new interests and talents, and have decided to follow these rather than the fields in which they worked before coming here. For instance, we have two men on the kibbutz who used to be top lawyers. One of them, who is from South Africa, was in charge of landscaping at the kibbutz for quite some time. During the last few years he has devoted full time, very successfully, to a large regional laboratory, developing new methods of preserving fruit. The cold storage and controlled atmosphere systems used at our own kibbutz and in many other places are largely the work of our member, the lawyer. Our other lawyer, who came here from Boston, has been working in education for a number of years. He is now the principal of the district high school, which happens to be right on our kibbutz. For many years before that, he worked in our vegetable garden.

We have an economist who was with the regional college, but before that he worked as an automobile mechanic. One of our girls who studied psychology and philosophy—or was it history?—is now running our guest house. Two other *haverot*, who studied psychology and child care, have worked for many years at tutoring children in various school subjects. One of these two, who has been doing this job for twenty-five years, also works in our guest house, and conducts English courses during the winter months.

What about our youngsters who have gone to universities, studying such subjects as history, biology, agriculture, psychology and engineering? What do they do after they graduate? Three of those who studied agricultural economics are back on the kibbutz working in that field. One of the girls who took a degree in psychology is working with disturbed children. One of the boys who studied engineering is an engineer at our factory. Another one of our young engineers decided to leave the kibbutz. A young entomologist also left so that he could do advanced studies in his field.

SAADIA   There are many things which bother people about us. It is important to keep in mind that the kibbutz is a multifaceted society, so that it is worth while examining it from many angles. Let us consider, for instance, the contribution of the kibbutz to socialist thought. The one contribution the kibbutz has been able to make in his respect is the practical expression it has given to the ideals of socialism. One would be hard put to say that the kibbutz has made some unique theoretical or ideological contribution. The idea of communal living has been around a long time, in many parts of the world. There have been communes that were in existence longer than the life span of the kibbutz thus far. But in the case of most of these communes, it became evident quite early in their development that they would not last. In the case of the kibbutz, on the other hand, the combination of nationalism and socialism, humanitarianism and individualism, augurs well for the permanence of the kibbutz, even if some of its forms may change.

The Kibbutz— A Glass House

The kibbutz is not a missionary movement; it does not propagandize or try to recruit new members. This may be all to the good. An active public relations campaign is not always a sign of strength. Sometimes an organization will fling itself into missionary activities to cover up its shortcomings or its self-doubts. But despite our poor public relations efforts, visitors come in large numbers. This means that the attraction of the kibbutz does not depend on its publicity.

We live in a glass house and we find it disturbing. It would be nice, sometimes, to be a little less conspicuous. We try to maintain a degree of privacy, but maintaining our privacy without seeming rude is quite a problem. Not every visitor understands that we simply cannot keep answering the same questions over and over again: How many of you are there? When did you start? How did it all begin? And so on.

These glass house surroundings are not conducive to serenity. Not everyone who comes to see us here has the same attitude. Some of our visitors conceive of the kibbutz as a vision of the messianic era; now, they want to take a closer look at the Messiah, to touch his hands and feet—to find out what the Messiah really looks like. This is always embarrassing because not a single person in a kibbutz really feels he is a hero, or somehow "different." None of us likes to be treated like a hero, or stared at.

It is very embarrassing because we really are not heroes at all. We are a group of individuals trying to do a job and to live in a way which, for reasons of our own, we have come to regard as the good life, the proper life.

Of course, great things have been done here; there have been acts of valor. But they came from very ordinary individuals. This is a most significant aspect of our lives: Under certain circumstances very ordinary human beings, sometimes even weak people, can perform heroic deeds. There are times when the entire group can find self-expression through the act of some individual, but without the group the individual alone might not have been able to perform that act.

On the other hand, it is also not very pleasant to have visitors come and look for our faults, to see just exactly where we have the cracks that will ultimately cause our demise. It is not pleasant for the average human being to be told about his shortcomings. If our shortcomings become painfully obvious to us, then we will deal with them when the need arises. But it is not at all pleasant to have somebody watching all the time and pointing out to us where we have failed.

YOSEF

There is a problem of privacy also within the kibbutz community itself. I wish I could say it was not a problem, but it is. A kibbutz is a small and intimate community so everybody knows what everybody else is doing. After all, if you eat with a person in the dining hall every day, you get to know his eating habits, and if you work with him you know how he does his work. People here rarely lock their doors. Insofar as our personal lives are concerned, we are free , within certain limits, of course, to live as we please without having to ask anybody else's approval, but privacy is a problem.

New Immi- grants and the Kibbutz

The lack of privacy which is associated with the kibbutz explains why so few newcomers from the mass immigration immediately following World War II have joined kibbutzim. Most of these people have survived the war in Nazi concentration camps, or in hiding, or with partisan groups—in short, in a manner which almost completely destroyed their personal and family lives. Naturally, these experiences had a traumatic effect upon them. One man who came here and saw the fence around our kibbutz said, "I never want to see another fence again. I won't come to this kibbutz. I know this is not a concentration camp but I shall never be able to think of a place with a fence as my home."

Many of these people who had lost their families or had been separated from them by the war—sometimes for as long as ten or twelve years—had only one goal in life: to be reunited with their families or to start new families, and to live together with their closest kin in small, tight, intimate groups, to have direct and complete control over their children, and to experience the privacy which the kibbutz appeared to deny them.

In recent years, however, the picture has begun to change. We have been getting immigrants from the Western countries, for instance, who have tried the kibbutz way of life and found that they liked it enough to stay with us.

Kfar Blum today is a mixture of *haverim* and *haverot* from many different countries. We have an American group, a British group, and a group from the Baltic countries. We also have two Yugoslavs, and several people from India and Burma. All in all, I think we have some thirty countries represented on our kibbutz. Before long, however, I think the majority of our members will be native-born Israelis and we are very happy about that.

With all these *haverim* from so many different backgrounds, SAADIA you can understand that while we do have certain basic rules and principles, we do not have rigid behavior patterns. It is a constant struggle to adhere to the rules; time and again we find ourselves backsliding. Thus, we have endless meetings and debates about such questions of principle as whether or not a kibbutz should hire workers from the outside. There is far more to this than just passing a resolution once and for all and letting it go at that. The price of liberty is eternal vigilance; the price of being a kibbutznik is also eternal vigilance, but with a certain sense of humor. Vigilance without humor becomes intolerable.

The kibbutz is the application of desirable goals to reality; **Kibbutz** hence, it is pragmatic. But it has certain implications that are **Pragmatism** quite revolutionary. One implication, which has been proven correct, is that within certain limits man can shape the society in which he lives. We are not supposed to remain passive and just assume that everything is predetermined, that whatever existed in the past or exists at present will endure forever and that there is nothing we can do about it.

However, we do recognize that the extent to which we can shape our destiny is limited. It would be quixotic for us to try to do anything about, say, the atom bomb. But there is a great deal we can do to influence the thinking of intelligent people and to run our own lives while we are still alive and mankind is still sane. If all mankind goes crazy, we will just go crazy along with them. But it is always possible to hope. As long as we are alive, and capable of thinking and dreaming, we will try to shape a better world and in that better world the kibbutz has a small but quite definite place of its own.

It has been proven time and time again that man cannot change himself fundamentally. Biology and evolution have demonstrated that whatever changes do occur in man take place not over tens but over millions of years. Some people had the naive idea that we could evolve a new breed of person here at the kibbutz. That is not possible. But it is not necessary to change the person. What we have to do is change his environment in such a manner that his behavior patterns will change for the better. We must create an environment which will stimulate him and which will help him resolve his conflicts. According to our Jewish tradition there is an eternal struggle within our souls between good and evil. If the kibbutz can help the good overcome the evil in the individual, then it has made its contribution to the growth of the individual. But this is not always possible. Not every kibbutznik responds to his environment in a "good" or positive manner. Very often the kibbutznik's response will be negative. But our effort as a society is to encourage the formation of positive responses.

Normal capitalist society today tends to tolerate new approaches; it will not necessarily do everything in its power to crush them. Thus, theoretically, a true capitalist should want to destroy the kibbutz movement because it represents socialism. But if our new kibbutz society will basically stick to its objective and prove to be a constructive force, then the larger society will not only tolerate it but will even show considerable interest in the venture. Some people from that larger capitalist society may, in fact, come to the aid of the kibbutz, and eventually even join it. This is a hopeful sign for humanity; not all progress is necessarily doomed.

The goals which the kibbutz sets for itself must serve real needs and be capable of giving personal satisfaction. A kibbutz cannot set standards which are designed for angels or which will subject the individual to inhuman physical or emotional strain. We must not permit our flexibility to be hampered by dogma. There can be guidelines but if they are too rigid they will be ignored.

The history of the kibbutz as it evolved over the years demonstrates that goals cannot just be arbitrarily set by the leader. They must be understood and accepted by the members. This does not mean that every member of the kibbutz has to be involved in every decision that is taken or even that every member has to obtain a complete understanding of either the decisions or their implications. But it is absolutely necessary that all the members understand and accept the basic goals of their kibbutz.

It must be remembered that the kibbutz way of life cannot be imposed upon its adherents, certainly not if the kibbutz is to remain a voluntary society. Perhaps you can do that in the *kolkhoz* in Soviet Russia, but you cannot be sure even there. The *kolkhoz* is not readily accessible to the world outside but those few individuals who have managed to leave the Soviet collective farms and to make their way to the free world report that the *kolkhoz* way has made for a very unsatisfactory relationship between the individual and the society in which he lives. A free society must be based on a membership that knows the principles of that society and accepts them of its own free will. That is why a certain minimum of intelligence must be a key requisite for membership in a kibbutz. The normal problems of day-to-day living on the kibbutz are such that unless the individual is aware of the significance of this whole way of life he or she will not be able to survive as a kibbutznik. No one on the outside can make you organize a kibbutz. The Zionist Organization cannot do that; neither can the Histadrut, nor even the State of Israel itself. Only my own personal needs and strivings can make me come to a kibbutz and keep me there.

What is true of me is true also of my family and friends. Every kibbutznik I know is here by his own decision. In a sense, this is true even of the "social cases," those who seem to have no other alternative, for no matter how bad your situation is, you can always place yourself on the mercy of the State, collect relief, or join the community of the urban underprivileged. If these individuals also stay with us it is because they have found that it is better to be a "social case" in a kibbutz than it is to be one on the outside.

One should never judge the kibbutz from a glimpse obtained at one given moment. The kibbutz does not stand still. In order to get the true picture you must see the kibbutz as it grows and evolves. Only on the basis of repeated study will you see the kibbutz in its true perspective. Your evaluation should also take into account the personality of the individual members, not as individuals in a collective but in terms of how the collective helps them fulfill themselves.

The mores of a kibbutz society are always a cross between the society in which it exists and the ideas and desires of the founders and members of the kibbutz. Controls within the kibbutz are social. No pressure from the police or from the law, no rigid rules, can be as effective as social pressure—the opinion of the members of the community.

The goals of the kibbutz have been clearly set forth. Whether or not the kibbutz will achieve its goals depends on both the people and the given circumstances.

Personally, for me as I look back on it, it has been a deeply satisfying life. What about you, Yosef?

YOSEF   I was born and raised in a Jewish home back in the United States. I belonged to Habonim. We have already talked about Habonim; it is a Labor Zionist youth organization which considers political ideology and social service an essential part of its life. I joined Habonim because I felt that young people should not only preach but should also practice what they preached. When I was in high school and in college, I spoke on street corners and carried picket signs for Labor Zionism. I believed in the Socialist Zionist ideology. I was sincerely and honestly imbued with the idea that one of the functions of life was to do good and to bring about a better world.

But, as I said before, I always felt that talking was just not enough, and so I asked myself: When I grow up, will I simply graduate from walking around with a blue and white Jewish National Fund box to carrying committee cards and going to people's houses asking them for checks? Will that be the logical summation of my Zionist activity? I felt there was something wrong.

Coming to the kibbutz, and coming to Palestine, as Israel was then called (I first came to this country back in 1939), was a natural outgrowth of this feeling. I had to carry out the things in which I believed.

Since I have been in this country I have not stood on any soap boxes, nor have I walked in any picket lines. And here at the kibbutz I have been living socialism, not preaching it. There is no one here whom I have to convince—every one is already convinced. I do not even have to argue about basic Zionism any more, with the exception of the odd tourist who starts a discussion. The majority of the people here are Zionists; that is why they are living in Israel.

I understand why you, Yosef, want to live in Israel. But why do you want to stay here on the kibbutz?   SAADIA

Because after thirty years I feel that the things I have just said still hold true. Despite all the difficulties and disappointments (and there have been many of them), despite the fact that we are living in a border area and have been forced to fight for our lives more than once, I feel that nothing has happened to make me change my mind.   YOSEF

I still believe in the things in which I believed when I first came here, and I think that basically the kibbutz has remained within the framework in which it began thirty years ago.

Perhaps within my own lifetime the kibbutz will change so that old-timers will no longer recognize it. Maybe the State of Israel will have prosperity, or perhaps we will have a depression. But remember, all these things can happen anywhere, not just in

Israel. However, there is one thing that distinguishes us from workers in many other parts of the world: We are building up a new country, a new society. Whatever the future may bring, at least I have had the privilege of participating in this effort. I fought in the War of Independence back in 1948. I was in the Israeli army from the very beginning. When history records the names of those who helped set up a homeland for the Jewish people after 2000 years of wandering and dispersion—and there were only a few paltry hundreds of thousands of us out of the billions of people in the world—my name will be on the list. I think that is something of which I can be very proud.

To sum it all up, I came here, and I have stayed here, because I had a dream and this is about as close as I have been able to get to translating that dream into reality. Whatever the future may bring, whatever else I may do in my life, I have the satisfaction of knowing that I have been able to work and to live for ideals in which I believe.

11

THE YOM KIPPUR WAR

From Saadia's Diary

Kfar Blum
October 29, 1973

The war burst on us at 2 p.m. [on October 6] with the roar of planes which some of the alert recognised as Migs. That was a surprise but not taken seriously until we heard menacing explosions in the distance and received a telephone communication announcing an alert. By 3 p.m. we set in motion the self-defense and civilian defense apparatus and within minutes some of our members received notification to report for army service. The radio called up reserves and that involved more members. Within two days one hundred of our youth were in the services.

Like the rest of Israel we were surprised, but since we live close enough to Syria it was not very long before we realigned every aspect of Kibbutz life to the emergency. First we cleared all the air raid shelters for the children. That meant transferring beds, mattresses, toys and other essential equipment so that the children would sleep with minimal discomfort. No one knew whether this was an incident, a short war or, God forbid, a real war. Not until the late afternoon, when the order arrived to keep adults in shelters as well, did we take the matter seriously. That meant taking another thirty or forty members away from production and involving them in local defense. Since many members are engaged in regional industries and in emergency transport, Kfar Blum was left to us oldsters, to the women and children. Fortunately we also had in our midst teenagers, volunteers and Ulpan students, so that we managed to keep up with all essential services. To complicate matters, the army mobilized our one truck, several of our tractors and other equipment.

The first three days were spent in limbo awaiting the possibility of going out into the fields to pick our ripening apples and pears, maturing cotton and the like. Every morning we were ready to go out and were told: "Not yet." The cows had to be milked but since there was no transport, the milk had to be spilled. We looked into our stock of food, fuel and other reserves and found ourselves in good shape. Never were there so many waiters, cooks and dishwashers available as during those first days. Naturally there was a blackout and we ate in small, frequent shifts so as not to congregate in large numbers at any one time in one place. There were reliable reports of Syrian helicopters landing in the area on sabotage and murder missions. Whereas we did not suffer from direct shelling as in the Six-Day war, enough fragments broke enough windows and roof tiles to require caution. For the veterans there was a strange reaction of "déja vu." Again we went through the familiar and unpleasant but tolerable experiences. For the newcomers it was all strange, unreal and quite incomprehensible.

Little by little a routine was established in which we edged out toward the fields and started to do agricultural work. We took care of all the branches within the built-up area, including our factory. Our workshops produced equipment for shelters, both for our use and for the kibbutzim in the area.

From the fifth day on, members and candidates who were abroad began to appear. Some arrived at Kfar Blum and others went directly to their army units. Reunions were intense but brief.

We got used to the nightly "orchestra" and learned to distinguish between intense sonic booms, the rattle of cannon and the ear-splitting explosions of Katyusha mortars—all this against the background of screeching Israeli planes and missiles exploding against them. Whoever wanted the sounds of war had his fill.

Telegrams and long distance phone calls deluged us from the beginning. The same with newspaper reporters, television crews and offers of volunteer help. In retrospect I can say with considerable satisfaction that the entire population stood up well under all pressures. The American Class[49] was well disciplined and mature in every respect. Their reaction to parental requests to "come home" were knowledgeable smiles. Volunteers and Ulpan students spent hours at the telephone explaining to anxious parents why they couldn't possibly return home at that time. No doubt their morale was far higher than that of their families. They obeyed the order to sleep in shelters despite their desire to follow the example of some of us who put our faith in statistics and slept calmly in our beds.

The fact is that except for the first two days, when the Syrians advanced their artillery to the edge of the Golan Heights, we were never in any real danger. By taking normal precautions the dangers were minimized to those of traffic accidents. The adventurous naturally increased the risks and it was against them that we had to wage constant internal warfare. Curiosity brought people out to watch air dog-fights or to pick up fragments or to check up whether the all-clear signal was not overdue. Fortunately, everyone developed a new sense of when danger was really imminent and behaved accordingly.

We had to reorganize the entire administration inasmuch as the farm manager, treasurer and work coordinator were all called up. An emergency Secretariat was set up with substitutes for each of the above. We set up a "war cabinet" to include those responsible for military defense activities.

Then reports of casualties began to arrive. The first few were light and we were relieved. On October 21, we heard that one of our brightest and most capable members, Muli Bashan, was killed in action. He was our chief engineer around whom all plans for electronic development hinged. He left a widow and three small children. The blow was stunning and the loss irreparable. The hurt is compounded by the fact that his army service did not entail special risks but he was caught by a shell and was killed instantly. As of this minute we have three wounded (not seriously) and two missing, whom we hope to trace.

One source of gratification for us is our special soldiers' service. Daily we keep the clubhouse open from noon to midnight, with

---

[49]The group of American students at the high school in the kibbutz.

volunteer effort on the part of our members. We serve snacks and drinks and provide relaxation. Whole bus-loads appear. First the soldiers dash to the telephone, then a hot shower and only afterwards food and drink. Our Guest House has been turned into a rest and recuperation centre. We are far enough behind the lines to serve as an oasis. Entertainers come to perform and our kids love it.

We are now reaching a stage of preparing for a long emergency situation. No one knows how long the cease-fire will last. No one can anticipate the immediate or the long-range future, and the likelihood that many of the reservists will stay with their units appears real. Accordingly, we are now undergoing our second reorganization and are requesting the release of key personnel so that we can gear our economy to whatever may come. We are now in need of an administration building, of concrete buildings to replace wooden bungalows. We have to complete the living quarters for the American Class and their parallel age group. We had started building on the promise of financial assistance from the Jewish Agency and are caught midway. It is necessary to finish our public hall. Most important, we must build several more underground shelters so as to be prepared for all future emergencies. Our factory will have to be reorganized, taking into account the available personnel. It may be necessary to revise all plans, both current and developmental. Unless we find a qualified engineer who is competent in electric and electronic matters, we might revise our line of production. Would that we could absorb more volunteers and find ways of accepting their heart-warming applications. We have neither the housing nor the technical manpower to absorb them.

Our community and social life has survived the stresses, but not without scars. It is not a simple matter to pretend to the children that all is well when wives and mothers know otherwise. The daily schedule of practically everyone had to be readjusted. Peacetime problems do not automatically disappear because of war.

Let this serve as a preliminary report; perhaps more will follow. I can add that fortunately in our immediate family all is well. Nothing would give me greater pleasure than to make all preparations for a long emergency seem utterly ridiculous. We are hoping for the best.

Kfar Blum
November 7, 1973

On October 29, we decided to take the children out of the shelters. It was a hard decision to make despite the official cease-fire, since we are within the range of both Syria and Lebanon. There was a meeting of our "war administration" (*Mazkirut*) together with the responsible educational authorities and we agreed to return to normal. Naturally provision was made in case of an alert or actual shelling. So far so good.

We had two very anxious days on October 20 and 21 when the army climbed up to the Hermon. The Syrians held our former outpost and poured in many troops to defend it. Not only are we familiar with the steep and rugged terrain but we also know many of the boys who are in the army unit involved. Imagine our feelings when we heard the explosions, saw the flashes and brush fires and knew that serious casualties were inevitable. Terrible.

The cease-fire, precarious as it is, has enabled many visits from our soldier members. Those who serve in the vicinity come more frequently. Others have not yet been seen. We have to be satisfied with hurried telephone messages or postcards. When one does show up it's a supreme holiday for the whole family and the kibbutz. A cluster of the curious gathers at once to listen, hear and share news. Most touching are the reunions of husbands and wives and most impressive is the brave show put on when they say good-by.

Two of our soldiers have been officially reported missing. The agony of the unknown is most cruel. Are they lying in some hospital as unidentified bodies, have they been taken prisoner, or were they killed? Parents cannot sleep. The kibbutz is worried. Day follows day and no word arrives. We brace ourselves for the worst. To clear the uncertainty we set up search teams who check army units, files, records, eyewitnesses. This is duplicating the function of the authorized army teams and it constitutes interference but *Tzahal*[50] has been indulgent. They and we know that we cannot sit idly by until even their efficient apparatus arrives at a report.

The Arabs know how sensitive we are about every individual and the extended delays in releasing the names of prisoners jangle our exposed raw nerves. What kind of people are the leaders of our neighbors? Reports of Arab cruelties are no longer rumors. Too many of our kids saw the results on the battlefield and still we preach humanity and restraint.

We are all puzzled about European reaction. We have long ceased to expect sympathetic understanding. What is inexplicable is that official Europe doesn't realize its own interests. Once the Arabs discover that blackmail is effective on the governmental level their demands will keep rising. They will raise [oil] prices arbitrarily, accumulate financial reserves to enable further blackmail and will be in a position to dictate policy to all of Europe. Russia, by controlling Arabs, will truly vanquish Europe and will be that much closer to ruling the world. All because Europe refuses to face one cold winter. It is risking the fires of hell thereafter as the ultimate price. We are praying that America will understand this threat on a long-range basis and will not weaken. If so, little Israel will do for the globe what England did in its finest hour against Hitler. But at what a price!

Like everyone, we follow the Kissinger travels. We tried to fathom the Henry-Golda conversations. We read and listen to news and to commentators. We are reminded over and over again of the parallel between 1947–48 and 1973. We were facing grave dangers then and we are facing them again today. We are stronger today but the shadow of Russia is menacing. Unless mankind has gone berserk, Russia will not hazard World War Three but it certainly follows a course of brinkmanship.

To us at Kfar Blum the behavior of the new nations of Africa is personally anomalous. Dozens of African students trained in all our economic branches. They stayed and lived with us for months and months. I personally acted as guide for over a year and became intimate with men who probably reached positions of

---

[50] *Tz'va Haganah L'Israel:* The Israel Defense Forces.

importance by now. We did our best to help them acquire skills and know-how. None of us expected gratitude then and no one expects it now, but neither did we look forward to a stab in the back.

And so we are now at an interlude with a respite from active firing. There is no absolute certainty that the guns and rockets will boom again but there is certainly no guarantee that they will not. In anticipation of a real ceasefire we already began to squabble a bit and indulge in internal recriminations. The best sign that we feel the gravity of our situation is that we are not pursuing that course now.

Joey [Yosef] was mobilized very early in the war and is busy with problems of transport, fuel, manpower training. He serves a very important function in the war effort because motor transport is of the essence.

Those of us who believe in basic human sanity are hopeful.

From An American Volunteer

This letter was written by an American boy who came to Kfar Blum as a volunteer and was inducted last year into the Israeli Army. He writes to the mother of an 18-year-old American boy who left his college studies to volunteer for service in Kfar Blum after the October War and who is now also in the Israeli Army. Both boys had originally participated in the high school program for American students conducted at Kfar Blum. The letter speaks for itself.

Greetings and Salutations,

I figured I'd help fill out this letter and say hello. I was sort of disappointed not to see J. this weekend. To see him come home for the first time in uniform. I remember what it was like for me. You feel a bit strange, but most of all, proud. I never tried to persuade him to stay and join the army. Such a big decision has to be made by one's self. But I always knew he'd arrive at it within the year. War or no war. Anyone who is true to himself would have to. J. sees himself as a Jew and knows his place is in Israel. Feels it is his real home. Along with this self identification comes obligation. Not just to country, but to friends; could he be at one with himself while all his *real* friends are serving—and when friends die. For anyone who is not a hypocrite with a basic sense of self-delusion, there's no other choice. One thing I remember from when we learned Camus is that running away from basic obligations is immediately comfortable, ultimately damning.

The army is a lousy thing for three years but J. would have been very miserable, lacking real self respect for a long time if he hadn't faced up to what *he* considered his biggest obligation to country, friends, and most of all, *himself.* I'm happy with life, while M. in school is downright miserable, for only these simple reasons. Three years is physically a long time. But that's the price we have to pay as Jews. Jews in Europe in the last generation didn't have the opportunity to pay it. I don't enjoy it, no one does. But I, and I know J. will consider it ultimately to be a privilege. Anyway, while he's in basic, he won't have much time to write, but besides exhaustion, he's okay. I'm sure that you, like everyone here, are proud of him. I may get to the States this summer; if so, I'll drop in. L'hitraot.

P.S. Excuse the dime store philosophy!

THE JORDAN RIVER AND MOUNT HERMON are part of the permanent vista of Kfar Blum.

AN OLDTIME HORA AFTER A DAY'S WORK—Kfar Blum, 1953

AUTHORS AND WIVES (from left: Yosef Criden, Ruth Criden, Helen Gelb, Saadia Gelb)

BEFORE SETTLING PERMANENTLY AT KFAR BLUM, the garin (nucleus) spent some time at Kibbutz Ramat Yochanan. In the photo, a younger Saadia Gelb "supervises" the cooks preparing food for the group heading for Upper Galilee.

WHEN THE SECOND GENERATION WAS YOUNG (1954):
playing on a "retired" tractor wheel

THE DAY'S HAUL OF FISH is brought from the ponds to the processing plant (1960).

LINE-UP ALONG THE FISHNETS in the ponds of Kfar Blum

*YEHUDIT AVNI, formerly of England, repairs shoes
for the Kibbutzniks.*

COTTON PICKING AT KFAR BLUM

*THE CHESS TOURNAMENT—a major recreational event
at Kfar Blum*

Most of the members of Kfar Blum live in apartments, two stories high; the lawns are handy for parking bicycles.

THE GUEST HOUSE for foreign visitors or Israeli vacationers

SHAVUOT FESTIVAL—welcoming the first fruits of the season

CELEBRATING HANUKKAH inside the Kibbutz dining hall (1972)

KIBBUTZ CHORALE in the open fields

IN A KIBBUTZ CLASSROOM—Helen Gelb is teaching.

UPPER GALILEE REGIONAL HIGH SCHOOL, at Kfar Blum

THE CHILDREN OF KFAR BLUM (1960)

THE OLYMPIC-SIZE SWIMMING POOL makes Kfar Blum a special attraction for travelers and a handy place for a refreshing moment in the day of the kibbutzniks.

KFAR BLUM CHILDREN enjoy a dip in the Jordan River.

Entrance to Underground Air Raid Shelter at Kfar Blum

THE THIRD GENERATION:
Kfar Blum's founders are now grandparents.

APPENDIX

The Kibbutz Movements

List of Kibbutzim

Kibbutz Enterprises

Regional Projects

Guest Houses

Map Showing Location of Kibbutzim

THE KIBBUTZ MOVEMENTS

The Federation of the Kibbutz Movements was founded in 1963 as a result of an increasing cooperating among the different kibbutzim movements. The "Federation" constitutes the roof organization of all trends incorporating about 240 kibbutzim all over the country and along all the borders. Incorporated in the "Federation", are: "Ichud Hakvutzot Vehakibbutzim", "Kibbutz Haartzi – Hashomer Hatzair", "Hakibbutz Hameuchad", "Hakibbutz Hadati", "Hanoar Hazioni" and the Kibbutzim of "Poalei Agudat Israel".

Today after 8 years of operation the "Federation" constitutes the central organization and address for all kibbutz affairs (side by side with those of the movements). Its operation extends over all kibbutz fields of activity which can be carried out jointly. Since 1963, the "Federation" has spread its wings over most fields of operation of the kibbutz. It seems that there is no kibbutz field of operation which does not receive expression in one of the "Federation's" projects or in the inter-kibbutz committees. The cooperation is expressed in two main ways:

a)   combined committees while the movement departments continue to operate independently.

b)   Projects founded as "Federation" activities and are under its complete patronage.

The "Federation's" economic committee operates in the household and economic field with the permanent participation of the secretaries of the economic committees of the various trends. It deals in the following fields: land, water, financing, housing, planning, costs, new settlements, taxes, marketing budgets, etc. and is the representation of the kibbutz-movement affairs for the government institutions, the Jewish Agency and other public institutions.

The industrial plants are federated in the "Association of Kibbutz Industry" which represents them externally. The inter-kibbutz unit for economic training is an institution of high standard and prestige in the kibbutz movement and outside it as well. Because of that unit the management and administration in the kibbutzim have reached a very high standard and serves as an example for other economic sectors in the country.

The "Federation's" Education and Research Authority is responsible for the whole wide-spread network of post-high-school and university education of the Kibbutz Movement.

The inter-kibbutz Research Committee coordinates between the different bodies inside and outside of the kibbutz movement which deal with research into different aspects of life in the kibbutz.

In the field of culture and art one may point out the following joint projects: The Kibbutz Stage, a central ensemble and three district workshops, a chamber orchestra with forty players, a central dancing group. A network of literature circles of about 1200 kibbutz members, an art and sculpture gallery of the kibbutz movement artists. All these are in addition to the movements' own cultural activities.

In the field of social and health education there are a consulting and rehabilitation station, a course for social workers, an infant and family welfare centre, a division for senior citizens, an inter-kibbutz education committee dealing mainly with training and extension studies and the supply of tutorial material.

The "Federation" serves as a forum for joint clarification of fundamental problems requiring inter-movement discussion, solutions of which may be found jointly from time to time.

The "Federation" participates in the decisive struggle for the existence of the kibbutz movement and its growth by means of absorption of children, youths and adults. A network of "Aliya Desks" in all countries led by the kibbutz movement emissaries (shlichim) direct the volunteers, the youth and the immigrants to settlement on the land and to the kibbutz. The inter-kibbutz absorption committee cares for their absorption in the country and the instructors' organisation of the youth departments arranges the absorption of the youths in the kibbutzim.

The interest in the kibbutz as a social phenomenon of universal value extends over the whole world and the "Federation" serves materially as a centre for information, communication and reference.

Recently, the Education Authority of the "Federation" has published a bibliography of publications on the kibbutz in foreign languages containing a list of hundreds of articles, brochures and surveys, in addition to the large amount of material available in Hebrew.

Also, the people who hoped to see in the "Federation" the realization of the kibbutz movement unification, have no ground to be disappointed at the impressive rate of cooperation and consolidation achieved so far.

And finally, some statistical data. In the kibbutz movement there are 240 kibbutzim with a population of 95,000 (52,000 members, 30,000 children and the rest candidates, parents, relatives and temporaries). The kibbutz movement constitutes 3.5% of Israel's population, but produces 30% of the agricultural production and 7% of the industrial production in Israel.

"ICHUD HAKEVUTZOT VEHAKIBBUTZIM"

It has today 83 settlements (five of which belong to the Noar Zioni Movement, and two to the Poalei Agudat Israel) with a population of 32,000 (50% male, and 50% female). There are 17,300 members and candidates, 10,500 children and youths and the rest Ulpan students, temporaries, parents, etc. The cultivated area is 460,000 dunams of which 200,000 is irrigated.

The Ichud includes the oldest settlements of the kibbutz movement, as well as new settlements set up by the pioneer youth movements in Israel and in the diaspora. In 1968 a new settlement joined the movement — Mevo Hamma — which was established after the Six Day War; in 1972 another settlement — Afik — was set up in the south of the Golan Heights.

The central economic operation of the Ichud is being implemented mainly by: a) "Keren Haichud Ltd." (Ichud Fund Ltd.) (it is the main financial instrument for mutual aid among the settlements — its capital fund is over nine million Israel pounds). b) "Mishkey Haichud Ltd." (a purchasing organization of the settlements).

Value of the agricultural production:

This amounted to 216.5 million Israel pounds which constitutes 59% of total production value. The rest falls upon the industrial plants and workshops (i.e. 25.1 million or 7%), the total amounts therefore to about IL. 365 million, and to that one has to add about IL. 20 million the output of industrial plants registered as separate companies.

Industrial Plants:

Lately the movement has begun to think about the planning of industry in the kibbutzim and set up a Department assigned to pave the way for a proper integration of the industry in the economy of the kibbutz.

Collective Education Institutions:

The children in the settlements of the Ichud, about 9,800, are being educated in various frameworks. Children of low ages (until the age of six) are relatively more numerous than children of the same ages in the other settlements. The high-school education is given in 13 district schools (about 3,100 pupils), most of which are jointly run by 2 or 3 kibbutz movements (Moshav children are also among the pupils). All the schools are open to external pupils and children from the youth Aliya — their share is about 30%.

In the settlements Garinim (nuclei) of youth movements assemble, and train themselves to complement existing kibbutzim and to set up new settlements. About 200 members are active in training and educational functions.

The Ichud periodicals are:

"Igeret Lachaver" (a weekly for internal information); "Yediot" (internal information for the movement's active members); "Niv Hakvutza" (an ideological quarterly); "Igeret Lachinuch" (a two monthly magazine on education); "Aleh" (a youth branch publication) and "Shadmot Lamadrich".

Remarks:

1) One may point out that the five kibbutzim of the "Hanoar Hazioni" have an attachement to the Ichud from the economic, educational, cultural and security point of view.

2) 13 Kibbutzim of the "Hakibbutz Hadati" are in close contact with the Ichud institutions.

3) 3 Kibbutzim of the "Poalei Agudat Israel", "Chefetz Haim", "Shalavim" and "Mevo Horon" are economically tied to the Ichud.

The Secretariat of the Ichud is in Tel Aviv at No. 10, Dubnov Street, Tel. 250231.

"HAKIBBUTZ HAARTZI" — "HASHOMER HATZAIR"

This is the Federation of the "Hashomer Hatzair" kibbutzim in Israel. It was established at the Foundation Council in Haifa on the 1st — 3rd April 1927. Its origin sprang from the youth movement organised on the eve of World War I in the Jewish section of Poland, Galicia and Austria by the name of "Hashomer Hatzair" (in 1913). During its whole existence, "Hashomer Hatzair" has consistently professed its faith in Zionism, Socialism and the kibbutz ideology. It loyally realizes its aspirations in joining the process of state building while paying particular attention to the movement's uniqueness. The Kibbutz Haartzi settlements are an integral part of the United Labour Party (MAPAM). The Kibbutz Haartzi has today 75 kibbutzim with a population of 31,055, of which there are about 18,000 members and candidates, about 10,000 children (among whom are included children from the outside and youth movement trainees, and about 1,500 temporaries and ulpan students).

After the Six Day War, the Kibbutz Haartzi has set up two new settlements: Kerem Shalom (in the Negev) and Snir (Golan Heights). In addition, it maintains two Nahal settlements, "Nachal Geshor" (Golan Heights) and Nachal Tzofer (Arava).

The scope of settlements in agriculture and industry:

At the end of 1969, the total area of the Kibbutz Haartzi settlements was 635 thousand dunams, of which the permanent area was 511 thousand dunams. The cultivated area was 448 thousand dunams. Side by side with agriculture there are also industrial plants in most Kibbutz Haartzi settlements which produce for the local market and for export. The annual export value of all the industrial plants of the kibbutzim is 102 million Israel pounds, out of which the share of the Kibbutz Haartzi is 22% (22 million Israel pounds).

Central Economic Institutions:

The central finance institute is "Keren Hashomer Hatzair", founded in 1937. Its capital fund is above 17 million Israel pounds.

"The Investment and Trust Company of Hashomer Hatzair Ltd." is a subsidiary company of the "Keren Hashomer Hatzair". Its aim is to encourage the development of industrial and agricultural plants in the Hashomer Hatzair Kibbutzim.

"Kibbutzei Hashomer Hatzair" is a central cooperative society which purchases products for all Kibbutz Haartzi settlements and concerns itself with training.

The **"Mifaley Techen"** Company imports and supplies equipment and raw materials, coordinates and trains the industrial plants set up by the kibbutzim or with their participation and it combines all industrial plants of the Kibbutz Haartzi. The annual financial turnover in 1970 amounted to 52 million Israel pounds.

"Mutzarey Techen" is a company marketing the industrial products of most Kibbutz Haartzi plants. Its financial turnover in 1970 was 60 million Israel pounds.

The Engineering Department deals with planning of new settlements by assisting them in construction and technical supervision.

The Construction Department executes construction works in the Kibbutz Haartzi kibbutzim.

The Economic and Household Department represents and trains the economic operation in the kibbutzim and it has a division for the planning and survey of the kibbutz economy.

Education and Culture:

The Kibbutz Haartzi maintains the following projects in this field: "Sifriat Hapoalim" has published until today over a thousand books (original and translation) in over 8 million copies. It has thousands of permanent subscribers in the cities and villages.

Periodicals:

"This week in the Kibbutz Haartzi" is an informative internal organ of the Kibbutz Haartzi. "Hedim" (Echoes) is a quarterly about problems of the kibbutz society. Another periodical is "Alon Hachinuch Hameshutaf" about the problems of communal education. In the Kibbutz Haartzi there operate associations of painters and sculptors, producers and musicians, authors, photographers and cameramen. "Givat Haviva" (in the name of the girl parachutist Haviva Reik) is a permanent seminary serving as a teaching and an ideological advanced study centre for members of the kibbutz and the educational movement. "Moreshet" is a project for perpetuation and memorial of the holocaust, and also publishes a periodical by the same name.

The Secretariat of the Hakibbutz Haartzi is in Tel Aviv at 15 Leonardo Da Vinci Street, Tel. 255133—51.

"HAKIBBUTZ HAMEUCHAD"

History and Development of the Movement

"Hakibbutz Hameuchad" was founded in Petach-Tikva in 1927 by the kibbutz Ein Harod, Gedud Haavoda (Labour Battalion), Plugat Hakovesh and Netzach U.S.S.R.

Its fundamental aims:

1) The settlement and productivization of the Jew in Israel as the main means of the Jewish national liberation.

2) The kibbutz population is big and growing, open to absorption and combines agriculture and industry.

3) The settlements are organised in a country-wide movement and come under its authority.

4) The settlements and the movement are intermingled in all country-wide affairs in the economic, political and security fields — as an organic part and as a stimulating force in the Labour and Zionist Movements (and later also in the State of Israel).

These ideas were developed by the men of the second Aliya whose main concentration was in kibbutz Ein Harod and its branches, and by the men of Gdud Haavoda of the Third Aliya.

After its inception, Hakibbutz Hameuchad began to open emissary offices abroad in the framework of the "Hechalutz Haklali", "Hechalutz Hatzair" and "Freiheit" (Freedom). During the World War II the Kibbutz Meuchad was the central factor in setting up the Palmach (shocktroops) and participation in rescue missions to Europe.

In the struggle against the British (1945–47) Hakibbutz Hameuchad constituted a considerable force through its settlements which served as bases for forces and operations and training of recruits for the Palmach. The operations were the bringing in of illegal immigrants, military actions against the British rule, settling people on the land as opposed by the "White Papers" policy and public activity for the masses.

From the political point of view, Hakibbutz Hameuchad was the driving factor for activism in all fields of the struggle. In the War of Independence, many settlements were in the line of fire. Its members fought as individuals and in Hagana and Israeli Army units and mainly in the "Palmach". "Kibbutz Meuchad" members fulfilled command functions far beyond their population percentage.

By the end of the War of Independence Hakibbutz Hameuchad, together with the other Kibbutz movements, started settling all parts of the country which had not yet been settled by Jews.

After the Six Day War Hakibbutz Hameuchad was among the initiators of new settlement projects. The contribution amounts to 3 Kibbutzim on the Golan Heights and three Nahal Settlements in other parts of the country. The entire cultivated area amounts to 513,000 dunams. Agricultural produce reached the figure of 203 million IL. in 1971. Industrial enterprises exist in most of the settlements; the industrial produce, in 1971, amounted to 128 million IL.

Settlements and Population.

In 1971, Hakibbutz Hameuchad had 58 settlements. The last one "Elrom" was set up in the north of the Golan Heights in July 1972.

Its population was 26,000, divided as follows:

14,000 members and candidates, 7,600 children, 1,100 youths, over 500 members' parents and the rest temporary people of various kinds. The adult kibbutz population constitutes 40% of all old settlements members and about 30% of the total kibbutz movement members.

Central Projects:

1) **The Central Seminary at EF'AL** is designed as an ideological and educational operation.

2) The **Hakibbutz Hameuchad Publishing House** deals in all publishing branches, literature-original and translated.

3) **Itzhak Katzenelson House at the Kibbutz "Lohamei Ha'Getaot"** contains the archives of the holocaust and heroism period.

4) The **Hakibbutz Hameuchad Settlements Ltd.** serves as a Central Purchasing Company.

5) **"Marketings & Supply – Hakibbutz Hameuchad Ltd."** serves a central purchasing company from additional settlement factors.

6) The **Hakibbutz Hameuchad Fund Ltd.** is the financial institution of the kibbutz movement.

7) **Oniot Tarshish Ltd.** is the Hakibbutz Hameuchad shipping company and its own 4 cargo ships.

8) **"The Planning Department of Hakibbutz Hameuchad" and "Ichud Hakvutzot Vehakibbutzim"**: The Department contains planning divisions for all engineering branches.

9) **The Investments and Projects Co. Ltd.** is a financing and Investment Company.

10) **Economic and Household Seminaries**: Hakibbutz Hameuchad was the initiator of courses for household coordinators (secretaries) and for high economic and agricultural education. Since 1962, the other kibbutz movements have joined these courses.

Youth Movements connected with Israel:

"Hanoar Haoved", "Hamachanot Haolim" and "Histadrut Hatzofim", which is called the "Dror" (Liberty) Movement abroad.

The Secretariat of the Kibbutz Meuchad is at 27, Soutin Street, Tel Aviv 64684, Tel. 245271.

"HAKIBBUTZ HADATI"

This movement comprises all "Hapoel Hamizrahi" religious kvutzot. The first Kvutzot arrived from Poland and Germany forty years ago. Settlements were founded on the borders in the southern Beisan Valley, Etzion Block and in the Negev. In the War of Independence and in the disturbances before it these settlements stood in the first line of fire. The Etzion Block, the glory of the religious kibbutz settlements, fell into the hands of the enemy and the Kvutza Kfar Etzion was completely destroyed.

"Keren Hakibbutz Hadati" (The Religious Kibbutz Fund)

At the end of 1971 on completion of the 30th years of its existence, the capital fund reached the amount of one million and 300 thousand Israel pounds. The total amount on the fund's balance sheet was IL. 4,500,000.

The Fund was established in 1940 with the aim of giving mutual assistance to the settlements of the Hakibbutz Hadati.

New Settlements:

Recently, 4 settlements have been established:

a)   "Alumim" in the Negev, near to Kvutzat Saad.

b)   "Kefar Etzion", the pioneer of the renewed settlement in the liberated Etzion Block.

c)   "Maale Gilboa" which changed from a military to a civilian settlement.

d)   "Rosh Tzurim" the second settlement in the Etzion Block was established on 15th of Ab, 1969.

Thus, the settlement of the Hakibbutz Hadati reached the number 13, so may they increase! In addition "Hakibbutz Hadati" keeps Nahal settlements in Kefar Darom and "Nahal Masua" in the Jordan Valley.

Absorption from Abroad:

The flow of absorption from abroad is steady. The Kibbutz Hadati attained achievements in this field with the help of Hebrew ulpanim and six training groups from abroad, which are maintained in our settlements.

The Youth Movement:

Hakibbutz Hadati sees itself responsible for the fate of the religious youth movement "Bnei Akiva" and the Kibbutz emissaries operate in its countrywide management.

Religious and Cultural Life:

In most of the settlements fine synagogues were built, which serve as a spiritual centre to the whole population. A rich and diverse cultural activity is maintained in all settlements, mainly in the winter season. It includes holy teachings, the Talmud (the Oral Law), as well as languages, agriculture, craftsmanship and artistic work, history, economy, sports, etc.

Education:

The children of the Kibbutz Hadati study in local schools in the framework of state religious education. In Sde Eliyahu there is a common school to all the settlements in the Northern District, and in

Yavne, there is a common school for the Southern District. The institutions prepare the pupils for the state examinations.

Publications:

The Kibbutz Hadati organ is the monthly "Amudim". It serves as a means of expression for the members and in it are discussed topical problems and those belonging "above the world"

The offices of the Kibbutz Hadati are in Tel Aviv, at 7 Dubnov Street, Tel. 257231.

"HANOAR HAZIONI"

The "Hanoar Hazioni" movement was set up in 1928, in Poland, Rumania, Hungary, Austria, Czechoslovakia. The first realizing "Garin" (nucleus) in the kibbutz framework dwelt in Petah Tikva departing for settlement on the land. Additional phases in the development of the movement after World War II, were the establishing of a movement in South American continent and in Canada.

The number of registered trainees and participants in organizational-educational and cultural activity is 6,000. Each year at least two "garinim" go out and thereby complement young settlements or constitute a foundation for settling up new settlements. The movement has 6 kibbutzim, 22 Moshavim and Moshavim Shitufeem, 5 educational institutions and it also operates in some educational institutions (Kefar Silver, Pardess Hana, Mikve Israel).

The movement issues a weekly in Hebrew "Daf Hatenua" which is an information organ, for problems of the world movement. "Orot" is a bulletin for clarification of ideological problems.

Every three months, a brochure "Alim" is published, dealing with state and community problems. An information bulletin in Spanish, French and English is also published. The movement belongs to the Independent Liberal Party and at the "Histadrut" (General Federation of Labour) it is represented by the Liberal Labour movement. In the inter-kibbutz framework it is connected to the "Ichud Hakvutzot Vehakibbutzim" by special agreement.

The Secretariat of the movement is in Tel Aviv, at 48 King George Street, Tel. 787374.

KIBBUTZEI POALEI AGUDAT ISRAEL

This is a religious Kibbutz movement which is not included in the Federation of the Kibbutz Movements.

It has three settlements – Hefetz Haim, Sha'alavim and Mevo Horon.

Economically, these kibbutzim are connected to the "Ichud Hakvutzot Vehakibbutzim"

The movement's secretariat is in Tel Aviv, Tel. 242126.

LIST OF KIBBUTZIM

HOW TO USE THE INDEX

The 250 Kibbutzim and Nahal Settlements in Israel, shown on the Map overleaf, are listed alphabetically in the Index below. Each name is marked by a number and a letter. The number directs the reader to corresponding numbers on the sides of the map; the letter corresponds to one of the letters along the top or bottom margin of this reverse side of the map.

To locate a kibbutz, roll the map upwards from the bottom (or downwards!), until the edge with the row of letters reaches the desired index number on the vertical borders of the map.

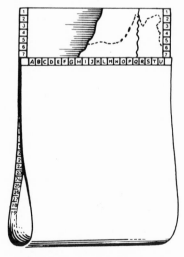

Then find the desired letter on the horizontal scale. The desired kibbutz will be within the imaginary square above (or below) this letter.

(To find Kibbutz GADOT 9.AD, roll the map upwards until the edge reaches No. 9 on the vertical scale, look for the letter AD – and you have located the Kibbutz!)

KIBBUTZ MOVEMENT is indicated by one of the following symbols:

◆ Hakibbutz Haartzi
● Hakibbutz Hameuchad
■ Ichud Hakevutzot Vehakibbutzim
✹ Hakibbutz Hadati
▲ Hanoar Hazioni
▼ Kibbutz Poalei Agudat Israel

DESCRIPTION OF THE KIBBUTZ: The first line contains name and geographical location of the kibbutz; the second line — official address (M.P. = Mobile Post; P.O. = Post Office); the third line — population, year of foundation, and the year of settling on the soil at the final location, marked by an *.

OTHER MARKINGS (on the right of the Index): the respective kibbutz possesses . . .

⚙ Industrial Enterprise
🏨 Guest House
📖 Ulpan for New Immigrants
📖 Other Ulpanim
☆ Historical site

◆ **ADAMIT** (W. Galilee)   7.U   ⚙
Galil Maaravi M. P., tel. 04—968034
pop. 85; fd. 1958; *1958

● **AFEK** (Zevulun Valley)   14.S ⚙
Afek P.O., tel. 04—710261
pop. 450; fd. 1936; *1939

■ **AFIK** (Ramat Hagolan)   15.AH
Ramat Hagolan M.P., tel. 067—50412
fd. 1972.

■ **AFIKIM** (Jordan Valley)   18.AC ⚙
Afikim P.O., tel. 067—50451
pop. 1400; fd. 1924; *1932.

● **ALONIM** (Yizreel Valley, 21 klm. SE Haifa)   17.T ⚙
Alonim P.O., tel. 04—431001, 932290   ☆
pop. 560; fd. 1935; *1938
Youth Aliyah House & Exhibition

✹ **ALUMIM** (Western Negev)   50.E
Hanegev M.P., tel. 051—94114
pop. 100; fd. 1966; *1967.

ALUMOT (Lower Galilee)   17.AB
Galil Tachton M.P., tel. 067—50200
pop. 134; fd. 1936; *1946;
Cult. House named after Peretz Naphtali.

AMIAD (Upper Galilee)   12.AB
Hevel Khorazim M.P.; tel. 067—37332
pop. 300; fd. 1946.

AMIR (Upper Galilee)   5.AD
Galil Elyon M.P., tel. 067—40492
pop. 450; fd. 1933; *1939.

ASHDOT YAAKOV/Ihud (Jordan Valley)   18.AC
Emek Hayarden M.P., tel. 067—50205
pop. 550; fd. 1924;

ASHDOT YAAKOV/Me'uhad (Jordan Valley)   18.AC
Emek Hayarden M.P., tel. 067—50262
pop. 530; fd. 1924;
Art Museum named after Uri & Rami Nechushtan.

AYELET HASHACHAR (Upper Galilee)   9.AC
Galil Elyon M.P., tel. 067—37313-4
pop. 800; fd. 1916; *1918
Museum of Hazor finds; Yad Lebanim;
Culture Hall w. 1100 seats.

BAHAN (Emek Hefer)   26.Q
Shomron M.P., tel. 053--98296
pop. 303, fd. 1954; *1954.

BAR'AM (Upper Galilee, nr. Lebanon frontier)   8.Z
Merom Hagalil M.P., tel. 067—39263
pop. 380; fd. 1949.*1949.

BARKAI (13 km. from Hadera)   23.Q
Menashe M.P., tel. 063—7106
pop. 350; fd. 1949; *1949.

BEERI (North-Western Negev)   51.E
Negev M.P., tel. 057—94051
pop. 550; fd. 1944; *1946.

BE'EROT YITZHAK (15 klm. E. Tel-Aviv)   35.N
Tel-Aviv Yafo P.O., tel. 03—915821-2
pop. 350; fd. 1935; *1943 (Western Negev,
nr. Gaza); *1948 (at present site).

BET ALPHA (Yizreel Valley)   22.Z
Gilboa M.P., tel. 065—77650

pop. 775; fd. 1920; *1922
Hall for sports and performances. ☆

BET GUBRIN (nr. Hebron Hills)　　　46.N
Lachish Darom M.P., tel. 051−91172
pop. 150; fd. 1949.
Nearby: large ancient caves.

BET HA'EMEK (Western Galilee)　　11.S
Ma'ale Hagalil M.P., tel. 04−922664-5
pop. 380; fd.1949.; *1949.

BET HASHITA (Eastern Yizreel Valley)　21.Z
Bet Hashita M.P., tel. 065−77762
pop. 960; fd. 1928; *1935.

BET KAMA (30 klm. N. Beer Sheva)　50.K
Negev M.P., tel. 057−2671
pop. 300; fd. 1946; *1949.

BET KESHET (Lower Galilee, nr. Mt. Tabor)　17.Y
Galil Tachton M.P., tel. 065−37207
pop. 370; fd. 1944; *1944.

BET NIR (Lachish District)　　　45.N
Sde Gat M.P., tel. 02−911260
pop. 150; fd.1955 ; *1955.

BET OREN (Mt. Carmel)　　　16.P
Bet Oren M.P., tel. 04−222111
pop. 250; fd. 1935; *1939
"Heichal Hacarmel".

BET ZERA (Jordan Valley)　　18.AC
Emek Hayarden M.P., tel. 067−50235-6
pop. 820; fd. 1927; *1927.

BROR CHAIL (7 klm. from Sderot)　47.H
Lachish Darom M.P., tel. 051−94126
pop. 600; fd. 1948; *1948
Osvaldo Oranha Cultural Hall.

CARMIA (11 klm. S. Ashkelon)　　46.F
Hof Ashkelon M.P., tel. 051−2412
pop. 250; fd. 1950.

DALIA (Megiddo District)　　20.R
Dalia P.O., tel. 04−993277
pop. 650; fd. 1934; *1939.

DAN (Upper Galilee)　　4.AE
Galil Elyon M.P., tel. 067−40930

pop. 466; fd. 1933; *1939
"Ussishkin House", archaelog. exhibit.

DAPHNA (Upper Galilee)　　　　　**3.AD**
Galil Elyon M.P., tel. 067–40937
pop. 660; fd. 1934; *1939.

DEGANIA A' (Jordan Valley)　　　**17.AC**
Emek Hayarden M.P., tel. 067–50248
pop. 500; fd. 1910 – first kibbutz in Israel –
"Mother of the kibbutzim".
"Bet Gordon" for agriculture & nature.

DEGANIA B' (Jordan Valley)　　　**18.AC**
Emek Hayarden M.P., tel. 067–50376
pop. 600; fd. 1914; *1920.

DOROT (Shaar Hanegev District)　**49.H**
Hof Ashkelon M.P., tel. 051–94127
pop. 450; fd. 1936; *1941.

DOVRAT (8 klm. from Afula)　　　**19.X**
Hevel Megiddo M.P., tel. 065–22132
pop. 350; fd. 1939; *1946.

DVIR (Negev, Hebron Hills)　　　**51.L**
Negev M.P., tel. 057–2605
pop. 205; fd. 1951; *1957.

EILON (W. Galilee)　　　　　　**8.U**
Galil Ma'aravi M.P., tel. 04–968151
pop. 650; fd. 1935; *1938; ("Tower & Stockade kb.").

EILOT (4 klm. N Eilat)　　　　　**98.P**
Hevel Eilot M.P., tel. 059–2252
pop. 140; fd. 1955; *1962.

EIN CARMEL (Carmel Slopes)　　**18.P**
Hof Hacarmel M.P., tel. 04–942071
pop. 460; fd. 1936; *1948.

EIN DOR (Lower Galilee)　　　　**19.Y**
Galil Tachton M.P., tel. 065–37226
pop. 600; fd. 1940; *1948.

EIN GEDI (Dead Sea Shore)　　　**50.Y**
Dead Sea P.O., tel. 057–96007, 96071
pop. 284; fd. 1956.

EIN GEV (On Eastern shore of Sea of Galilee)　**15.AD**
Jordan Valley P.O., tel. 067–50251

pop. 380; fd. 1937
"Kinneret" concert hall.

EIN HACHORESH (Emek Hefer)   26.O
Ein Hachoresh P.O., tel. 063–22943
pop. 650; fd. 1929; *1931.

EIN HAMIFRATZ (Zevulun Valley)   12.R
Asherat M.P., tel. 04–910018
pop. 638; fd. 1930; *1938.
Regional Sports Hall.

EIN HANATZIV (Bet Shean Valley)   23.AA
Bet Shean M.P., tel. 065–88533
pop. 460; fd. 1938; *1946.

EIN HAROD/Ihud (Eastern Yizreel Valley)   21.Y
Ein Harod / Ihud P.O.; tel. 065–77700
pop. 730; fd. 1921.
Bet Lavi

EIN HAROD/Meuhad (Eastern Yizreel Valley)   21.Y
Ein Harod / Meuhad P.O., tel. 065–77736
pop. 830; fd. 1921.
Art gallery & Jewish art collection; Zisling
House – Auditorium & Perpetuation Hall;
Sturman House – Institute for the Geography of
Israel (joint institution of Ein Harod/Ihud &
Meuhad).

EIN HASHLOSHA (Western Negev)   53.B
Hanegev M.P., tel. 057–93077
pop. 260; fd. 1948; *1950

EIN HASHOFET (Ephraim Mountains)   20.S
Ein Hashofet P.O., tel. 04–933266
pop. 650; fd. 1933; *1937.
Memorial hall for fallen soldier.

EIN SHEMER (Shomron)   24.P
Menashe M.P., tel. 063–77040
pop. 600; fd. 1927; *1933.

EIN TZURIM (6 kms. from Malachi Rd. Junction) 44.J
Lachish Tzafon M.P., tel. 055–96351
pop. 370; fd. at Gush Etzion, destroyed during
War of Liberation 1948.

EIN ZIVAN (Ramat Hagolan)   7.AH
Kuneitra P.O., tel. 067–30936
pop. 120; fd. 1968; *1968.

◗ **ELROM** (Ramat Hagolan)   **5.AG**
Ramat Hagolan M. P. Tel. 067-37495
pop. 60; * 13.7.1971

■ **EREZ** (S. of Ashkelon)   **47.F** ⚙
Hof Ashkelon M.P., tel. 051—2415
pop. 315; fd. 1949; *1950.

◆ **EVRON** (W. Galilee)   **10.S** ⚙
Asherat M.P., tel. 04—922443
pop. 450; fd. 1936; *1945.

● **EYAL** (Sharon)   **30.P** ⚙
Hasharon Hatichon M.P., tel. 03—923344
pop. 95; fd. 1949; refounded 1967 by kibbutz
children & "Mahanot Olim".

■ **EYNAT** (East of Petach Tikva)   **33.O** ⚙
Eynat P.O., tel. 03—414381
pop. 520; fd. 1952.

● **FAROD** (Central Galilee)   **11.Z** 📖
Merom Hagalil M.P., tel. 067—39371
pop. 260; fd. 1949.

◆ **GA'ASH** (Sharon, nr. the Sea)   **30.L** ⚙
Ga'ash P.O., tel. 03—937018
pop. 440; fd. 1949; *1951.

◆ **GA'ATON** (Western Galilee)   **9.U** ⚙
Ma'ale Hagalil M.P., tel. 04—924185   📖
pop. 320; fd. 1948; *1948.

● **GADOT** (Upper Galilee, on Jordan River)   **9.AD** 📖
Hevel Khorazim; tel. 067—37347
pop. 240; fd. 1949; *1949
(Absorption of Immigrant families).

■ **GAL'ED** (Shomron)   **21.R** ⚙
Hevel Megido M.P., tel. 04— 993285   📖
pop. 320; fd. 1939; *1945
Culture Hall named after G. Yosephtal.

◆ **GAL'ON** (Lachish District)   **45.M** ⚙
Sde Gat M.P., tel. 051—91074
pop. 130; fd. 1939; *1946.

◆ **GAN SHMUEL** (Shomron, nr. Hadera)   **24.O** ⚙
Shomron M.P., tel. 063—4197   📖
pop. 800; fd. 1921; *1929.

◆ **GAT** (nr. Kiryat Gat)   **45.L**
Sde Gat M.P., tel. 051–91171
pop. 470; fd. 1934; *1942.

◆ **GAZIT** (Lower Galilee)   **19.Z**
Yizreel M.P., tel. 065–37215
pop. 450; fd. 1948 *1950.

● **GESHER** (On Jordan River)   **19.AB**
Emek Bet Shean M.P., tel. 067–50229-31
pop. 400; fd. 1939; destroyed & rebuilt 1948.

■ **GESHER HAZIV** (W. Galilee, N. Naharia)   **9.S**
Galil Ma'aravi M.P., tel. 04–921734-5
pop. 435; fd. 1949; *1949.

■ **GEVA** (Yizreel Valley)   **21.Y**
Geva P.O., tel. 065–77744
pop. 600; fd. 1921; *1921.

■ **GEVIM** (N. W. Negev)   **49.G**
Hof Ashkelon M.P., tel. 051–94331
pop. 300; fd. 1947; *1947.

■ **GINEGAR** (Emek Yizreel)   **18.V**
Ginegar P.O., tel. 065–40740
pop. 460; fd. 1920; *1922.

■ **GEZER** (7 klm. from Ramleh)   **39.N**
Nachal Eylon M.P., tel. 03–961129
pop. 40; fd. 1940; *1945; refounded 1970 by
American new immigrants
Under Jewish Agency supervision.

● **GINOSSAR** (on Sea of Galilee)   **14.AB**
Ginossar P.O., tel. 067–22321-2
pop. 500; fd. 1934; *1937.

● **GIV'AT BRENNER** (nr. Rehovot)   **39.L**
Giv'at Brenner P.O., tel. 03–952891-2
pop. 1700 (Israel's largest kibbutz);
fd. 1928; *1928. Sanatorium; Culture House
named for Enzo Sireni; Absorption Ctr.

■ **GIV'AT CHAIM/Ihud** (Emek Hefer)   **25.O**
Giv'at Chaim/Ihud P.O., tel. 063–4896
pop. 746; fd. 1925; *1952
Large Cultural Hall.

● **GIV'AT CHAIM/Me'uhad** (Emek Hefer)   **25.O**
Giv'at Chaim/Me'uhad P.O., tel. 063–24443
pop. 800; fd. 1925; *1932.

● **GIV'AT HASHLOSHA** (N. E. of Petah Tikva)   33.O ⚙
Giv'at Hashlosha P.O., tel. 03–911288
pop. 500; fd. 1925; *1940.

◆ **GIV'AT OZ** (Ta'anach Valley)   21.U ⚙
Hevel Megido M.P., tel. 065–23025   📖
pop. 420; fd. 1949.

● **GLIL-YAM** (nr. Herzlia)   31.L ⚙
Glil Yam P.O., tel. 03–982242
pop. 360; fd. 1934; *1943.

■ **GONEN** (Upper Galilee, E. of Lake Hule)   6.AD
Galil Elyon M.P., tel. 067–40955
pop. 130; fd.1951; *1953.

■ **GROFIT** (Arava, N. Eilat)   89.R
Eilot M.P., tel. 059–2726.
pop. 90; fd. 1963; * 1966

● **GVAR'AM** (12 klm. from Ashkelon)   46.H 📖
Hof Ashkelon M.P., tel. 051–2419
pop. 260; fd. 1935; *1942.

● **GVAT** (Western Yizreel Valley)   18.U ⚙
Gvat P.O., tel. 065–66105   ☆📖
pop. 700; fd. 1922; *1926.

◆ **GVULOT** (Negev)   56.D
Negev M.P., tel. 057–93100
pop. 95; fd. 1943; *1946.

● **HACHOTRIM** (on Mediterranean, S. Haifa)   16.O ⚙
Hof Hacarmel M.P., tel. 04–94715
pop. 350; fd. 1942; *1948.

● **HAFETZ CHAIM** (15 klm. from Rehovot)   41.L ⚙
Hafetz Chaim P.O., Tel. 055–91029
pop. 420; fd. 1934; *1944.

● **HAGOSHRIM** (Upper Galilee)   4.AD
Galil Elyon M.P., tel. 067–40731
pop. 510; fd. 1948; *1948.

◆ **HAMA'APIL** (East Emek Hefer)   26.P ⚙
Hama'apil P.O., tel. 063–2309   📖
pop. 500; fd. 1938; *1945.

■ **HAMADIA** (Bet Shean Valley)   22.AB ⚙
Bet Shean M.P., tel. 065–88423
pop. 390; fd. 1942; *1942.

HANITA (Western Galilee)   7.T
Galil Elyon M.P., tel. 04—968024
pop. 460; fd. 1938 ("Tower & Stockade" period)
Museum Hanita.

HA'OGEN (Emek Hefer)   26.O
Ha'ogen P.O., tel. 053—98140
pop. 520; fd. 1939; *1947

HA'ON (Jordan Valley)   17.AD
Emek Hayarden M.P., tel. 067—50204
pop. 200; fd. 1949;

HAREL (Jerusalem Corridor)   40.O
Shimshon M.P., tel. 02—911221
pop. 170; fd. 1948;

HASOLELIM (Lower Galilee)   16.U
Natzrat Elit P.O., tel. 065—56291
pop. 250; fd. 1947; *1949.

HATZERIM (6 klm. W. of Beer Sheva)   55.J
Hanegev M.P., tel. 057—2253
pop. 360; fd. 1946; *1946.

HATZOR (Ashdod) (18 klm. S. W. Gedera)   42.J
Hatzor (Ashdod) P.O., tel. 055—94321
pop. 570; fd. 1937; *1946.

HAZOREA (Yizreel Valley)   19.S
Hazorea P.O., tel. 04—933168-9
pop. 650; fd. 1933; *1936.
Wilfried Museum for Middle & Far East cultures
& local archaelogy.

HEFZI-BA (Eastern Yizreel Valley)   22.Z
Gilboa M.P., tel. 065—77675
pop. 540; fd. 1922; *1922.

HORSHIM (N. E. of Petah Tikva)   32.P
Sharon Tichon M.P., tel. 03—927825
pop. 160; fd. 1955; *1955.

HUKUK (Lower Galilee)   13.AA
Hevel Khorazim M.P., tel. 067—20248
pop. 300; fd. 1945; *1946.

HULATA (Hule Valley)   8.AD
Galil Elyon M.P., tel. 067—37446
pop. 400; fd. 1937; *1946.

HULDA (12 klm. from Rehovot)　　　**40.N**
Nachal Eylon M.P., tel. 03–955012
pop. 355; fd. 1909; re-establ. 1930.

KABRI (Western Galilee)　　　**9.T**
Ma'ale Hagalil M.P., tel. 04–922321
pop. 620; fd. 1939; *1949.

KEREM SHALOM (Western Negev)　　　**56.A**
Negev M.P., tel. -57–93193
pop. 60; fd. 1956; *1958.

KFAR AZA (32 klm. S. Ashkelon)　　　**49.F**
Negev M.P., tel. 051–94138
pop. 260; fd. 1951; *1956.

KFAR BLUM (Hule Valley)　　　**5.AD**
Galil Elyon M.P., tel. 067–40721
pop. 620; fd. 1938; *1943
"Yad Nehemia" sports house & swimming pool;
English Ulpan.

KFAR ETZION (Etzion Block)　　　**45.S**
Har Hebron M.P., tel. 02–942588, 02–942793
pop. 120; fd. 1967; *1943; for second time 1967
Permanent exhibition of struggle of Etzion Block.

KFAR GIL'ADI (Upper Galilee)　　　**3.AC**
Kfar Gil'adi P.O., tel. 067–40706
pop. 700; fd. 1916; *1916
Museum for History of "Hashomer";
reconstructed Tel Hai court yard.

KFAR GLICKSON (Shomron Plain)　　　**22.Q**
Menashe M.P., tel. 063–88017
pop. 300; fd. 1935; *1939.
Culture Hall named after Dr. Marton

KFAR HACHORESH (Nazareth Mountains)　　　**17.V**
Kfar Hachoresh P.O.; tel. 065–56560
pop. 280; fd. 1929; *1949
(Kupat Holim rest house).

KFAR HAMACCABI (Zevulun Valley)　　　**15.S**
Kfar Hamaccabi P.O., tel. 04–721150
pop. 350; fd. 1936;
Swimming training center.

KFAR HANASSI (Upper Galilee)　　　**11.AD**
Hevel Khorazim M.P., tel. 067–37534
pop 450; fd. 1948
Room of Dr. Weizmann, Israel's first president.

◆ **KFAR MASARYK** (Zevulun Valley)   12.R
Asherat M.P., tel. 04–910024
pop. 580; fd. 1932; *1939.

◆ **KFAR MENAHEM** (15 klm. from Gedera)   43.M
Emek Sorek M.P., tel. 055–91522
pop. 600; fd. 1933; *1939
Museum for Art & Archaelogy.

■ **KFAR RUPPIN** (Bet Shean Valley)   24.AB
Bet Shean M.P., tel. 065–88355/6/7
pop. 300; fd. 1934; *1938.

● **KFAR SZOLD** (Hule Valley)   4.AE
Galil Elyon M.P., tel. 067–40924
pop. 500; fd. 1934; *1942.

■ **KINNERET** (Jordan Valley)   17.AC
Emek Hayarden M.P., tel. 067–50384
pop. 810; fd. 1913.

■ **KIRYAT ANAVIM** (Judean Mountains)   40.S
Kiryat Anavim P.O., tel. 02–524072
pop. 400; fd. 1920.

● **KISSUFIM** (50 klm. W. Beer Sheva)   52.B
Negev M.P., tel. 057–93078
pop. 310; fd. 1951; *1951.

■ **KVUTZAT SCHILLER** (Sorek Valley)   39.L
Rehovot P.O., tel. 03–951251
pop. 300; fd. 1925; *1927.

◆ **LAHAV** (Eastern Negev)   52.M
Negev M.P., tel. 057–4368
pop. 230; fd. 1952
Museum for Bedouin folklore & archaelogy.

◆ **LAHAVOT BASHAN** (Estern Hule Valley)   6.AE
Galil Elyon M.P., tel. 067–40853
pop. 400; fd. 1940; *1945.

◆ **LAHAVOT HAVIVA** (Shomron)   25.Q
Shomron M.P., tel. 063–2311
pop. 250; fd. 1949.

★ **LAVI** (Lower Galilee)   15.Z
Galil Tachton M.P., tel. 067–22280
pop. 350; fd. 1949;

LOCHAMEI HAGETA'OT (Western Galilee)   **10.R**
Asherat M.P., tel. 04–924162/3
pop. 450; fd. 1949 (by partisans & ghetto fighters)
Museum of the Holocaust.

MA'ABAROT (Emek Hefer)   **26.N**
Ma'abarot P.O., tel. 053–25131
pop. 650; fd. 1927; *1933.

MA'AGAN (Jordan Valley)   **17.AD**
Emek Hayarden M.P., tel. 067–50216
pop. 270; fd. 1941; *1949
Parachutists' House.

MA'AGAN MICHAEL (33 klm. S. of Haifa)   **21.O**
Hof Hacarmel M.P., tel. 063–99611
pop. 880; fd. 1941; *1949
Field School & Nature Reserve.

MA'ALE GILBOA (Gilboa Mountains)   **23.Z**
Gilboa M.P., tel. 065–88306
pop.110; fd. 1962; *1968.

MA'ALE HACHAMISHA (Jerusalem Mountains)   **40.S**
Harei Yehuda M.P., tel. 02–524382
pop. 320; fd. 1934; *1938.

MA'ANIT (12 klm. E. Hadera)   **24.Q**
Menashe M.P., tel. 063–77142
pop. 500; fd. 1936; *1942.

MA'AYAN BARUCH (Upper Galilee)   **3.AD**
Galil Elyon M.P., tel. 067–40927
pop. 330; fd. 1947; *1947.

MA'AYAN ZVI (nr. Zichron Yaakov)   **21.O**
Hof Hacarmel M.P., tel. 063–99018, 99398
pop. 653; fd. 1936; *1938.

MAGAL (Shomron)   **26.Q**
Shomron M.P., tel. 063–22319
pop.245; fd. 1953; *1938.

MAGEN (Western Negev)   **54.C**
Negev M.P., tel. 057–93252
pop. 185; fd. 1949; *1949

MAHANAIM (Upper Galilee)   **10.AC**
Hevel Khorazim M.P., tel. 067–37424
pop. 400; fd. 1939.

● **MALKIA** (Upper Galilee)   **7.AB**
Merom Hagalil M.P., tel. 067—40072
pop. 230; fd. 1949 (Palmach veterans).

● **MA'OZ CHAIM** (Bet Shean Valley)   **23.AB** ⚙
Bet Shean M.P., tel. 065—88447/8/9
pop. 560; fd. 1932; *1937
Culture center & hall "Bet Yavnieli".

■ **MASADA** (Jordan Valley)   **18.AC** ⚙
Emek Hayarden M.P., tel. 067—50212
pop. 326; fd. 1930; *1937
"Arlozorov" Cultural House.

● **MASH'AVEI SADE** (30 klm. S. Beer Sheva)   **62.K** ⚙
Ramat Negev M.P., tel. 057—2032
pop. 450; fd. 1947; *1949

■ **MATZUVA** (Western Galilee)   **8.T** ⚙ 📖
Galil Ma'aravi M.P., tel. 04—968105
pop. 386; fd. 1937; *1940.

■ **MEFALSIM** (Shaar Hanegev District)   **48.F** ⚙
Hof Ashkelon M.P., tel. 051—94052
pop. 466; fd. 1949; *1949.

◆ **MEGIDDO** (Western Yizreel Valley)   **21.T** ☆
Hevel Megiddo M.P., tel. 065—23021
pop. 300; fd. 1949.

● **MENARA** (Upper Galilee)   **4.AB** ⚙ 📖
Galil Elyon M.P., tel. 067—40653
pop. 300; fd. 1940; *1943
Sports Hall.

◆ **MERHAVIA** (Yizreel Valley)   **20.W** ⚙ 📖
Merhavia P.O., tel. 065—22946
pop. 600; fd. 1911 (first Jewish settlement in
Yizreel Valley)
Yad Lebanim; "Hashomer Hatzair" Archives.

● **MEROM GOLAN** (Ramat Hagolan)   **6.AH** ⚙
Kuneitra°P.O., tel. 067—37542/5
pop. 300; fd. 1967; *1970.

◆ **MESILOT** (Bet Shean Valley)   **23.AA** ⚙ 📖
Gilboa M.P., tel. 065—88075/7
pop. 550; fd. 1932; *1938.

◆ **METZER** (Shomron)   **24.Q** ⚙
Shomron M.P., tel. 063—7107
pop. 290; fd. 1953; *1953.

■ **MEVO HAMA** (Southern Ramat Hagolan)   16.AE ⚙
Ramat Hagolan M.P., tel. 067—50414
pop. 158; fd. 1968.

◗ **MEVO HORON** (7 km. north of Latrun)   39.Q
Tel. 03962061
pop. 80; fd. 1968.

● **MISGAV AM** (Upper Galilee)   3.AB 📖
Galil Elyon M.P., tel. 067—40631
pop. 220; fd. 1945.

■ **MISHMAR DAVID** (15 klm. S. Rehovot)   40.N
Nahal Eylon M.P., tel. 03—961021
pop. 140; fd. 1948.

◆ **MISHMAR HA'EMEK** (Yizreel Valley)   20.S ⚙📖
Mishmar Ha'emek P.O.; tel. 04—933164/5
pop. 780; fd. 1922; *1926
Memorial "Pinat Hagola".

● **MISHMAR HANEGEV** (20 klm. N. Beer Sheva)   52.J ⚙📖
Negev M.P., tel. 057—2402
pop. 540; fd. 1938; *1946
Culture House with archaelogical collection.

■ **MISHMAR HASHARON** (Sharon)   27.O ⚙📖
Mishmar Hasharon P.O., tel. 053—24703
pop. 470; fd. 1925; *1933.

■ **MISHMAROT** (Northern Sharon)   23.P ⚙
Pardes Hanna, POB 4, tel. 063—77006
pop. 250; fd. 1933;

◆ **MIZRA** (Yizreel Valley)   19.W ⚙📖
Mizra P.O., tel. 065—23074/5
pop. 670; fd. 1920; *1923
Nr. Mizra: "Ohel Sara" Institute for Art &
Adult Education; Educat. Inst. "Amakaim".

● **NAAN** (7 klm. from Rehovot)   39.M ⚙📖
Naan P.O., tel. 03—950645, 03—963491
pop. 950; fd. 1926; *1930.

● **NACHSHOLIM** (10 klm. N. of Zichron Yaakov)   19.N ⚙
Hof Hacarmel M.P., tel. 04—942021
pop. 300; fd. 1948.

◆ **NACHSHON** (Jerusalem Corridor)   40.O ⚙
Shimshon M.P., tel. 03—965273
pop. 300; fd. 1950; *1950.

◆ **NACHSHONIM** (10 klm. from Petach Tikva)   34.O
Hamerkaz M.P., tel. 03−914139, 03−919675
pop. 290; fd. 1946.

■ **NAHAL OZ** (3 klm. from Gaza)   49.E
Negev M.P., tel. 051−94271
pop. 400; fd. 1953.

■ **NA'OT MORDECHAI** (Hule Valley)   6.AC
Galil Elyon M.P., tel. 067−40950
pop. 670; fd. 1946; *1946.

◆ **NEGBA** (26 klm. S. of Gedera)   45.I
Lachish Tzafon M.P., tel. 051−4111
pop. 500; fd. 1933; *1939.
Monument to the fighters of the War of Liberation.

● **NETIV HALAMED-HEY** (Hebron Mountains)   44.P
Ha'ala M.P., tel. 02−911217
pop. 350; fd. 1949.
Halamed-Hey House and Memorial.

■ **NETZER SIRENI** (Judaean Plain)   38.L
Beer Yaakov P.O., tel. 03−961235
pop. 580; fd. 1948
Memorial to the Holocaust.

■ **NEVE EYTAN** (Bet Shean Valley)   23.AB
Bet Shean M.P., tel. 065−88530
pop. 290; fd. 1938.

● **NEVE UR** (Bet Shean Valley)   20.AC
Bet Shean M.P., tel. 065−88361/2
pop. 150; fd. 1949; *1954.

■ **NEVE YAM** (2 klm. S. of Athlit)   18.O
Hof Hacarmel M.P., tel. 04−942016
pop. 175; fd. 1938; *1939.

■ **NIR-AM** (3 klm. from Sderot)   48.G
Hof Ashkelon M.P., tel. 051−94134
pop. 300; fd. 1934; *1943.

◆ **NIR DAVID** (Bet Shean Valley)   23.Z
Gilboa M.P., tel. 065−88084
pop. 623; fd. 1931; *1936 (First "Tower &
Stockade" settlement)
Museum for Mediterranean Archaelogy.

■ **NIR ELIAHU** (Sharon)   30.O

Hasharon M.P., tel. 03—923366
pop. 220; fd. 1950; *1950.

NIRIM (Negev)   **53.B**
Negev M.P., tel. 057—93070
pop. 350; fd. 1946 (destroyed & rebuilt).

NIR OZ (Western Negev)   **54.C**
Negev M.P., tel. 057—93080
pop. 200; fd. 1955; *1957
Monument to the Fallen of the Six-Day War.

NIR YITZHAK (Western Negev)   **55.B**
Negev M.P., tel. 057—93007
pop. 270; fd. 1949.

NiTZANIM (14 klm. S. of Ashdod)   **43.H**
Evtach M.P., tel. 051—2379
pop. 270; fd. 1939; *1943 (destroyed in
War of Liberation, and rebuilt)
Remembrance Hall for the Fallen of the
War of Liberation.

OR HANER (nr. Shaar Hanegev)   **47.G**
Hof Ashkelon M.P., tel. 051—94029
pop. 294; fd. 1957; *1957.

PALMACHIM (9 klm. from Rishon Lezion)   **37.J**
Rishon Lezion P.O., tel. 03—941149
pop. 310; fd. 1949
Antiquities Museum.

RAMAT DAVID (Yizreel Valley)   **18.U**
Ramat David P.O., tel. 065—66270/1
pop. 326; fd. 1922.

RAMAT HAKOVESH (30 klm. N. of Tel Aviv)   **30.O**
Ramat Hakovesh P.O., tel. 03—923115, 925362,
925058, pop. 610; fd. 1925
"Yad Lemeginim" auditorium and memorial hall.

RAMAT HASHOFET (Ephraim Mountains)   **20.R**
Ramat Hashofet P.O., tel. 04—993282
pop. 600; fd. 1934; *1941.
Bet Menahem

RAMAT RAHEL (South of Jerusalem)   **43.U**
POB 98, Jerusalem, tel. 02—37919
pop. 100; fd. 1926, destroyed 1929, 1948, *1951.

■ **RAMAT YOHANAN** (Zevulun Valley)   15.S
Kfar Hamaccabi P.O., tel. 04—721094
pop. 598; fd. 1924; *1932
"Times & Way of Life" Archives.

◆ **RAMOT MENASHE**(Ephraim Mountains)   20.Q
Hevel Megiddo M.P., tel. 04—993186
pop. 500; fd. 1948.

● **REGAVIM** (Menashe Region)   22.Q
Menashe M.P., tel. 063—8134
pop. 380; fd. 1947; *1949
Folklore corner of North African Jewry.

● **RE'IM** (W. Negev)   52.D
HaNegev M.P., tel. 057—94052
pop. 230; fd. 1949.

◆ **RESHAFIM** (Bet Shean Valley)   23.AA
Bet Shean M.P., tel. 065—88331
pop. 450; fd. 1944; *1948.

◆ **REVADIM** (S. E. of Gedera)   42.L
Emek Sorek M.P., tel. 055—91063
pop. 300; fd. 1947; destroyed; *1950
Archaeological collection.

● **REVIVIM** (40 klm. of Beer Sheba)   61.J
HaNegev M.P., tel. 057—4896-7, 71283
pop. 550; fd. 1938; *1943
Culture House named after Eliyahu Golomb.

■ **ROSH HANIKRA** (Western Galilee)   7.S
Galil Ma'aravi M.P., tel. 04—968051
pop. 365; fd. 1949.

★ **ROSH TZURIM** (Etzion Block)   44.S
Harei Hevron M.P., tel. 02—942775
pop. 110; fd. 1969.

◆ **RUHAMA** (Northern Negev)   48.J
Hof Ashkelon M.P., tel. 051—94128
pop. 570; fd. 1936; *1944.

★ **SA'AD** (Negev)   49.F
HaNegev M.P., tel. 051—94110
pop. 600; fd. 1938; *1947.

◆ **SA'AR** (W. Galilee)   9.S
Galil Maaravi M.P., tel. 04—923265

pop. 260; fd. 1948; *1951.
Collection of Maritime Archaeology.

◆ **SARID** (Yizreel Valley)　　　　　　　**18.U**
Sarid P.O., tel. 065—40066-7
pop. 750; fd. 1926.
Monument & Memorial House

◆ **SASA** (Upper Galilee)　　　　　　　　**8.Y** ☆
Merom Hagalil M.P., tel. 067—39067
pop. 220; fd. 1949.
Museum.

■ **SDE BOKER** (Ramat Hanegev)　　　　**65.L**
Sde Boker P.O., tel. 057—2262
pop. 115; fd. 1952.

★ **SDE ELIYAHU** (Bet Shean Valley)　　**24.AB**
Bet Shean M.P., tel. 065—88452
pop. 450; fd. 1936; *1939.

● **SDE NAHUM** (Bet Shean Valley)　　**22.AA**
Gilboa M.P., tel. 065—88316
pop. 330; fd. 1929; *1937.

■ **SDE NEHEMIA** (Hule Valley)　　　　**5.AD**
Galil Elyon M.P., tel. 063—8162-3
pop. 336; fd. 1937; *1940.

◆ **SDE YOAV** (Hevel Lachish)　　　　　**45.I**
Sde Gat M.P., tel. 051—2495
pop. 60; fd. 1956; *1966.

● **SDOT YAM** (6 klm. N. of Hadera)　　**23.N**
Shomron M.P., tel. 063—8162/3
pop. 600; fd. 1936; *1940
Antiquities Museum; culture hall named after
Hanna Senesh.

◗ **SHA'ALAVIM** (between Jerusalem and Tel Aviv)　**39.P**
Emek Ayalon M.P., tel. 03—916180, 963052
pop. 210; fd. 1951.

◆ **SHA'AR HA'AMAKIM** 915 klm. from Haifa)　**16.S**
Sha'ar Ha'amakim P.O., tel. 04—932083
pop. 660; fd. 1929; *1935
Sport hall; culture hall in memory of the fallen.

◆ **SHA'AR HAGOLAN** (16 klm. from Tiberias)　**18.AD**
Emek Hayarden M.P., tel. 067—50401
pop. 620; fd. 1930; *1937
Prehistoric Museum of Yarmuk Culture.

SHAMIR (Upper Galilee)   5.AE
Galil Elyon M.P., tel. 067–40920
pop. 470; fd. 1936; *1944 .
Perpetuation project, football field with
amphitheatre.

SHFA'IM (Sharon Coast)   30.L
Shfa'im P.O., tel. 03–937746
pop. 680; fd. 1927; *1935.

SHLUCHOT (Bet Shean Valley)   23.AA
Bet Shean M.P., tel. 065–88348
pop. 400; fd. 1941; *1948.

SHOMRAT (Western Galilee)   11.R
Asherat M.P., tel. 04–910096
pop. 375; fd. 1946; *1948.

SHUVAL (N. W. from Beer Sheba)   51.J
HaNegev M.P., tel. 057–2601, 6596
pop. 240; fd. 1944; *1946.

SNIR (Upper Galilee)   4.AF
Galil Elyon M.P., tel. 067–40401
pop. 60; fd. 1967; *1968.

TEL KATZIR (Jordan Valley)   17.AD
Emek Hayarden M.P., tel. 067–50223
pop. 174; fd. 1949.

TEL YITZHAK (Sharon)   29.M
Sharon Tichon M.P., tel. 053–99281
pop. 230. fd. 1930; *1938
Project for perpetuation of the Holocaust and
Heroism.

TEL YOSEF (Yizreel Valley)   21.Y
Tel Yosef P.O., tel. 065–77603
pop. 540; fd. 1921
Bet Trumpeldor.

TIRAT ZVI (Bet Shean Valley)   25.AB
Bet Shean M.P., tel. 065–88353
pop. 500; fd. 1935; *1937.

TZE'ELIM (30 klm. S. W. of Beer Sheba)   56.E
HaNegev M.P., tel. 057–93148
pop. 200; fd. 1947.

■ **TZORA'A** (Jerusalem Coridor)   **42.P**
Shimshon M.P., tel. 02–911334
pop. 466; fd. 1948.

● **TZOVA** (Jerusalem Corridor)   **41.S**
Harei Yehuda M.P., tel. 02–526424
pop. 350; fd. 1948.

■ **URIM** (W. Negev, 30 klm. from Beer Sheva)   **54.E**
Ofakim P.O., tel. 057–93017
pop. 450; fd. 1945; *1946.

▲ **USHA** (Zevulun Valley)   **15.S**
Kfar Maccabi P.O., tel. 04–721014
pop. 350; fd. 1930; *1937.

YAD HANNA (Sharon)   **27.P**
Lev Hasharon M.P., tel. 053–98185
pop. 120; fd. 1950.
Only kibbutz with Communist majority.

● **YAD HANNA SENESH** (Sharon)   **27.Q**
Lev Hasharon M.P., tel. 053–98166
pop. 80 ; fd. 1950.

◆ **YAD MORDECHAI** (12 klm. S. Ashkelon)   **46.F**
Hof Ashkelon M.P., tel. 051–2414
pop. over 500; fd. 1933; *1944; destroyed
1948 and rebuilt.
Museum of Negev Defence & Ghetto Rising.

● **YAGUR** (Zevulun Valley)   **17.R**
Yagur P.O., tel. 04–952291
pop. 1200; fd. 1922; *1922
Theatre & culture hall.

◆ **YAKUM** (11 klm. S. Netanya)   **29.M**
Yakum P.O., tel. 03–938185
pop. 450; fd. 1938; *1947.

◆ **YAS'UR** (Zevulun Valley)   **12.T**
Asherat M.P., tel. 04–910115
pop. 340; fd. 1949.

★ **YAVNE** (Betw. Gedera & Ashdod)   **41.J**
Avtach M.P., tel. 055 91381
pop. 760; fd. 1929; *1941; one of Israel's largest
chicken breeders & exporters.

◆ **YEHIAM** (Western Galilee)   **10.U**

Ma'ale Hagalil M.P., tel. 04−923484, 922715
pop. 500; fd. 1946; *1946.

■ **YIFTACH** (Upper Galilee)   **6.AB**
Galil Elyon M.P., tel. 067−40151
pop. 300; fd. 1948 (by Palmach veterans) *1948.

■ **YIF'AT** (Western Yizreel Valley)   **18.U**
Yif'at P.O., tel. 065−66362, 66248/9
pop. 875; fd. 1926; *1952
Culture Hall; Exhibition of agricult. implements.

● **YIR'ON** (Upper Galilee)   **8.Z**
Merom Hagalil M.P., tel. 067−39365
pop. 195; fd. 1949.

■ **YIZREEL** (6 klm. from Afula)   **21.W**
Yizreel P.O., tel. 065−23049
pop. 482; fd. 1948; * 1948

■ **YOTVATA** (Arava, N. Eilat)   **91.Q**
Yotvata P.O., tel. 059−2511
pop. 375; fd. 1957.

◆ **ZIKIM** (12 klm. S. Ashkelon)   **46.E**
Hof Ashkelon M.P., tel. 051−2413
pop. 250; fd. 1949;
Cult. Hall.

NAHAL SETTLEMENTS

● **GILGAL** (Jordan Valley)   **35.Z**
Tel. 02−922621

◆ **GSHUR** (Golan Heights)   **11.AH**
Tel. 067−31160

■ **KETURA** (Arava)   **86.R**
Tel. 059−3736

■ **KALLIA** (N. of Dead Sea)   **42.AB**
Tel. 02−922338

★ **KFAR DAROM** (Gaza Strip)   **51.B**

★ **MASSU'A** (Jordan Valley)   **33.AA**
Tel. 02−922623

■ **MORAG** (Gaza Strip).   **11.H**

MITZPE SHALEM (W. of Dead Sea)   **46.Y**
Tel. 02–23261

NA'ARAN (Jordan Valley)   **37.Z**
Tel. 02–922662

NAHAL SINAI   **12.F**

NAHAL YAM (Northern Sinai)   **12.E**
Tel. 057–23640

TZOFAR (Arava)   **75.T**
Tel. 057–960481.

KIBBUTZ ENTERPRISES

KIBBUTZ INDUSTRIES

The Union of Kibbutz Industries is the industrial arm of the Federation of Kibbutz Movements. It was founded in 1963 as a roof organisation for all Kibbutz industrial projects.

The rapid development of Kibbutz industry has aroused a great deal of interest and it has begun to play a large part in the economic progress of the State, just as the Kibbutz plays its part in the development of modern agriculture.

There are already 220 projects in 160 Kibbutzim. Each year some 15 to 20 new industrial projects are set up. Kibbutz industry already produces 5% of the national industrial product, and its total produce reached IL. 750 million in 1972. About 25% of Kibbutz industrial produce is exported, and its value reached $ 45 million in 1972.

The address of Kibbutz Industries: 8 Shaul Hamelech Blvd., Tel Aviv, Tel. 252171.

A. METAL INDUSTRY

AFEK	Mego Afek	Industr. measuring instruments	Afek P. O.
ALONEI ABA	Alrom	Metal furniture	Haifa P. O.
ALONIM	Alum	Anodized aluminium, building hardware	Alonim P. O.
AMIR	"Amir"	Metal Works	Galil Elyon M. P.
ASHDOT YAAKOV/ Ihud	Metal Works	Metal constructions	Emek Hayarden M. P.
ASHDOT YAAKOV/ Meuhad	Almat	Stainless steel polishing	Emek Havarden M. P.
BET ALPHA	Nigrarim Metal Industry	Carts, mobile devices	Gilboa M. P.
BET HASHITA	Ashalim	Farm machinery, packing equipment	Bet Hashita P. O.
BET KAMA		Staplers for office & industry	Hanegev M. P.
CABRI	Cabiran	Non-ferrous precision castings	Galil Maaravi M. P.
DALIA	Arad Ltd.	Water meters & plastic parts	Dalia P. O.
DEGANYA A'	Toolgal Deganya	Diamond tools	Emek Hayarden M. P.
DEGANYA B'	Metal Works	Liquid fertilizer equipment, sprayers	Emek Hayarden M. P.
DOROT	Foundry & Metal Works	Irrigation valves, castings	Hof Ashkelon M. P.
EILON	Eshet-Evlon	Agricultural machinery	Galil Maaravi M. P.
EIN HACHORESH	Pachmas	Steel drums, mobile storage	Emek Hefer M. P.
EIN HAROD/Ihud	Palbam Ltd.	Stainless steel equipment	Ein Harod Ihud P. O.
EIN HAROD/Meuhad	Steel Industries Ltd.	Stainless steel equipment	Gilboa M. P.
EIN HASHOFET	Mivrag Ltd.	Wood & sheet metal screws	Ein Hashofet P. O.
EVRON	Bermad	Metering, pressure regulating & hydraulic valves; irrigation systems	Asherat M. P.
GA'ATON	"Ga'aton" Metal Works	Precision parts on automatic lathes	Maale Hagalil M. P.
GA'ASH	Matar	Lighting poles, sports equipment	Ga'ash P. O.
GIV'AT BRENNER	Limit	Irrigation equipment, castings	Giv'at Brenner P. O.
GIV'AT CHAIM/Meuhad	Metal Works	Electro-chem, metal polishing	Giv'at Chaim Meuhad P. O.
HANITA		Cutting tools	Galil Maaravi M. P.

Settlement	Company	Products	Location
HATZOR	Omen	Pressure die casting, irrigation & electr. equipment	Tel Aviv P. O.
HEFZIBA	Mad-Takin	Water meters — servicing & repairs, meter covers.	Gilboa M. P.
KFAR BLUM	Electro-mech products	Control panels, controlled atmosphere installations	Galil Elyon M. P.
KFAR DANIEL	Danny	Metal furniture, pingpong tables	Hamerkaz M. P.
KFAR ETZION	Spark Processing	Spark processing	Gush Etzion M.P.
KFAR HANASSI	Habonim	Stainless steel castings, nirosta, valves.	Galil Elyon M. P.
KFAR MENAHEM	Metal Works	Automotive spare parts, automatic lathe work; equipment for poultry breeding; high tension accessories.	Emek Sorek M. P.
KFAR SZOLD	Lordan Ltd.	Spiral heat exchangers, air coolers, unit heaters	Galil Elyon M. P.
KINNERET	Metal Works	Waste wagons.	Emek Hayarden M. P.
KIRYAT ANAVIM	Metal Works	Agricult. machinery, fruit sorting equipment	Kiryat Anavim P. O.
LEHAVOT HABASHAN	Metal Works	Agricult. sprayers, fire-fighting equipment	Galil Elyon M. P.
MA'AYAN ZVI	Garage	Motor vehicles repair workshop	Hof Hacarmel M. P.
MAHANAIM	Diyuk Hydraulica	Metal Industry	Hevel Khorazim M. P.
MASH'AVEI SADE	"Shaviv"	Automatic lathe work	Hanegev M. P.
MENARA	Metal Works	Agricult. & general purpose wagons	Galil Elyon M. P.
MESSILOT	Wire Rope Works	Wire ropes & slings	Gilboa M. P.
MIZRA	Ta'amal Mizra	Hydr. presses, fork lifts	Mizra P. O.
NA'AN	Metal Works	Sprinklers & irrigation equipment	Na'an P. O.
NAHAL OZ	Ozat	Electro-chem. metal works	Hanegev M. P.
NETZER-SIRENI	Metal Works	Agricult. platforms; field kitchens	Beer Yaakov P. O.

NIR AM	Michsaf	Stainless-steel & silver-plated cutlery	Ashkelon M. P.
NIR DAVID	Metal Works	Sprinklers & irrigation equipment	Gilboa M. P.
NITZANIM	Paltechnika	Efficiency & health chairs	Avtach M. P.
NORDIA	Springs	Techn. springs for agriculture & industry	Netanya P. O.
RAMAT DAVID	Metal Works	Agricult. wagons, constructions for cotton: fertilizers	Ramat David P. O.
ROSH TZURIM	"Or Tzurim"	Metal Works	Harei Hebron M.P.
SHAAR HA'AMAKIM	Chromagen	Electr. & sun boilers; threshing drums	Shaar Ha'amakim P. O.
SHUVAL	Spark Processing	Associated with Beer Sheva Aeronautical Works	Hanegev M. P.
TEL YOSEF	Metal Works	Fertilizer dispensers; vegetable unloaders; tanks for liquid manure pumping	Tel Yosef P. O.
TIMORIM	Tomer	Metal & wood furniture	Hevel Lachish Zafon M. P.
TZOR'AH	Israel Cycle Man. Ltd.	Bicycles, mopeds; toys; metal works; electrolythical welding & coating	Bet Shemesh P. O.
URIM	Michsaf	Knives forging	Hanegev M. P.
YAGUR	Lageen	Tin boxes	Yagur P. O.
YEHIAM	Metal Works	Packing equipment for roses, ladders for citrus & fruit picking	Maale Hagalil M. P.
YIF'AT	Agricult. Machinery	Fork lifts, loaders, mowers, vegetable washing machines	Yif'at P. O.
YIFTACH	Mechanical Works	Associated with the Aeronautical Works	Galil Elyon M. P.

B. PLASTIC AND RUBBER PRODUCTS

AMIAD	Labour Saving Equipment	Irrigation and Filtration System	Hevel Khorazim M. P.

ASHDOT-YAAKOV/ Ihud	Log	Plastic & expanded packing products	Emek Hayarden M. P.
BARKAI	"Barkai"	Polyethelene films	Asherat M. P.
BE'EROT YITZHAK	Chetzem	Protective coatings; fibreglass	
BET ZERA	Ar-Kal	Techno-plastic products & container packing; boxes for bottles	Emek Hayarden M. P.
DAFNA	"Dafna"	Plastic shoes & sandals	Galil Elyon M. P.
DAN	Dan Pal	Techno-plastic building materials, doors, etc.	Galil Elyon M. P.
EIN CARMEL	Kal-Kar	Molded polystyrene products for packaging, building & camping	Hof Hacarmel M. P.
EIN SHEMER	Rubber Industries	Rubber products	Manasse M. P.
EIN ZIVAN	"Dafna-Ein Zivan"	Plastic shoes	Kuneitra P. O.
GINEGAR	Plastica	Polyethelene products	Ginegar P. O.
GLIL YAM	Madgal	Plastic injection moulding	Gil Yam P. O.
GVAT	Plastro-Gvat	Pipes for building, agricult., industry	Gvat P. O.
HACHOTRIM	Reshet-o-Plast	Plastic nets	Hof Hacarmel M. P.
HAMADIYA	Inbar	Containers & sinks; boats made of reinforced plastic	Emek Bet Shean M. P.
HA'OGEN	Ha'ogen-Plast Ltd.	Calendered rolls & continuous plastic materials; P.V.C. coated linen.	Lev Hasharon M. P.
HATZERIM	Netafim	Droplet irrigation (Blass system)	Hanegev M. P.
HAZOREA	Plastopil Ltd.	Polyethelene for agricult. & packing	Hazorea P. O.
HULATA	Hulata Shoes	Home & gymnastics shoes	Galil Elyon M. P.
MA'AGAN MICHAEL	Plasson	Injections moulding for industry, agricult. & building	Hof Hacarmel M. P.
MA'OZ CHAIM	Polyraz Thermoplastic Articles	P.V.C. & polystyrene rolls & sheets; packaging bands.	Emek Bet Shean M. P.
MERHAVIA	Plassim Ltd.	Plastic pipes & accessories for agricult.,	Merhavia P. O.

Settlement	Company	Products	Location
METZER		industry & building Polyethylene bags	Shomron M. P.
MISHMAR HA'EMEK & GAL'ED	Tama	Household ware; synthetic strings; extrusion & injection moulding	Mishmar Ha'emek P. O.
MISHMAR HANEGEV	Polybid	Expanded polystyrene products for insulation & packaging	Hanegev M. P.
NACHSHOLIM	Tefen	Plastic injection moulding	Hof Hacarmel M. P.
NEGBA	Z. L. P.	Lamination & Polypropylene	Nahal Lachish Zafon M. P.
NEVE EITAN	"Pas On"	Reinforced Plastics	Bet Shean M.P.
NIR DAVID	Shafrit	P.V.C. & Polyethylene tubes; packing for liquids	Gilboa M. P.
RAMAT HAKOVESH	Duram	Gaskets for water & oil	Ramat Hakovesh P. O.
RAMAT YOHANAN	Palram	Rigid P.V.C. profiles & sheets; vacuum forming products	Kfar Hamaccabi P. O.
REGAVIM	Plastic Works	Plastic injection moulding	Manasse M. P.
RESHAFIM	Teraflex	Plastic products	Emek Bet Shean M. P.
REVIVIM	Raviv	Precision plastic moulding	Halutza M.P.
SDE NEHEMIA	Huliot	Plastic for industry & household; containers	Galil Elyon M. P.
SHAAR HAGOLAN	Golan	Plastic coated metal profiles; shutters, profiles; flexible pipes.	Emek Hayarden M. P.
YAGUR	Lageen-Tuboplast	Plastic tubes & wrappings	Yagur P. O.
YAKUM	Plastiv Yakum	Plastic products, containers, toys, etc.	Yakum P. O.
YESODOT	Plasdot	Plastic napkins, table cloths & tapes	Emek Sorek M. P.

C. ELECTRONIC, ELECTRICAL & CONTROL PRODUCTS

Settlement	Company	Products	Location
BARAM	Elcam	Hard metals, dies	Merom Hagalil M. P.

BET ALPHA	Kav Kor	Thermostats, control lamps	Gilboa M. P.
BET KESHET	Electronika	Electronic products	Galil Tachton M. P.
EILON	Perles-Eilon	Electronic Products	Galil Maaravi M.P.
EILOT		Thermostats	Eilot M.P.
EIN DOR	Teldor	Cables & wires for telecommunication, electronics & electricity	Yezreel M. P.
EIN HASHOFET	Electr. Appliances	Ballasts	Hevel Megiddo M. P.
FAROD	Farod Radiophone	Internal Communication	Merom Haglil M.P.
GA'ASH	Lighting Works	Lighting fixtures	Ga'ash P. O.
GAL'ON	"Gal'on"	Fans, exhaust fans, electr. appliances	Sde Gat M. P.
GEVA	Baccara	Automation & control	Geva P. O.
GINOSSAR	Agar	Electronic control products	Ginossar P. O.
HEFZIBA	Tagal	Electronic products	Gilboa M. P.
KFAR BLUM	Electronic Works	Electronic assembly for industry	Galil Elyon M. P.
KFAR MASARYK	Salora	Television sets & electronics	Asherat M. P.
LOCHAMEI HAGETA'OT	K. M. A. Ltd.	Cables & electronic equipment	Asherat M. P.
MAGEN	Electronics	Stereo amplifiers, radios	Hanegev M. P.
MASSUOT YITZHAK	M. H. Ltd.	Electrical household appliances	Lachish Zafon M. P.
MAVO HAMMA	El Hamma	Acid measuring instruments	Galil Elyon M. P.
NACHSHONIM	Electro-Nim	Electronic Works	Hamerkaz M. P.
NAHAL OZ	"Ozat"	Electrochemical Works	Hanegev M.P.
NETIV HALAMED-HEY	"Tana"	Electronic Works	Ha'ela M. P.
NIRIM	Nirim Electronics	Electronic instruments for agriculture	Hanegev M. P.
ROSH TZURIM	Or-Tzurim	Motorcar electrical products	Jerusalem P. O.
YAD MORDECHAI	Eldar	Electronic products	Hof Ashkelon M. P.
YAS'UR	Yas'ur Electronics	Teaching appliances – electronic assembly	Asherat M. P.
YEZREEL	Yezreel Electronics	Teaching appliances – electronic assembly	Gilboa M. P.

BET HASHITA	Bet Hashita	Olives & vegetable pickling	Bet Hashita P. O.
BET HERUT	Hod-Lavan Ltd.	Turkey processing	Bet Herut P. O.
BROR CHAIL	Deco	Dehydrated vegetables	Ashkelon, P.O.B. 257
EYNAT	Ein-Bar	Bakery	Eynat P. O.
GAN SHMUEL	Canning Factory	Canned food, citrus concentrates	Shomron M. P.
GIV'AT BRENNER	Rimon Ltd.	Citrus juices & concentrates; canned food & jams	Giv'at Brenner P. O.
GIV'AT CHAIM/Ihud & Meuchad	Gat	Frozen juices & concentrates, canned vegetables	Giv'at Chaim P. O.
HAFETZ CHAIM	Mata'm	Suppliers of kosher food for airlines & tours	Hafetz Chaim P. O.
KFAR HACHORESH	Oranim	Bakery	Kfar Hachoresh P. O.
MA'ALE HACHAMISHA	Carmit	Caramels & other sweets	Harei Yehuda M. P.
MA'ANIT	Gal'am Ltd.	Edible & industrial starches, glucose, caramel	Menashe M. P.
MISHMAR HASHARON	Regional bakery	Bakery	Mishmar Hasharon P. O.
MIZRA	Ma'adanei Mizra	Sausages & meat products	Mizra P. O.
NA'OT MORDECHAI	Naot Ltd.	Fruit juices & concentrates	Galil Elyon M. P.
NEVE YAM	Noon	Canned fish, vegetables & fruit	Hof Hacarmel M. P.
RAMAT HAKOVESH	Rama	Bakery	Ramat Hakovesh P. O.
SHA'AR HA'AMAKIM	Kama	Flour mill	Sha'ar Ha'amakim P. O.
SHAMIR	Galil	Royal jelly	Galil Elyon M. P.
TIRAT ZVI	Tiv	Sausages & smoked meat	Emek Bet Shean M. P.
YEHIAM	Ma'adanei Of	Meat and poultry products	Maale Hagalil M. P.
YOTVATA	Dairy	Pasteurized milk & citrus beverages	Eilot M. P.

E. WOOD PRODUCTS AND FURNITURE

Location	Company	Product	P. O.
AFIKIM	Kelet	Plywood & veneers; panels for wall covering	Afikim P. O.
EIN HAROD/Ihud	Carpentry	Office furniture	Ein Harod Ihud P. O.
EIN HAROD/Meuhad	Carpentry	Mechanical carpentry, "String" furniture	Gilboa M. P.
GAT	Wood Works	Wood turning	Sde Gat M. P.
GEVIM	Zamir	Wooden flutes for teaching purposes	Lachish Zafon M. P.
GIV'AT BRENNER	Carpentry	Furniture for institutions; "Kol Gil" furniture	Giv'at Brenner P. O.
HAMADIA	Hamadia Doors	Wooden doors for building; decorative partitions	Emek Bet Shean M. P.
HAZOREA	Furniture	Teak furniture	Hazorea P. O.
LAVI	Wood Works	Furniture for synagogues & institutions	Galil Tachton M. P.
MISHMAROT	Taal Ltd.	Plywood, furniture, boxes, "Sibit" panels	Pardes Hanna, P.O.B. 28
NETZER SIRENI	Carpentry	Office & institutions furniture	Beer Yaakov P. O.
RAMAT HASHOFET	Wood Works	Packing boxes, containers, loading pallets	Ramat Hashofet P. O.
REGBA	Kitchen cupboards	Kitchen furniture, built-in wardrobes	Asherat M. P.
SDOT YAM	Masponat Keisaria	Wood, metal & fibreglass products, refrigerators	Sdot Yam P. O.
SHOMRAT	Furniture	Libraries, furniture	Asherat M. P.
JORDAN VALLEY COMMON ENTERPRISE	Sefen Ltd.	Masonite, formica, insulating panels	Emek Hayarden M. P.

F. TEXTILE AND LEATHER PRODUCTS

Location	Company	Product	P. O.
AMIR	Adin	Shirts	Galil Elyon M. P.

Settlement	Company	Product	Address
CARMIA	Blankets	Blankets & sleeping bags	Hof Ashkelon M. P.
DAPHNA	Daphna	Shoes	Galil Elyon M.P.
EIN SHEMER	Nardi	Belts & leather products	Shomron M.P.
EIN TZURIM	Tadmor	Leather coats, leather products	Lachish Zafon M. P.
EINAT	Shoe Factory	Shoes	Eynat P. O.
GIV'AT HASHLOSHA	Noga	Military & work boots, shoes	Giv'at Hashlosha P. O.
GLIL YAM	Giza	Covers, curtains, dresses	Gil Yam P. O.
HAMA'APIL	Taga	Stretch stockings, synthetic fibre	Hama'apil P. O.
MATZUVA	Weaving Plant	Weaving products	Galil Maaravi M. P.
NA'OT MORDECHAI	Naot	Sports boots, shoes & sandals	Galil Elyon M. P.
NEGBA	Sewing Shop	Children's clothing	Lachish Zafon M. P.
ROSH TZURIM	Sewing Shop	Linnen sewing	Jerusalem P. O.
SCHILLER	Shiltex Ltd.	Elastic bands, shoelaces	Emek Sorek M. P.

G. CHEMICAL & PHARMACEUTICAL PRODUCTS

Settlement	Company	Product	Address
DALIA	Zohar	Detergents for home & industry	Dalia P. O.
EREZ	Novis Ltd.	Pharmaceuticals, Dietetic food, beverages, honey	Hof Ashkelon M. P.
MA'ABAROT	Isr. Pharmaceut. Products Ltd.	Pharmaceutical & veterinary products	Ma'abarot P. O.
MA'ABAROT	Halavit	Cattle feed, veterinary products	Ma'abarot P. O.
NIR YITZHAK	"Chemada"	Bromides (delicate chemicals)	Hanegev M. P.

H. BUILDING MATERIALS & QUARRIES

Settlement	Company	Product	Address
ALONIM	"Alum"	Aluminium Products	Alonim P.O.
BET ALPHA	Sand & Stone equipment	Gravel; road building	Gilboa M. P.
GESHER	Quarries	Gypsum quarries	Emek Bet Shean M. P.

Location	Company	Product	Address
GESHER	Gypsum Works "Hachotrim"	Gypsum panels	Emek Bet Shean M. P.
HACHOTRIM	Quarries	Building sand	Hof Hacarmel M. P.
KFAR GILEADI	Gur Umga	Asphalt, gravel, "kurkar", building sand	Kfar Gileadi P. O.
KFAR GLICKSON	Quarries	White & coloured chalk	Menasse M. P.
KINNERET	Tof Quarries	Building & road building material	Emek Hayarden M. P.
MEROM GOLAN	Mechora	Gravel for building & roads	Kuneitra P. O.
PALMACHIM		Building sand & "kurkar"	Rishon Lezion P. O.
SDOT YAM	Caesarea Tiles	Mosaic & marble tiles	Sdot Yam P. O.
TEL YITZHAK	M. L. T. Ltd.	Prefabricated products	Lev Hasharon M. P.

I. DECORATIVE AND ART PRODUCTS

Location	Company	Product	Address
BET ZERA	Matan	Musical boxes	Emek Hayarden M. P.
BROR CHAIL	Ceramics	Artistic ceramic products	Lachish Darom M. P.
EILON	Mosaics	Wall decorations, mosaic table tops	Galil Maaravi M. P.
EIN GEDI	Photographic Laboratory	Decorative Photos	
GIV'AT BRENNER	Bangali	Wooden fabrics	Giv'at Brenner P. O.
GIV'AT HASHLOSHA	Mosaics	Decorative mosaics	Giv'at Hashlosha P. O.
KFAR ETZION		Decorative candles	Har Hebron M.P.
KFAR HAMACCABI	Maccabi Works	Metal, wood & plastic gifts	Kfar Hamaccabi P. O.
KFAR MENAHEM	Ceramics	Decorative ceramic products	Emek Sorek M. P.
MA'AYAN ZVI	Hatzvi	Decorative & publicity articles, embedding of flowers & butterflies in polyester, etc.	Hof Hacarmel M. P.
NACHSHON & REVADIM		Crystals, gem polishing	Lachish Zafon M. P.

J. MISCELLANEOUS

Location	Company	Product	Address
AMIR	"Amir"	Paper products	Galil Elyon M. P.

BE'ERI	Be'eri Printing Press	Printing	Hanegev M. P.
BET HERUT	Shohar Print Enterprises	Silkscreen, publicity items, packaging	Bet Herut P. O.
EILOT	Mechanical Laundry	Laundry	Eilot P. O.
EIN HAMIFRATZ	"Yitzur Motzrei Ariza"	Corrugated Cardboard	Asherat M. P.
EIN HAROD/Ichud	"Ricor"	Cryogenic & Vacuum Systems	Ein Harod/Ihud P.O.
HASOLELIM	Linero	Drawing equipment	Natzrat Elit P.O.
KFAR RUPPIN	Banetiv	Auxil. equipment for physics teaching	Emek Bet Shean M. P.
KFAR SZOLD	Lordan & Co.	Heat Exchangers	Galil Elyon M.P.
MERHAVIA	Dfus Hashomer Hatzair	Printing	Merhavia P. O.
NA'AN	Na'an Laundry	Laundry	Naan P. O.
NEOT MORDECHAI	Alpha Neot	Dehydrated alfalfa meal	Galil Elyon M. P.
RUHAMA	Hamivreshet Ltd.	Industr. & household brushes	Hof Ashkelon M. P.
SARID	Gamal	Grindstones	Sarid P. O.
SHAMIR	"Shamir"	Optical lenses	Galil Elyon M. P.
TEL YOSEF	Dfus Tel Yosef	Printing	Tel Yosef P. O.
KIBBUTZ ARZI MOVE-MENT ENTERPRISES	Hadfus Hachadash Ltd.	Printing	Tel Aviv P. O.

REGIONAL PROJECTS

In the last few years the regional projects have become an integral part in the processes of Kibbutz agricultural produce, and play an important part in production efficiency and market control.

Today there are 26 regional organisations with 115 projects: 8 animal fodder plants (700,000 tons per year), 5 lucerne-drying plants, 10 chicken slaughter-houses, 11 cotton-gins, 26 packing-plants for vegetables, fruit and flowers, 2 canning factories for fruit and citrus-juices, 16 cold-storage plants for fruit and potatoes, and about 30 service stations for heavy machinery, workshops, garages, laundries, etc.

Up till today about IL. 300 million have been invested in the projects. There are about 3,500 employees, of whom about 800 are Kibbutz members.

Recently the idea of the regional factory has found interested parties among Moshav farmers, and they want to join in the existing projects.

The regional factories are represented by the Central Council of Regional Projects at the Agricultural Centre, and this body represents the regional projects for the Government Offices, Bank Hapoalim, and other national institutions.

Address of the Central Council of Regional Projects: Central Agricultural House, 8 Shaul Hamelech Blvd., Tel Aviv, Tel. 252171.

LIST OF REGIONAL ENTERPRISES

"AVSHALOM". Bnei Shim'on Region for Development & Mechanization, Bnei Shim'on Road Junction; tel. 057–2624/5.
Fd. 1958: 84 employees; serving 6 kibbutzim.
Enterprises: Agricult. equipment; fruit cold storage & packing house; sorting of flowers & potatoes.

BIK'AT BET SHEAN. Bik'at Bet Shean M. P.; tel. 065–88282.
600 employees; serving 14 kibbutzim.
Enterprises: Alfalfa drying; regional garage; heavy equipment; cotton gin; drying & packing of dates.

GALIL DEVELOPMENT. Galil Elyon M.P., tel. 065–40660-3.
148 employees; serving 26 kibbutzim.
Enterprises: "Galil" – cold storage; "Of Hagalil" – poultry slaughter house; T. G. – fruit; cotton; "Kabul Hahule" – meat.

GILBOA. Tel Yosef, Gilboa M.P., tel. 065–7678/9.
Enterprises: "Of Gilboa" – poultry slaughter house; citrus packing house; potato sorting; agricult. equipment.

"GRANOT". Regional enterprises for Hefer Valley, Sharon & Shomron; tel. 063–25090.
250 employees; serving 40 kibbutzim.
Enterprises: "Ambar" – cattle feed; "Aspeset" – alfalfa drying; "Sivan" – cotton; "Kirur" – cold storage & packing house.

HA'EMEK ENTERPRISES. Migdal Ha'emek, P.O.B. 73; tel. 065–40660-3.
290 employees; serving 32 kibbutzim.
Enterprises: "Pri Ha'emek" – fruit & citrus produce; "Of Ha'emek" – poultry slaughter house; cotton gin; Workshop & gasoline station.

HEVEL MA'ON. Ma'on Region settlements; Hanegev M.P., tel. 057–93058.
110 employees; serving 11 kibbutzim.
Enterprises: Sorting of potatoes, peppers & carrots; regional garage; agricultural equipment.

JORDAN VALLEY ENTERPRISES. Emek Hayarden M.P., tel. 067–50421.
400 employees; serving 19 kibbutzim.
Enterprises: Heavy equipment; regional garage; spare parts stores; drainage; banana export; dehydration of dates, vegetables & fruit; citrus packing house.

MEROM HAGALIL. Meron: Merom Hagalil M.P., tel. 067–39381.
Serving 4 kibbutzim and moshavim.
Enterprises: Cold storage; packing house; agricultural equipment & garage; poultry breeding.

MILU'OT. Enterprise for the development of the Haifa Bay Kibbutzim.
Asherat M. P., tel. 04–713282.
650 employees; serving 26 kibbutzim.
Enterprises: "Milubar" – cattle fooder; Miluof – poultry slaughter house; "Milopri" – cold storage & packing; "Miloz" – fruit & citrus

produce; "Milomoz" – banana packing; "Milosiv" – cotton.

RAM. Ramat Hashofet, Ramat Hashofet P.O., tel. 04–1933181.
150 employees; serving 10 kibbutzim.
Enterprises: Packing house; cold storage; agricultural equipment.

SHA'AR HANEGEV ENTERPRISES. Hof Ashkelon M.P., tel.
051–94311.
400 employees; serving 12 kibbutzim.
Enterprises: Cotton gin; "Of-Kar" – poultry slaughter house; laundry;
packing house; agricult. equipment & garage; fruit sorting & packing;
meat & potato flour, & also potato products.

YIZREEL. Yizreel M.P., Tel. 065–22956.
150 employees; serving 20 settlements.
Enterprises: Fruit packing house; cold storage; sorting & packing of
flowers; agricultural equipment.

GUEST HOUSES

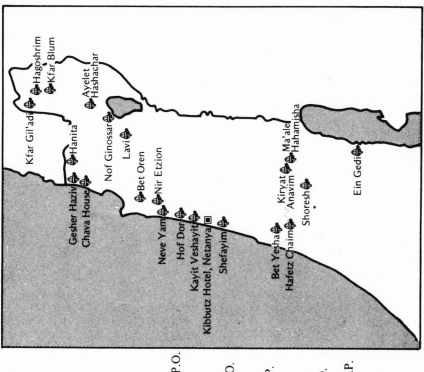

Ayelet Hashachar, (Upper Galilee), Galil Elyon M.P.
Bet Oren, (Mount Carmel), Haifa, P.O.B. 701
Bet Yesha, Giv'at Brenner (nr. Rehovot), Giv'at Brenner P.O.
Chava House, Shavei Zion
Ein Gedi, (Dead Sea), Beer Sheva P.O.
Gesher Haziv, (Western Galilee)
Hafetz Chaim, (15 klm. from Rehovot), Hafetz Chaim P.O.
Hagoshrim, (Upper Galilee), Galil Elyon M.P.
Hanita, (Western Galilee), N. Naharia, Galil Ma'aravi M.P.
Hof Dor, Nachsholim (Mediterranean), Hof Hacarmel M.P.
Kayit Veshayit, Sdot Yam
Kfar Blum, (Upper Galilee), Galil Elyon M.P.
Kfar Gil'adi, (Upper Galilee), Kfar Gil'adi P.O.
Kiryat Anavim, (Judaean Mountains), Kiryat Anavim P.O.
Lavi, (Lower Galilee), Galil Tachton M.P.
Ma'ale Hahamisha, (Judaean Mountains), Bnei Yehuda M.P.
Neve Yam, (Mediterranean), Hof Hacarmel M.P.
Nir Etzion, Carmel Mountains
Nof Ginossar, Ginossar, Sea of Galilee, Ginossar P.O.
Shefayim, (Sharon Coast), Shfa'im P.O.
Shoresh, Judaean Mountains

Temple Israel

Minneapolis, Minnesota

In Honor of the Bat Mitzvah of
ELIZABETH ANNE GLASSBERG

by
Mr. & Mrs. John M. Glassberg
February 12, 1977